Social Security Law in India

Social Security Law in India

Second Edition

Debi S. Saini

This book was originally published as a monograph in the International Encyclopaedia of Laws/Social Security Law.

Founding Editor: Roger Blanpain
General Editor: Frank Hendrickx
Volume Editor: Willy van Eeckhoutte

Wolters Kluwer

Published by:
Kluwer Law International B.V.
PO Box 316
2400 AH Alphen aan den Rijn
The Netherlands
E-mail: international-sales@wolterskluwer.com
Website: lrus.wolterskluwer.com

Sold and distributed by:
Wolters Kluwer Legal & Regulatory U.S.
7201 McKinney Circle
Frederick, MD 21704
United States of America
E-mail: customer.service@wolterskluwer.com

ISBN 978-94-035-3871-6

e-Book: ISBN 978-94-035-3872-3
web-PDF: ISBN 978-94-035-3873-0

The Author

Debi S. Saini is presently Adjunct Professor of HRM, Management Development Institute, Gurgaon. Earlier he has been an Emeritus Professor at the Indian Institute of Management, Ranchi for two years. He obtained his Master's degree in Commerce (business studies) from the Delhi School of Economics, and LLB, LLM and PhD degrees from the Faculty of Law, University of Delhi. He has been certified as a Global Professional in Human Resource (GPHR) by the Society for Human Resource Management (SHRM), USA. His PhD thesis in the area of Sociology of Labour Law was supervised by the eminent jurist Dr Upendra Baxi. Dr Saini worked in the area of social security law for his LLM thesis. Starting his academic career in 1971 as a Lecturer at Delhi College of Arts and Commerce (renamed), University of Delhi, Delhi, he later on served as, among others, Professor of Labour Law (1992–1994) at Gandhi Labour Institute, Ahmedabad; and Professor of HRM at IILM, New Delhi (1996–1999); Professor of HRM at the Management Development Institute, Gurgaon (2004–2016). He has been the first Isambard Kingdom Brunel Fellow at the business school of the University of Portsmouth, Portsmouth, UK (June 2016); a visiting professor at Aarhus School of Business, University of Aarhus, Aarhus, Denmark; IAE Aix-en-Provence Graduate School of Management, Université Paul Cezanne, Aix-Marseille, France; and SP Jain Centre of Management, Dubai, UAE.

Professor Saini's areas of interest are labour and social security law, employee relations, strategic HRM and law and society. He has been teaching courses in these areas at MBA and PhD levels in India and overseas. He has edited or authored seven books in these areas. He has authored ninety-three papers/book chapters/management cases in his area of expertise. His papers have been published, among others, in *Asia-pacific Management Review*, *Human Resource Management*, *Journal of World Business*, *Asia-Pacific Business Review, Zeitschrift fur auslandisches and internation- ales Sozialrecht* (Review of Foreign and International Social Law), *Asia-Pacific Business Review, Journal of Indian Law Institute, Delhi Law Review, Cochin University Law Review, Economic & Political Weekly, Indian Journal of Labour Economics, Asia Case Research Journal,* and *Indian Journal of Industrial Relations.* He has published 153 book reviews in areas of his interest. Five of Dr Saini's teaching cases in HRM are being sold by the Harvard Business School Publishing online, Asia Case Research Centre and European Case Clearing, two of which are in the 'Popular' category.

The Author

Dr Saini was the editor of *Vision: The Journal of Business Perspective*; and the Founding-Editor of *Management & Change* (1997–1999). He is on the editorial boards of many journals and has earlier been on the Editorial Board of *Industrial Relations Journal*, Blackwell, Oxford (1998–2002). He has done consulting assignments for the ILO, GTZ (Germany), and SHRM. Among others, Dr Saini received 'Best Professor in Human Resource Management' award from CMO Asia in Singapore (July 2013); 'The Best Researcher of MDI Award for 2005' from MDI; and 'Best HRM Faculty Award' from Amity University, NOIDA, India, in 2007.

Professor Saini has been delivering lectures/chairing seminars and making presentations in HRM and Labour Law areas in conferences and workshops in different countries. Among others, he has been invited as a keynote speaker at many international fora, including Portsmouth Business School, University of Portsmouth, UK (June 2016); Faculty of Management Studies, University of Sri Jayewardenepura, Sri Lanka, (October 2015); the National Congress of Italian Association for Personnel Management in Sorrento, Italy (May 2008); invited speaker at three SHRM annual meetings in USA, and by Boston College Centre for Work & Family, Boston College London, U.K. (September 2006).

Details of Dr Saini's publications, interest areas and involvements can be known from his website <http://sites.google.com/view/debisaini/> and he can be reached on the following e-mail address: debissaini@gmail.com.

Table of Contents

List of Abbreviations

AB-NHPM	Ayushman Bharat Yojana: National Health Protection Mission
ABY	Ayushman Bharat Yojana
AIR	All India Reporter
ALC	Assistant Labour Commissioner
AMC	Asset Management Company
APL	Above Poverty Line
ATC	Administrative Tribunal Cases
BIFR	Board for Industrial and Financial Reconstruction
BMSP	Basic Minimum Services Programme
BOCWA	Building and Other Construction Workers (Regulation of Employment & Conditions of Service) Act, 1996
BOCWWCA	The Building and Other Construction Workers' Welfare Cess, Act, 1996
BOT	Board of Trustees
BPL	Below Poverty Line
CA	Controlling Authority
CBOT	Central Board of Trustees
CEO	Chief Executive Officer
CGHS	Central Government Health Service
CHC	Community Health Centre
COW	Code on Wages 2019
CPA	Consumer Protection Act, 1985
CPC	Civil Procedure Code
CPFC	Central Provident Fund Commissioner
CPI	Consumer Price Index
CSRE	Crash Scheme for Rural Employment
Cur.LR	Current Law Reports
DG	Director General
DGLW	Director General–Labour Welfare

List of Abbreviations

DRDA	District Rural Development Agency
ECA	Employees' Compensation Act 1923
EAS	Employment Assurance Scheme
EDLIS	Employees' Deposit-Linked Insurance Scheme
EIC	Employees' Insurance Court
EPF	Employees' Provident Fund
EPFA	Employees' Provident Fund and Miscellaneous Provisions Act
EPFO	Employees Provident Fund Organization
EPFS	Employees' Provident Fund Scheme
EPS	Employees' Pension Scheme
ERP	Enterprise Resource Planning
ESB	Extended Sickness Benefit
ESI	Employees' State Insurance Act 1948
ESIC	Employees' State Insurance Corporation
ESIS	Employees' State Insurance Scheme
FLR	Factories Law Reports
FPS	Family Pension Scheme 1971
FRUs	First Referral Units
FWP	Food for Work Programme
GIC	General Insurance Company
HRM	Human Resource Management
HSCs	Health Sub-centres
IAS	Indian Administrative Service
IAY	Indira Awas Yojana
ICDS	Integrated Child Development Services
ICS	Indian Civil Service
IDA	Industrial Disputes Act
ILC	Indian Labour Conference
ILO	International Labour Organization
ILO–SAAT	International Labour Organization–South Asian Advisory Team
IMO	Insurance Medical Officer
INR	Indian Rupee (1 INR = 44.37 USD in October 2010)
IOMC	Iron Ore, Manganese Ore and Chrome Ore
IP	Insured Person
IRC	Industrial Relations Code 2020
IRDP	Integrated Rural Development Programme
ISM	Indian System of Medicine
IT	Information Technology

JRY	Jawahar Rojgar Yojana
JSY	Janani Suraksha Yojana
Lab. IC	Labour and Industrial Cases
LC	Labour Commissioner
LEO	Labour Enforcement Officer
LIC	Life Insurance Company
LLJ	Labour Law Journal
LLN	Labour Law Notes
LLR	Labour Law Reporter
LSDM	Limestone and Dolomite Mines
LWO	Labour Welfare Organization
MBA	Maternity Benefit Act
MBC	Maternity Benefit Council
MFIs	Micro-Financial Institutions
MNC	Multinational Corporation
MNP	Minimum Needs Programme
MNREGA	Mahatma Gandhi National Rural Employment Guarantee Act, 2005
MNREGS	Mahatma Gandhi National Rural Employment Guarantee Scheme
MWA	Minimum Wages Act
NCEUS	The National Commission for Enterprises in the Unorganized Sector
NCL-I	National Commission on Labor-I
NCL-II	National Commission on Labor-II
NEP	New Economic Policy
NFBS	National Family Benefit Scheme
NGOs	Non-governmental Organizations
NHIA	National Health Insurance Agency
NICSI	National Informatics Centre Service Institute
NLLA	National Labour Law Association
NMBS	National Maternity Benefit Scheme
NOIDA	New Okhla Industrial Development Authority (Name of a town in the state of U.P.)
NREGA	National Rural Employment Guarantee Act, 2005
NREP	National Rural Employment Programme
NRF	National Renewal Fund
NRHM	National Rural Health Mission
NSAP	National Social Assistance Programme

List of Abbreviations

NSS	National Sample Survey
NSSAI	National Social Security Authority of India
OAP	Old Age Pension
OBCs	Other Backward Classes
OOPE	Out of Pocket Expenditure
OPD	Out-Patient Department
OSHWCC	The Occupational Safety, Health and Working Conditions Code, 2020
PASS	Personal Accident Insurance Social Security Scheme
PDB	Permanent Disablement Benefit
PDS	Public Distribution System
PF	Provident Fund
PGA	Payment of Gratuity Act
PHC	Primary Health Centre
PIL	Public Interest Litigation
PM-JAY	Pradhan Mantri Jan Arogya Yojana
PMRPY	Pradhan Mantri Rojgar Protsahan Yojana
PMSBY	Pradhan Mantri Suraksha Bima Yojana
PPD	Permanent Partial Disablement
PPF	Public Provident Fund
PPP	Public-Private Partnership
PREP	Pilot Rural Employment Project
RGSKY	Rajiv Gandhi Shramik Kalyan Yojana
RIHS	Revised Integrated Housing Scheme
RSBY	Rashtriya Swasthya Bima Yojana (National Health Insurance Scheme)
SBI	State Bank of India
SBR	Standard Benefit Rate
SC	Supreme Court of India
SCC	Supreme Court Cases
SCs	Scheduled Castes
SEWA	Self-Employed Women's Association
SICA	Sick Industrial Companies (Special Provisions) Act 1985
SLP	Special Leave to Appeal
SSC	Social Security Code 2020
STs	Scheduled Tribes
TDB	Temporary Disablement Benefit
ULPs	Unfair Labor Practices
UPA	United Progressive Alliance

UWSSA	Unorganized Workers Social Security Act, 2008
VRC	Vocational Rehabilitation Centre
VRS	Voluntary Retirement Scheme
WCA	Workmen's Compensation Act

List of Abbreviations

General Introduction

1. This part aims to provide to the reader a brief background to and a context of the development of social security law in India. It seeks to outline India's economic and social situation, the key features of the social protection system as they have evolved over the years and the sources of the social protection law. There are several problems and limitations that a developing country like India faces in conceptualizing and operationalizing a comprehensive social security programme. An overview of the historical background of the social and economic life of the Indian people as also the composition of Indian population in terms of its general profile, income level, occupational structure and its social characteristics will help fully comprehend India's limitations and compulsions in providing a meaningful social protection to people in general.

§1. Social and Economic Background

2. India is a republic in Southern Asia, with the second highest population in the world after China, which stood at 1.21 billion as per 2011 census. In May 2018, it is estimated to have reached 1.35 billion. The country's area is 3.28 million square kilometres which is the seventh largest in the world. India is known to have a wide range of diversities. Its social and cultural diversity, in fact, is the source of its real strength. India is also the largest democracy in the world, which is governed by a Constitution passed by the Constituent Assembly on 26 November 1949 that came into force on 26 January 1950. The Preamble of the Constitution of India was elaborated and fine-tuned by the forty-second amendment in 1976. This resulted in a more articulate 'sovereign', 'democratic', 'socialist' and 'secular' character of the Republic of India. The integration of 500 princely States of India was done in 1956, when they were reorganized within administrative boundaries as States.

3. India today comprises a Union[1] of twenty-nine States and six Union Territories. The country is a multi-party parliamentary democracy. The Head of the State is the President in whom is vested all executive power. In actuality, however, the

1. While constitutional *pundits* like to call India a federation, the Indian Constitution describes it as a Union of States. The Central (federal) Government enjoys tremendous powers over the State Governments. Its power extends to dismissal of a duly elected State Government in certain circumstances if found necessary, though lately the Supreme Court has intervened in misuse of this power.

real power is vested in the Prime Minister who heads the Central (federal) Government consisting of his Council of Ministers. The Central (federal) legislative power is vested in Parliament which consists of the President and the two houses: House of People (Lok Sabha) – also known as the lower house – and the Council of States (Rajya Sabha) – also known as the Upper House. Both these houses consist of elected members. The Prime Minister is appointed by the President and other ministers are appointed by the President on the advice of the Prime Minister. The Constitution provides that the President shall act on the aid and advice of the Council of Ministers, which is headed by the Prime Minister. Each State is administered by a Governor appointed by the President for a term of five years, while each Union Territory is administered by the President through a Lt. Governor or an administrator appointed by him/her. For every State there is a legislature, which consists of a Governor and a Legislative Assembly. In some States there is a Legislative Council as well. The real power in a State is vested in the Chief Minister, who heads a Council of Ministers at the State level. Like the Prime Minister at the Central level, the Chief Minister advises Governor to exercise the executive power.

4. The Constitution provides that the official language of the Union shall be Hindi, even though English language enjoys an important place both in Government and outside. English is also a connecting link for multi-lingual India, having eighteen official languages in the Eighth Schedule of the Constitution. A British authority Sir George Grierson listed 723 main languages and dialects[2] in India.

5. As per the 2011 census, the following data may be noted: of the total population, 68.84% lives in 649,481 villages. Also, there were 384 urban agglomerations and 5,161 towns in 2001. The rural section of the population is most neglected so far as the provision of basic amenities of living and social security are concerned. Of the total population, people in the category of workers were 402.5 million of which 275.5 million are males and 127.0 million females. Relatively speaking, males comprise 68.4% and females 31.6%.

6. Women form an integral part of the Indian workforce. As can be seen in Table 1, as per census 2011, the total number of female workers in India was 149.8 million comprising 121.8 and 28.0 million in rural and urban areas, respectively. Out of total 149.8 million female workers, 35.9 million females were working as cultivators and another 61.5 million were agricultural labourers. Of the remaining, 8.5 million were in the household industry and 43.7 million were classified as other workers. As per census 2011, the work participation rate for women is 25.51% as compared to 25.63% in 2001.

---

2. *See* 'India', *Encyclopaedia Britannica*, vol. 21 (Chicago, IL: The University of Chicago, 1987), 10.

Table 1 Total Workers in India: 2011 Census

Populations/Workers		*Persons*	*Males*	*Females*
1	2	*3*	*4*	*5*
Population	Total	1,210,569,573	613,121,843	5,874,477,30
Workers		481,743,311	331,865,930	149,877,381
Percentage of Workers		39.79	53.26	25.51
Population	Rural	833,463,448	427,632,643	405,830,805
Workers		348,597,535	226,763,068	121,834,467
Percentage of Workers		41.83	53.03	30.02
Population	Urban	377,106,125	195,489,200	181,616,925
Workers		133,145,776	105,102,862	28,042,914
Percentage of Workers		35.31	53.76	15.44

I. Origin of Modern India

7. India remained under foreign rule for nearly 200 years. The British conquest of India started in 1757 with the Battle of Plassey and got completed only by 1858 with the defeat of the rebellious factions of the Indian army in the Great Mutiny of 1857 and when the British enacted the Government of India Act 1858. The British Rule ended on 15 August 1947. A day before this, the country was partitioned into India and Pakistan. India had been conquered before but usually the invaders settled in India itself. Whereas the early invaders Indianized themselves, the British kept a distance between themselves and the Indian populace. The conquest of India by the British and the pre- and post-conquest trade relations with Europe can be said to have considerably influenced the key socio-economic postulates of Indian development. The British Rule exacerbated the disintegration of the Indian village community by the introduction of the new land revenue systems and also by the process of commercialization of agriculture. Despite this, however, the British contributed to the administrative consolidation of the country through their conquests. These conquests led to administrative regroupings of territories into presidencies and provinces.

8. To understand the socio-economic structure of pre British India, it is essential to know the structure of the village community, which was based on simple division of labour. The farmers cultivated the soil and tended cattle. The country has been caste-ridden since long. Various castes have been carrying on different occupations. There still exist classes of people called, among others, weavers, carpenters, goldsmiths, ironsmiths, cobblers, barbers, scavengers, washermen and oilpressers. These occupations were hereditary and passed by tradition from father to son. These craftsmen were paid remuneration for their work rendered throughout the year by way of a stipend in kind, out of the crops at the harvest time. The food produced by the village was consumed by the village population itself. And the handicraft industry in the village also got its raw material produced at the village level. Thus, Charles Metcalfe labelled the Indian village communities as 'little Republics'[3] having everything they want within themselves. There were the following three types of classes in village India: (a) the agriculturists consisting of landlords and tenants; (b) the village artisans and menials who were servants of the people; and (c) the village officials. The towns were the places of pilgrimage or sacred religious centres or were seats of a court or the capital of a province. Some towns were also trading or commercial centres; hence they were mostly situated on important trade routes.

9. India's chief industry in the pre-British period was textile handicrafts. The Indian exports consisted mainly of manufactures like cotton and silk fabrics, calicos, artistic wares, silk and wool cloth, pepper and cinnamon, opium, indigo, etc. Europe was one of the main customers of India during the seventeenth and eighteenth centuries.

10. The first phase of industrial revolution that originated in Britain had come to an end around 1850. Industry was blooming there. The British found India an important source of its raw material and a market for its finished products. However, the British period had a crippling effect on the Indian handicraft industry, which could not withstand competition from machine-made goods, and had to close down. The British thus took steps to commercialize Indian agriculture, so as to enhance exports of raw materials from India to England.

11. As the British rule was getting established, a new social class was emerging in India. This class of people was keen to imitate Western dress, manners, fashions and customs so as to identify itself with the British officials. This helped to generate the demand for British goods. However, the destruction of Indian handicraft led to unemployment on a vast scale, and the British had no alternative plan of action to settle those who became unemployed in the process. The artisans shifted to land, which in any case was limited. This process was known as progressive ruralization or deindustrialization of India. Around 1850, only 55% of the Indian population was dependent on agriculture, which rose to 68% in 1901 and 72% in 1931. Thus the number of landless workers grew at a fast rate.

12. Another relevant point for discussion here is the impact of the British on the land system in India. So as to bring stability in agriculture, the British introduced the *zamindari* system by converting the status of revenue collectors to that of private landlords called *zamindars*. The *zamindars* were now required to pay an enhanced land revenue to the State. In some parts a system called *ryotwari* was introduced, whereby each peasant who was holding a plot of land was recognized

3. Quoted by Jawaharlal Nehru, *Discovery of India* (Delhi: Oxford University Press, 1947), 302.

as a landlord and made directly responsible to the State for paying the land revenue. But in both cases, the British fixed excessive land rents. Eventually, the net result of their land policy was the emergence of subsistence agriculture.

13. Since 1850, a policy of commercialization of Indian agriculture was spread. Thus, production of crops took place largely for sale rather than for family consumption. This was done by offering to the peasants bait of higher market price. The policy resulted in fall of food production, which also led to the occurrence of some of the most terrible famines in the economic history of India.

14. The British period also saw a large-scale adoption of the British legal and judicial system in the country. The Western liberal values influenced Indian administrative and political formations. University education was designed exactly on British patterns. An elaborate system of bureaucracy was set up through the institution of the elitist Indian Civil Service (ICS). Even though the ICS was symptomatic of an integrated administrative system, it mainly served the colonial interests of the British *Raj* and was so trained as to keep people's participation in the governance structure at bay. After independence the ICS gave way to the now prevalent Indian Administrative Service (IAS), which is largely similar to the former and is often criticized for being indifferent to the people's needs and problems. IAS is known to be the most powerful class in the country which keeps its class interest at the top priority and has been instrumental at bureaucratizing the governance structure, even as the enormity of socio-economic problems in the country need a people-involvement model of governance so as to be effective. That is how, many pieces of social legislation have become merely symbolic, including many labour and social security laws.

15. During the British period India witnessed development of the largest railway network in the world along with the key infrastructure such as post and telegraph, national highways, ports and harbours, among others. This period also saw development of several new cities as per the requirements of trade and commerce. The development of industries and plantations was also intimately related to India's trade relations with Europe. Concurrently, agriculture was commercialized on a fairly large scale. Both these steps helped the colonial goals of the British. After 1870, foodgrains' exports increased because the railway was extensively used to transport food surplus.

16. One of the earliest industries to develop was plantations. In the 1860s and 1870s indigo, tea and coffee plantations grew rapidly. However, the wage labour was employed in these industries on highly exploitative conditions. The tea plantations indulged in large-scale employment of indentured labour. The method of transportation in them was so exploitative that many workers died in the transit. There were a large number of coffee plantations in the south, where labour was imported from the neighbouring districts. However, the terms and conditions of employment in these plantations were comparatively better than those prevailing in the tea industry.

17. About a dozen of cotton textile mills came into existence during the period 1850 to 1860. The setting up of these mills reflected the emergence of the modern factory system. By 1879 there were fifty-six mills employing 43,000 workers. During this period jute industry also developed. Twenty jute mills were in operation by 1882 which employed 20,000 workers. Most cotton mills were located in the Bombay region, whereas the jute mills were located mostly in the Calcutta region. Around the last quarter of the nineteenth century, Indian railways had a mileage of about 8,000 and the country produced one million tonne coal per annum. By the end of the nineteenth century, 194 cotton mills and thirty-six jute mills were in operation and coal production had risen to a figure of over 6 million tonnes per annum.

18. During the nineteenth century, British business pioneered industrial enterprises in India. Apart from the British, the Parsis, the Jews and the Americans were also prominent in the country first as merchants and later as industrialists. Especially Parsis were very progressive in adapting themselves to the demands of European business methods. British merchants and craftsmen were the two principal groups who set up factories in England. But in India these two groups did not take interest in setting up factories. The merchants found themselves more comfortable in their traditional occupations and hence did not give them up to take to factories. The craftsmen, on the other hand, did not have money and training to set up factories. Gradually, however, many communities came forward to set up industries by giving up their trading. Thus, Parsis, Gujaratis, Marwaris, Jains and Chettiars set up industrial ventures.

19. Bombay and Calcutta were the two early principal industrial centres. Both were created by outside capital and immigrant labour. In the industrial centres that developed later, however, the majority of workers were drawn either locally or from the neighbouring areas. These included Ahmedabad, Kanpur and Sholapur, among others. Most factory workers today are also not long-distance migrant workers and are generally drawn from local or neighbouring areas. In some industries such as construction, the incidence of migrant labour is very high. In general, however, growing demographic pressure is visible in increasing number of landless workers through eviction and acquisition of marginal lands. The process of migration of rural labour to urban areas has continued almost incessantly in the post-independence period.

20. Employment in factories has been rising fairly rapidly. The factory employment in 1895 was over 3,81,000, which exceeded the figure of one million by 1931. In 1951, it got more than doubled since 1931 to 2.9 million. The figure was around 4 million in 1961. As per the 2001 census, 41.8 million workers were employed in the manufacturing sector. As per the Census 2011, the total Indian workforce in all sectors was over 487 million.

II. People and Labour Force

21. The issues in social security are intimately related with population growth, literacy rate, the place of females in society, composition of population, poverty line and urbanization. India ranks second in the world in terms of its population, which continues to grow quite rapidly. India today possesses only 2.4% of the total land area of the world but has to support about 17.5% of the world population. The density of population has increased from 230 persons per square kilometre in 1981 to 273 persons per square kilometre in 1991 to 382 in 2011. The density was seventy-seven persons per square kilometre in 1901.

22. A disturbing revelation since the beginning of the twentieth century is the decline in the ratio of females per 1,000 males. There is a decline in sex ratio from 972 in 1901 to 946 in 1951 to 940 in 2011. The decline in sex ratio is largely attributable to poverty in the country. The general condition of the poor people is marked by high infant mortality, extremely poor medical facilities, unhygienic conditions of living, absence of pre-natal and post-natal care and high death rate among women. The poor also prefer to provide better food to the breadwinner who is always male, as it is he who is a source of economic security to the family. In the absence of any effective old age social security schemes, the presence of a son is considered to be an insurance against old age. Thus, comparatively speaking males get better diet and medical care, and so do male infants. This accounts for different mortality rates among males and females. High mortality rates among women in the reproductive age group are also responsible for the declining sex ratio. There are hardly any facilities for especially the rural women for hospitalization for delivery and pre- and post-natal care, which results in more maternal deaths.

23. Labour force participation rate as per 2011 census is 39.79. For females it is 25.51% against 53.26% for males. The rural sector has a better female workforce participation rate of 30.02% compared with 53.03% for males.

24. Most women from poor households participate in labour force, but as the household income rises, they may withdraw from it. They may again join the labour market at a higher level of income when they have acquired a better level of education. As per the 66th round of National Sample Survey Office (NSSO) data released in 2011, over 50% of India's workforce is self-employed. Only 15.5% of employees are regular wage earners and 33.5% are casual labourers. The number of people who are self-employed is higher in rural areas at about 54.2%, against 41.4% in urban areas. The incidence of child labour is also high. As per 2011 census,10.1 million (3.9% of total child population in India) are working, either as 'main worker' or as 'marginal worker;' and more than 42.7 million children in India are out of school. Unofficially, it is believed that it is much higher if we keep in view children studying in schools but also working on fields.

25. The size of the organized sector has been declining in India too as in other countries. The National Sample Survey (NSS) (68th Round) showed that the total workforce in the country was 472.9 million in 2011–2012. In the mid-1970s the organized sector employed 17% employees, but by the 1990s its share had come down to about 10%; it further came down to about 7% in 2020–2021.

Since the late 1990s all new employment is either in the informal sector or in informal jobs in the organized sector. The people who are employed in these informal activities are owners of highly profitable though small enterprises, large farmers, high-income professionals, casual workers below subsistence level wages, marginal farmers, owners of tiny businesses, and street vendors. Those employed as informal workers are characterized by unsecured jobs, unstable employment, low earnings and lack of social security. Their social security needs are quite different and have to be so looked.

As an economy grows, employment declines in agriculture and rises in industry, and then declines in industry too and rises in services. This is how it has happened in most developed countries. Most developed countries have a product structure similar to their employment structure. Mostly GDP contribution of agriculture in these economies constitutes less than 5%. Agriculture in India, however, contributed 59% of GDP in 1950, but only 21.82% in June 2021; the industry contribution figures as on this date were and 29.34% and 54.27% respectively. In terms of employment of workforce in these three sectors, the percentage across sectors in 2020 was: 41.49% in agriculture 26.18% in industry and 32.33% in services.

III. Constitutional Framework of Social Development

26. India is the largest democracy in the world. Its Constitution has stood the test of time for the last seventy years, even as it has been amended one hundred and four times (the last one was in January 2020). One of the latest amendments relates to the new tax regime that is goods and services tax. Several more amendments are expected, including those relating to reservation of seats in Parliament for women. Various political parties in power see hindrances in the constitutional framework for realizing their political, social or economic agenda. Therefore, they have been instrumental in having the Constitution amended so as to pave the way for reform. The Supreme Court of India (SC) had decided[4] by a majority of 7 to 6 judges that the basic structure of the Constitution cannot be changed simply by following the procedure of amendment. It will, perhaps, require the appointment of another Constituent Assembly.

27. The Constitution has its most important parts in Chapters III and IV. The former is titled Fundamental Rights and the latter Directive Principles of State Policy. The Fundamental Rights are modelled after the American Bill of Rights enforceable through the higher judiciary. They limit the power of the legislature to enact laws. The higher judiciary can issue five types of writs to provide remedy to citizens whose fundamental rights are violated. These include the writs of habeas corpus, *mandamus, certiorari,* prohibition and *quo warranto*. These writs can be issued against the State and its agencies when they violate, among others, any of the fundamental rights of citizens. The word State is used very widely to include

4. *Kesavananda Bharti v. State of Kerala*, AIR 1973 SC 1461.

not only Governments and the legislatures of the union and the States, but also local and other authorities including public corporations, Government companies, universities and colleges run with funding from public exchequer or privately through State regulation. The Fundamental Rights pertain to right to equality before law, along with rights to particular freedoms. These particular freedoms include speech; association; movement; residence; profession, trade and business; protection of life and personal liability and religion. The Constitution prevents employment of children below 14 years of age in hazardous employments. It also prevents traffic in human beings and employment of 'forced labour' – a term which has been given quite an extended connotation by a piece of legislation titled Bonded Labour System (Abolition) Act in 1976. Citizens have been guaranteed freedom of conscience and religion. Minorities have been guaranteed the right to culture, script and language and the right to administer educational institutions.[5] Earlier, the right to property was provided as a Fundamental Right, but it is now merely a legal right. In a landmark judgment[6] in 1982 the Supreme Court laid down that poor people, persons in custody or simply women and children can seek enforcement of their Fundamental Rights merely by writing a letter to any Supreme Court judge without an accompanying affidavit. This category of cases has been labelled as public interest litigation (PIL). After this judgment, a large number of cases have been decided by the higher judiciary involving PIL. The Court also pointed out that it could appoint socio-legal commissions or devise some similar procedures to enforce fundamental rights of people. It can also award compensation to the aggrieved where the infringement of rights is gross and patent or it is 'unduly harsh on account of their poverty, disability or socially or economically disadvantaged position'. In a sense, this development of judicial availability to the poor can also be said to be a form of social security to the poor in the Indian context.

28. In its Preamble, the Constitution promises to secure to the people 'justice, social, economic and political; liberty of thought, expression, belief, faith and worship; equality of status and of opportunity; and to promote among them all fraternity assuming the dignity of the individual and the unity and integrity of the Nation'. From a reading of Part IV along with the Preamble the philosophy of the Constitution is discernible. The Directive Principles contained in Part IV are said to be the 'soul of the Constitution'. They represent certain key values which are to be rooted in the 'reconstruction of Indian society and Government along lines of a modern welfare state'.[7] However, these directives are not enforceable in a court of law. But the higher judiciary has declared from time to time the binding nature of some of these directives (i.e., right to primary education). Some of these directives relate to

5. D.K. Agarwal, *INDIA. Constitutional Law*, International Encyclopaedia of Laws (The Netherlands: Kluwer, 1993), Ch. 2.
6. *S.P. Gupta v. Union of India*, AIR 1982 SC 149. It was in this judgment that the strict rule of *locus standi*, or standing was relaxed. A seven-judge Constitution bench, by a majority ruled that any member of the public acting bonafide and having sufficient interest in instituting an action for redressal of public wrong or public inquiry, but who is not a busy body or a meddlesome interloper, could move the court. This judgment is described as the 'Charter of Public Interest Litigation'.
7. M. Galanter, *Law and Society in Modern India* (Delhi: Oxford University Press, 1989).

promotion of welfare of people[8] including minimizing inequalities,[9] directing the State's policy towards securing fulfilment of certain minimum needs,[10] right to work, provision of just and humane conditions of work and maternity relief, living wage, participation of workers in management of industries, free and compulsory education for children, promotion of educational and economic interests of the Schedule Castes (SCs), Schedule Tribes (STs) and other weaker sections and raising the level of nutrition and the standard of living of people and to improve public health.[11] Interestingly, much of the development of labour jurisprudence in the country owes to the provisions contained in Part IV. This part in a way legitimizes the labour's demands raised through demand charters submitted to managements. The judiciary has frequently reminded the executive and the legislature to enact laws to provide for basic needs of the people and to enforce them as per the spirit in which they have been created.

29. Based on the framework of the Directive Principles of State Policy, a fairly large number of pieces of labour legislation (including those on social security) have been enacted by the Central and State legislatures. These laws are broadly classified into the following: employee relation laws; laws of wages and monetary benefits; laws of social security; and laws relating to conditions of work. Labour being a subject in the Concurrent List in the Indian Constitution, the States and Union Territories of India have in some cases enacted their own labour laws over and above the Central laws to suit local situations and power realities.[12] Central and State labour enactments in the country add up to nearly 200. In fact, it has been generally argued that labour class is over-protected in India through labour laws. Despite that, however, the cases of violation of labour and social security laws are too many; so much so that often when one sees working conditions of the unorganized workers, one

---

8. Art. 38(1) obliges the State to: 'strive to promote the welfare of the people by securing and promoting as effectively as it may a social order in which justice, social, economic and political, shall inform all the institutions of national life'.
9. Art. 38(2) provides that: 'the State shall, in particular, strive to minimize the inequalities in income, and endeavour to eliminate inequalities in status, facilities and opportunities, not only amongst individuals but also amongst groups of people residing in different areas or engaged in different vocations'.
10. Art. 39 envisages State policies to be directed towards ensuring: (a) that the citizens, men and women equally, have the right to an adequate means of livelihood; (b) that the ownership and control of the material resources of the community are so distributed as best to subserve the common good; (c) that the operation of the economic system does not result in the concentration of wealth and means of production to the common detriment; (d) that there is equal pay for equal work for both men and women; (e) that the health and strength of workers, men and women, and the tender age of children are not abused and that citizens are not forced by economic necessity to enter vocations unsuited to their age or strength; (f) that children are given opportunities and facilities to develop in a healthy manner and in conditions of freedom and dignity and that childhood and youth are protected against exploitation and against moral and material abandonment.
11. Art. 47 provides that the State shall regard: 'the raising of the level of nutrition and the standard of living of its people and the improvement of public health as among its primary duties'.
12. Debi S. Saini, 'Labour Legislation and Social Justice', *Economic and Political Weekly*, 25 Sep. 1999, L-32–L-40.

wonders whether any such laws exist for them at all.[13] In fact, in the era of globalization, the number of such violations has substantially increased, as state agencies are often seen siding more with the interests of employers. The hire and fire policies of employers have substantially increased, despite the fact that old pieces of labour protection legislation remain unaltered.

30. Overall, the Constitution envisages an egalitarian conception of development. It commands law for production of policies and programmes of action for empowering the poorer and the disempowered sections of society. Areas in which such action has been undertaken through State efforts include unorganized labour, women, children, SCs and other backward classes (OBCs). Given the hierarchical, feudal nature of Indian society, one is expected to witness in it prevalence of evils such as slavery, bonded labour, untouchability, deprivation of childhood to working children, illiteracy and subordination of women. All these problems arise because of the presence of acutely hegemonic groups in our society where people exploit others due to their superior power of money, muscle, rank or position. Taking a cue from the constitutional mandate to the State to muster proactive efforts in eradication of the above evils, we will briefly discuss how these problems have been acted upon.

31. Primary education is the basic *sine qua non* for the disempowered so that they can appreciate the framework of empowerment to which they are being subjected through State action. Education provides the basic foundation for good citizenship, and it is a primary vehicle for imparting cultural values in children, and making them adjust to the fast-changing environment around them. Article 45 of the Constitution promises free and compulsory education for all children till the age of 14 years. The article provided to achieve complete literacy by 1960 but the country still has miles to go to achieve that goal. As per the 2011 census the *literacy* rate for the population seven years and above was 74.04% [Males: 80%; and Females: 65.4628%]. Article 46 obliges the State to promote with special care the educational and economic interest of the weaker sections of the people and in particular those belonging to the SCs and Scheduled Tribes (STs). Keeping the saliency of these rights in view, the Supreme Court, in one of its judgments, held the right to education to be a fundamental right.[14] This judgment led to amendment of the Constitution making the right to education a fundamental right. The Right to Education Act 2009 is a landmark legislation which gives right to free and compulsory education for children between the ages of 6 and 14. It also provides 25% reservation for students from the weaker sections in private schools.

A very serious problem in operationalizing compulsory primary education is high rate of drop-outs. A national programme of nutritional support to children in primary education commonly called the Midday Meal Scheme was launched by the Central Government. This scheme is aimed to improve enrolment, attendance and retention as well as upgrading the nutritional status of students in primary classes.

13. Arjun Patel & Kiran Desai, 'Rural Migrant Labour and Labour Laws', in *Labour Law, Work and Development*, ed. Debi S. Saini (New Delhi: Westwill, 1995).
14. *Unni Krishnan J.P. v. State of A.P.* (1993) 1 SCC 645.

Under the scheme, students studying in classes I to V in all primary schools run by Government and local bodies are provided cooked/processed food. It envisages central assistance for reimbursing the cost of food grains. Provision has also been made for special assistance for education of women, SC/ST candidates, minorities and adults.

32. Untouchability is another important area in India that needs proactive action of the State. India is a largely caste-ridden society. The lowest of the four broad categories of social divisions, i.e., *shudras* consist of those who work manually, usually for the benefit of higher castes. Out of the *shudras* some castes have been treated for centuries as untouchables. These include mainly scavengers, sweepers, skin-flayers, apart from several other categories of untouchables. They have been referred to as the SCs. They are the most unfortunate social categories of Hindu caste hierarchy and are scattered throughout India. They have been exploited economically and oppressed socially by other castes including the higher categories of *shudras*. The SCs are usually landless and bonded workers with the landed aristocracy or with other category of farmers; or they work in factories or small-scale industries. The incidence of illiteracy among them is appalling – in some cases it is as high as 95% of the population belonging to SCs.

Providing social protection to these classes of people is a more complex issue in India, for they are both economically as well as socially deprived citizens. Article 17 of the Constitution confers upon the SCs a fundamental right against the practice of untouchability vis-à-vis them. Its practice is made punishable by law. So as to uplift their social status by uplifting their economic status, the Constitution provides a positive discrimination in their favour in Government jobs. Reservations have benefited the SCs substantially; at least it makes provision of an opportunity to be availed of by them. Taking a cue from the central spirit of the Constitution, the independent India enacted the Untouchability Offences Act (UOA) in 1955. This law, which was renamed as the Protection of Civil Rights Act (CRA) in 1976, outlaws untouchability directly or indirectly. Later on, the Government realized that the atrocities on the SCs were rising phenomenally. This was more so due to their greater assertion of right consciousness created because of their empowerment. Therefore, a new law was enacted so as to provide for more stringent punishment for commission of such practices. It was titled the SCs/STs (Prevention of Atrocities) Act 1989. The Act defines untouchability precisely and introduces stringent measures for preventing commission of atrocities on these castes and tribes. This law also envisages a special court to be appointed by the State Government for each district to try offences under the Act.

33. Due to low literacy, SCs and STs do not have much access to the job market. If they get education, they find it difficult to compete with the candidates from the higher castes especially for more sought-after jobs in Government and public sector enterprises. Article 15(4) of the Constitution provides that special provisions can be made for SCs/STs and OBCs (Other Backward Classes) in relation to job reservations. Article 46 talks about promotion of educational and economic interests of weaker sections especially SCs/STs, and protecting them against social injustice and all forms of exploitation. The Government has provided 15% and 7.5% reservations respectively in favour of SCs and STs in jobs, as also in admissions to colleges and universities.

34. Article 16(4) empowers the State to make provision for reservations in appointments or posts in favour of 'any backward class' of citizens which in the opinion of the State is not adequately represented in services under the State. A Commission (The Mandal Commission) appointed by the Janata Party Government, in its report submitted in 1980, found that Other Backward Classes (OBCs) can be Hindus and non-Hindus both, and such castes/occupations were found to be numbering about 3,743. Later, the Janata Dal Government led by the then Prime Minister V.P. Singh implemented the job reservations for OBCs; 27% Government jobs are now reserved for this category of people. This is believed to be a revolutionary step in uplifting the status of these communities in the caste-ridden India. This step has immensely aroused the rights consciousness in these communities, which has also led to a redefinition of socio-political agendas in the country. In the post-Mandal era, major political parties are competing to project OBC candidates as the Chief Minister in various States.

35. In a country like India where poverty and unemployment are acute, workers are likely to offer themselves for wage employment at very low or even starvation wages. There have been several cases where these workers took loans from the traditional money-lender but could not pay the interests and principal amount, and agreed to provide them labour until the repayment of the loan. Such instances created the institution of bonded labour, the incidence of which was very high at one time. Especially, the workers from the lower castes including the SCs/STs and children are more susceptible to become victims of the bonded labour system. This system is highly exploitative and cannot be accepted in any enlightened society. The Constitution of India through Article 23 abolished the bonded labour system throughout the length and breadth of the country. But since the problem still prevailed, the Bonded Labour System (Abolition) Act was enacted in 1976. This Act is supplementary to Article 23 of the Constitution. It prohibits making of any advance to a worker which can become a bonded debt and prohibits compelling any person to render bonded labour. It declares any custom of bonded labour in a family void, abolishes liability to pay bonded debt, and frees any attachment of the bonded worker. The District Magistrate has been obliged to promote welfare of freed bonded workers and protect their economic interests. It creates Vigilance Committees to identify and ensure abolition of bonded workers. An important social protection question in the country is the rehabilitation of bonded workers.

36. No enlightened society can allow its children to be subjected to work at a tender age. But in a land of poverty such as India, the incidence of child labour is bound to be high. As per the 1991 census the number of child workers was 11 million, which as per 2011 census came down marginally to 10.1 million. But unofficial data suggest a much higher figure. It is estimated that about 80% child workers in India are from SCs/STs, and they are mostly those who live below the poverty line. Article 24 of the Constitution envisages a Fundamental Right of children, i.e., not to be required to work in factories or hazardous occupations. The Supreme Court has taken the provisions of these articles quite seriously, and has provided that this Article is enforceable not just against Government and its agencies but even against individual citizens. Article 39 provides certain principles of policy to be followed by the State. These principles, among others, include that health and strength of workers including that of children is not abused and children are given facilities for developing in a healthy manner with freedom and dignity. Even as the best friends of children were waiting for compulsory primary education to become a reality, the Government of India in 1986 enacted the Child Labour (Prohibition and Regulation) Act, which in a way has considerably harmed the child labour abolition agenda. Rather it has accepted the legitimacy of child labour by providing for its regulation in most cases and its abolition in only some. The Act regulates the work of children who are below 14 years in cases they are permitted to work. It provides stringent punishment for violation of the law.

37. Article 40 of the Constitution gives a directive to the Indian State to take steps to organize *Gram Panchayats* (village councils) and endow them with powers, so that they can function as units of self-government. So as to be in consonance with the spirit of this article, India effected revolutionary changes in its laws relating to village and local governance. In 1992, the Constitutional Amendments (73rd and 74th) were enacted to this effect. The 73rd amendment transferred power for determining priorities in planning at the grass-root level. It confers constitutional status on *panchayat* bodies (village councils) and endows them with powers of self-governance. One can also witness in the new dispensation decentralization of development activities, which among others, emphasizes active people-participation in such activities. Reservation of seats in these councils has been provided for women and people belonging to the SCs and STs.

38. Women empowerment should be an important issue in the social protection agenda in any society. India is presently witnessing a debate about reserving one-third of the seats for women in Parliament. Even as there is near unanimity among political parties about the percentage of such reservation, they have not been able to resolve connected issues. India needs to pursue policies that can affect fundamental change of attitudes in State and society towards women. Following are the major areas of action that we need to focus on improving wage conditions for women; equality of wages between men and women; protection of women from problems resulting from their biological situation and access to credit and training for the self-employed.

IV. The Economy and the Social Sector

39. Compared to other countries in Asia, such as South Korea, Taiwan, Singapore, Hong Kong, Malaysia, China and Thailand; India has experienced relatively slow economic progress in the 1990s. However, in the first decade of this century and even after that, the country has attained impressive rate of growth. In some respects, it is certainly better than most other developing countries. It has a well-developed economic and political structure, an experienced administrative system and a comprehensive network of transport and communication. Due to the importance given to the public sector in the post-independence period, India has been able to develop a fairly sophisticated industrial base. India opted for a planned economy and implemented five-year plans in this regard. The twelfth five-year plan completed its term in March 2017. The new government led by Prime Minister Narendra Modi, which assumed office in 2014, dissolved the Planning Commission, and replaced it by a think tank called the NITI Aayog (policy commission). On the social justice front, a comprehensive set of labour laws provide protection to especially industrial employees in many areas, which conform closely to international standards. But the employers in the huge small-scale sector indulge in unfair labour practices (ULPs) so as to negate the benefit of labour laws to employees.[15] In the modern era of globalization, however, Indian labour law is criticized for breeding inflexibility, resistance to change, over-protection to labour, and inefficiency. Most of the 245 odd public sector enterprises and 850 odd state enterprises in India are not running efficiently. India lags far behind in productivity and work culture. It has a large supply of educated manpower, but the problem of unemployment and under-employment is acute.

40. Some of the other key economic problems that the country faces include poverty, unemployment, inequalities in income, over-population, illiteracy, inadequate health care facilities for the majority of the population and poor nutritional status of the population. As per the World Bank's 2016 estimates 270 million of India's 1.3 billion population is poor, which is about 20%. But a small elite group enjoys an extremely high standard of living. India is estimated to have the largest middle class in the Third World. It is estimated that about 267 million people belonged to this class in 2016, which is likely to be doubled to 547 million by 2025–2026. This class of people is also the biggest beneficiary of State action including social security provisions. India undertook economic reforms as late as 1991. But it is argued that the reforms are not likely to solve the chronic problem of poverty and unemployment at least in the short run. It is argued by the champions of social justice that the key economic problems of India have become more acute in the post-reforms period, because of the reduced role that the State has assumed for itself in the social sector.

41. The problem of poverty in India is intimately related with unemployment and underemployment. The Government has come out with Mahatma Gandhi National Rural Employment Guarantee Act (MNREGA) which seeks to provide 100 days' employment in a year to adult members of the family failing which to give them unemployment allowance.

42. Education is the most crucial investment in human development. The illiteracy rate in the country is still very high. The Government has given a high priority to education, so as to promote human resources development. Its education

15. Debi S. Saini & Pawan Budhwar, 'Managing the Human Resource in Indian SMEs: The Impact of Indigenous Realities on Effectiveness', *Journal of World Business* 43, no. 4 (2008).

agenda includes total eradication of illiteracy; gradual increase in the governmental and non-governmental spending on education; making primary education free and compulsory up to 5th Standard and to improve the quality of education. Right to primary education has now been made a fundamental right, and Government is making all out efforts to put this into operation. The Central Government has framed in 2018 a health insurance scheme called Ayushman Bharat Yojana which is claimed to revolutionize the health protection system in the country. It is aimed at making the comparatively less well-off and poor people in the country in return of nominal premium eligible for cashless treatment in all government hospitals and also select private hospitals.

43. With the improvement in technology, people now have better access to health care which has resulted in a steep fall in mortality. Despite that, however, the burden of diseases and nutritional problems continues to be high. There is deterioration in rural and urban sanitation, and the system for liquid and solid waste disposal remains quite poor.

44. Besides the poor people in general, India has the peculiar caste-system related problems. Considerable social stigma is attached to the SCs which will take a long period to root out. Backward classes and minorities also suffer from a high incidence of social and economic backwardness. The Central Government is running several schemes for their welfare. The Government has also devised some schemes for the disabled and older persons.

45. India has a high incidence of poverty. The above issues in social and economic development get deeply intertwined with the social security agenda in developing countries. Especially, the social scientists in the Third World are not inclined to confine social security agenda to contingencies-related susceptibilities. Poverty-alleviation programmes, employment generation programmes, subsidies on food and other essential items, housing, etc. become deeply integrated in their social security agenda. Keeping in view the fact that a large section of the population needs state assistance in these areas, they have come to be treated as an inalienable part of social security system. However, lawyers confine themselves mainly to the statutory social security provisions.

§2. Salient Features of the Indian System

46. First of all, it is important to understand the structure of the Indian social security system as it has historically evolved. It is well known that developing countries have dualistic economies, which consist of formal and informal sectors. Those employed in the formal sector enjoy comparatively higher wages and better service conditions; better protection of labour law; and better bargaining power through associations and unions. In a way, people employed in this sector are an opinion-making class in society. Formal sector employees[16] are employed in comparatively larger establishments, Government departments and undertakings, autonomous corporations and multinational companies (MNCs). In India, some of the small enterprises also provide labour law benefits without attempting to violate them through commission of unfair labour practices (ULPs). Employees in the formal sector usually enjoy social security benefits, though they are not comparable to those available to citizens in the developed world. The informal sector represents the unprotected segment of the labour market. Employees belonging to this sector are usually casual or contract workers, low-paid workers having almost no labour law protection, home-based workers, and are usually employed in small establishments. The informal sector can be rural (including agricultural) as well as urban.

47. The traditional forms of social security were started so as to cover comparatively powerful occupational groups in the formal sector, who could influence public policy through well-organized associations and trade unions. The most notable among such groups are the Government employees who are in the most advantageous position to enforce social protection. Initially, social security measures were designed and developed to meet the needs of such groups of employees. Their main concerns have been preserving the value of their earning, job security, medical care, protection against old age, etc. That is why, traditional forms of social security are mainly of protective nature. At the international level, these protections have been standardized through the conventions and recommendations of the International Labour Organization (ILO).

48. At the national level social protection is made available through labour and social security laws, which can be guided by the standards set by the ILO. The employees in the informal sector have received such protection much later. Their needs are met only in piecemeal or through ad hoc State actions or voluntary organizations. International action in support of their problems is still in the experimental stage and defies concrete course of action.

49. The development of social protection framework in India as well has followed the above pattern of evolution. The Directive Principles of State Policy as enshrined in the Constitution of India recognize the right to social protection for all citizens. But these directives are not enforceable in any court of law. Interestingly, the Supreme Court has held them to be 'nevertheless fundamental in the governance of the country'. And, the judiciary has time and again expressed its advice to

16. The term employee is not uniformly used in all pieces of labour and social security legislation in India; and therefore, is quite problematic. Ideally, they should all use the term employee or worker. For example, ESI and ECA, PGA, EPFA use the term 'employee', MBA uses the word 'woman employed'; the Factories Act uses the word 'worker'; the IDA and CLA use the term 'workman'; UWSSA uses 'Unorganized Workers', 'home-based workers', and 'wage workers'. In this connection it may be noted that we have tried to use in this volume the same term as is used by the legislation being referred to. While talking of employed people in general the word worker is being used when the reference is to manual worker; and employee when reference is to all categories of workers.

the Government to apply them in making laws and policies. Following these directives, the legislature in India has provided social protection through statutory laws. Collective agreements in the formal sector also reflect provision of social security measures by the employers. The statutory social protection is provided usually through social insurance laws or by obliging the employers to provide protection through their unilateral efforts. The informal sector employees in India enjoy very little social protection through law. Some sections of these employees are, however, covered under laws such as the Employees' Compensation Act, 1923 (ECA) and the Minimum Wages Act, 1948. State Governments also provide for some amount of social protection, especially to senior citizens and disabled people, by way of social assistance. But these measures are highly inadequate. In some spheres of employment, welfare funds have been created by the Central Government for protecting the employees concerned.

50. There was no social security system in India before the British Indian Government enacted the Workmen's Compensation Act 1923 (WCA). However, the joint family system in India is well-known and could be viewed as an important source of social security in a broad sense of the term. Religious solidarity practiced by various religious groups can also be looked at as a supplement to the social security provided by the joint family system. We will be, however, concerned here largely with the formal system of social security available to Indian people.

51. The Constitution of India in its seventh schedule contains three lists – Central List (List I), State List (List II), and Concurrent List (List III) for the purpose of deciding legislation authority under various spheres of State responsibility. For matters contained in List I only Parliament, the Central Legislature, can enact a law; for matters in List II only the State Legislature concerned can enact a law; and for matters contained in List III, both Central and State Legislatures can enact a law. However, in case of repugnancy between the laws passed by the Central Legislature and the State Legislature in relation to a matter specified in List III, the Central law will prevail over State law unless President's assent has been accorded to such a State law. Most labour matters including social security find place in List III (Concurrent List). This includes trade unions, industrial and labour disputes; social security and social insurance, employment and unemployment; welfare of labour including conditions of work, provident funds, employers' liability, employees' compensation, invalidity and old age pensions and maternity benefits and factories. Regulation of labour and safety in mines and oilfields, however, is the exclusive domain of the Central Legislature. Likewise, relief of the disabled and unemployable is under the exclusive jurisdiction of the State Legislatures. Since most labour matters fall in the Concurrent List, Parliament has enacted labour laws in almost all these matters including social security. But many states have carried out amendments in these central laws keeping in view the labour policy of the state concerned.

52. The Indian system of social security can be divided into four broad types, namely employer's unilateral liability, social insurance, provident funds, and social assistance. The most usual type of social security with widest coverage envisages employer's unilateral liability as imposed by a legislation. This is also the most primitive and is sometimes described by academicians as the decaying form of social protection because it does not contain any insurance or assistance element in it. It merely involves a statutory liability of the employer to provide certain protection to the employee. The employer has the option to insure its liability under these laws or create a fund for meeting its liability. Four Indian laws come under this heading: Employees' Compensation Act 1923 (ECA); Maternity Benefit Act (MBA), 1961; Payment of Gratuity Act 1972 (PGA); and some portions of the Industrial Disputes Act 1947 (IDA).

53. The key social insurance law in the country is the Employees' State Insurance Act 1948 (ESIA), which envisages an employees' state insurance scheme (ESIS). The ESIS is contributory in character whereby employers, employees and to a certain extent the State contribute to a fund, out of which various types of benefits are provided to the beneficiaries. The amount of benefit is usually proportionate to the average daily wage of the employee concerned. The average daily wage of the employee also determines the contributions payable by him or her to the Employees' Provident Fund Scheme (EPFS). Contributions to the EPF scheme are made by the workers as well as their employers who pay regular contribution into a fund created under the EPF Scheme. Such contributions are credited to the accounts of the subscribers concerned. The fund is invested as per the norms laid down in this regard. Annual interest is credited to the account of the employee on the total amount of PF deposit in his or her account. When an employee superannuates or dies or seeks retirement, the balance standing to the account is refunded to him/her. One may argue that a provident fund is not a social security in the strict sense of the term. But this type of scheme provides significant protection during the old age. The main law in this regard is the Employees' Provident Fund and Miscellaneous Provisions Act 1952 (EPFA). The EPF Scheme has been framed under this Act. This Act also envisages an employee pension scheme (EPS) under which the covered employees receive monthly pension after retirement or death subject to certain conditions. Social assistance is provided by most State Governments to certain classes of people out of their own resources. A peculiar method of providing social assistance in India is through welfare funds. Such funds are created through levying of cess on goods manufactured or their exports in a specific industry. Various types of subsidies are provided to the beneficiaries from these funds. As observed earlier, relief to the disabled and unemployable is the exclusive domain of the State Governments.

I. Traditional System of Social Protection

A. *Compensation for Occupational Accidents and Diseases*

54. The enactment of the ECA[17] symbolizes the beginning of social security in India. It was passed in 1923 on the model of a similar Act in Britain. This Act came into operation in July 1924. It provides for payment of compensation by the employer to its/his employees in case of occupational accidents resulting into temporary or permanent disablement. Compensation is also payable to the dependants in case of death of the employee. Certain categories of occupational diseases are also covered under ECA. This Act provides for payment of compensation only in those cases where the disablement or death results from an injury due to an accident arising out of and in the course of employment. Injuries by accident also include contracting of some diseases in certain circumstances. Interestingly, the employer's liability is not based on any negligence on the part of the employer. However, cases covered must have a rational nexus with the employment and must normally take place during the working hours and at the employer's premises, except where the premises are notionally extended in some special circumstances. Thus, the ECA overrides the common law rule of voluntary assumption of risk under which the employer was mostly not responsible to pay damages to his employees as they were presumed to be working subject to the risk involved in the work.

B. *The Maternity Relief*

55. Maternity benefit for women is an important aspect of social security schemes almost all over the world. The first legislative attempt to provide maternity relief in India was made in 1929 when the Government of Bombay enacted the MBA in 1929. In 1930 the Central Province (now known as the State of Madhya Pradesh) also enacted a law to this effect. Later on, most other provinces enacted laws on similar lines. Apart from these State legislations, the Central Legislature also enacted the Mines MBA in 1941, which applied to women workers employed in mines. The ESI Act which was enacted by the Central Legislature in 1948 also provides for maternity benefit. In 1951, the Plantations Labour Act was enacted to provide for such benefit to plantation workers. With a view to reducing the disparities between the above State-enacted legislation, Parliament (the Central Legislature) enacted the MBA in 1961 (MBA). This law provides that all women employees shall be paid maternity benefit in case of child birth, miscarriage or sickness arising out of pregnancy. This Act also envisages a unilateral responsibility of the employer and the scheme has no insurance element in it. A worker when governed by the ESI Act cannot claim maternity relief under the MBA.

---

17. As originally enacted, this Act was named the Workmen's Compensation Act 1923 (WCA). This name has been altered in 2010; this Act has been amended and the new name is the ECA.

C. Retirement Benefits Including Pensions

56. There is no general scheme of retirement benefits payable to common people in the country. Retirement benefits are available only in the organized sector including government employment.

These benefits include provident funds, the pension scheme drafted under the main EPF law in the country, and gratuity. The Central as well as State Governments provide attractive retirement benefits to their employees.

57. The main legislation which provides for creation of the EPFS, the Deposit-linked Insurance Scheme and the Employees' Pension Scheme (EPS), is the EPFA which applies to establishments belonging to 180 industries or classes of businesses. For workers employed in coal mines, the relevant law is the Coal Mines Provident Fund and Miscellaneous Provisions Act 1948. The EPF Act has a wider applicability and has very wide scope and coverage.

The Family Pension Scheme (FPS) framed under the EPF Act in 1971 has been replaced by the EPS. The EPS provides for pension on superannuation, retirement, permanent total disablement and death. The Employees' Deposit-Linked Insurance Scheme 1976 (EDLIS) was framed under the EPF Act. This scheme provides added social security for those employees who are members of the EPF and the Coal Mines Provident Fund. This scheme provides an insurance cover to the persons covered without payment of any premium for this purpose. The insurance cover has been linked to the average balance in the provident fund account of the deceased during twelve months preceding his or her death subject to a ceiling.

58. Another important method in India to provide cash benefits is by way of payment of gratuity to replace at least partly the loss of income at the time of superannuation, retirement or resignation, and death or disablement due to accident or disease. Gratuity is a lump sum payment which is payable under a central law, i.e., the Payment of Gratuity Act 1972 (PGA). It is a benefit payable by the employer for termination of service of an employee. Ordinarily, for being entitled to gratuity, an employee must have completed with the employer concerned at least five years of continuous service.

D. Unemployment Benefits

59. Till recently, India had no system of providing social security in the contingencies of unemployment for common people. This is so, despite the 'right to work' having been provided for in the Constitution as a Directive Principle of State Policy. These directives as observed earlier, have been accepted as fundamental in the governance of the country. Perhaps, the unemployment and the underemployment situations in the country are so acute that no government has gone into the feasibility of introducing a system of unemployment insurance. In 2004, the then government evolved a scheme of employment guarantee of unskilled work to those living below the poverty line (BPL). This scheme was enacted into a legislation called the National Rural Employment Guarantee Act 2005 (NREGA). Later on the Act was renamed as Mahatma Gandhi National Rural Employment Guarantee Act. This Act has been seen as a historic one in a country like India, where a very large section of population suffers from very high incidence of under-employment. Under this Act, any person is eligible to get job guarantee if she/he is above the age of 18 and resides in rural areas. The scheme provides a 100 days' limit on the number of days of work that a household[18] can get in a year. Workers getting employment under this scheme are employed mostly in public works. They are entitled to the statutory minimum wage fixed for agricultural workers in the state concerned, unless the Central Government 'notifies' a different norm.

60. The IDA, mainly provides a settlement mechanism for industrial dispute resolution. However, it also contains Chapter V in it which provides some amount of benefits in case a worker concerned becomes unemployed due to lay off, retrenchment, or closure of the establishment concerned. The provision for lay off and retrenchment were introduced for the first time, when the Government of India promulgated an ordinance in October 1953 which made it obligatory for all establishments covered by the IDA to pay lay-off and retrenchment compensation to the workers concerned affected by such lay-off and retrenchment. Later on the IDA was amended in December 1953 to incorporate the ordinance. The idea underlying the retrenchment and closure compensation is to help the workers to maintain themselves until they are able to find alternative jobs.

II. Modern System of Social Insurance

61. Almost immediately after getting independence on 15 August 1947, India introduced an insurance element in the existing system of social protection through employer's unilateral liability. The ESIA, was enacted in 1948. The ESI Act has its genesis in the report of Professor B.P. Adarkar completed in 1944, who had been appointed as special officer to prepare a scheme of health insurance for industrial workers. On request from the Government of India, this report was reviewed by two experts from the ILO, who suggested certain modifications in it in view of the adoption of social insurance principles by other countries. The modified Adarkar Plan was introduced as Workmen's State Insurance Bill 1946, which was eventually passed by the Dominion Legislature in 1948 as ESI. It symbolizes the beginning of social insurance for industrial workers in India. This law has an all-India coverage and provides for a wide range of benefits, including sickness, disability, death, maternity, medical care, dependants' pension and reimbursement of funeral expenses. In fact, this is the main law providing social security to workers in India. But it applies to a very small section of the working class that constitutes the organized sector.

18. Each nuclear family counts as a separate 'household'.

As on 31 March 2020, data related to the ESIC was as follows:

State/Union Territories covered	35
No. of Employees	30,966,930
No. of Insured Persons/Family Units	34,144,140
No. of Insured Women	6,265,035
Total Beneficiaries	132,479,263
No. of Employers covered	1,236,565
Branch Offices/Pay Offices	559/185
Dispensaries cum branch offices	49
ESI Hospitals	159
ESI Annexes	42
ESI Dispensaries cum ISM units	1,502/308
Insurance Medical Officers	8,626
Insurance Medical Practitioners	1,287
Total Income	22,161.91 crores[19]

§3. SOURCES OF SOCIAL SECURITY LAW

62. Indian social security law can be locatable in the following sources:

(i) Primary Legislation – Acts of Parliament and State Assemblies
(ii) Secondary Legislation – Regulations and Rules to give effect to the legislations
(iii) Case Law – Decisions of the Supreme Court, various High Courts and the Employees Insurance Courts
(iv) Collective Bargaining
(v) Individual Contracts
(vi) International Standards
(vii) International Agreements and Conventions.

I. Legislation

63. The provision of some aspect of social security in India can be seen in the Fatal Accidents Act 1855. This law provides for payment of compensation to the family for loss occasioned to it by the death of a worker concerned. This law modified the common law. The right to compensation under the Act arises, if the death was due to the neglect or default of another person including the employer. Another

19. In India one crore is ten million.

legislation that modified the common law position about workers' vulnerability while they are on work is the Employers' Liability Act 1938. This Act as amended in 1951 declares that certain defences of common law shall not be raised by an employer in suits for damages filed against them in respect of injuries sustained by a worker concerned. These two pieces of social security legislation are the ones which modify common law about employment-related injuries.

64. Certain pieces of legislation envisage unilateral responsibility of the employer towards their employees in certain situations. Principally, the key law in this regard is the ECA, which envisages payment of compensation unilaterally by the employer to the employee concerned in case of death and disablement connected with the work. Likewise, the Maternity Benefits Act 1960 (MBA) provides for the payment of maternity benefit to women workers, subject to certain conditions, in case of child birth, miscarriage or abortion, and sickness arising out of pregnancy.

The IDA in its Chapters V-A and V-B provides for payment of compensation to the workman[20] concerned by the employer in case of involuntary unemployment resulting from lay-off, retrenchment and closure. These provisions also envisage unilateral liability of the employer; there is no insurance element in this protection.

Some pieces of legislation provide for retiral benefits. They include the EPFA Coal Mines Provident Fund and Bonus Scheme Act 1948; Seamen's Provident Fund Act 1966; and the Payment of Gratuity Act 1972. In this category of laws only the last one envisages a unilateral liability of the employer. Others involve joint liability of the employer and the worker to contribute to a fund that eventually seeks to provide protection in case a worker superannuates, resigns, dies or is discharged from service.

65. In addition to Acts of Parliament, which set out the basic policy framework, secondary legislative activity is carried out by the Government or the autonomous body created by a legislation on social security. Two well-known bodies of this type are the Employees' State Insurance Corporation (ESIC) as envisaged under the ESI Act and the Employees' Provident Fund Organization (EPFO) as envisaged under the EPF Act. The EPF legislation consists of schemes framed under specific social security legislation. For example, four schemes have been framed by the Central Government under the EPF Act. They are the Provident Fund Scheme; the Family Pension Scheme; the Deposit-Linked Insurance Scheme; and the Pension Scheme. Likewise, the Government has made rules under all the social security laws relating to administration of the protection envisaged by the concerned social security law. A law enacted by Parliament or State legislature is not complete unless it is read with the help of rules and regulations framed there under; the latter are called delegated legislation. It consists of all law-making which takes place outside the legislature and is generally expressed in the form of rules, regulations, byelaws, orders,

20. In India, while referring to the person covered, some pieces of legislation use the term worker, some use the term workman, and some use the term employee. The effort in this volume on India is to use the relevant term as has been used by the particular piece of legislation being referred to. The IDA uses the term 'workman'.

schemes, directions or notifications. The rules are not subject to detailed debate and voting in Parliament. They are just laid before Parliament. The ESI Corporation [envisaged under the ESI Act 1948] has enacted ESI (Regulations) for administering the ESI Scheme. The rules and regulations are enacted keeping in mind the operational needs for giving effect to the various provisions of the Act concerned.

66. So far, the social security system in the country mainly caters to the organized sector; the masses who work in the unorganized sector have no social protection worth the name. Of course, a few steps have recently been taken to mitigate the miseries of those living below the poverty line. Their needs are employment opportunities and minimum income support. Much of their expectations do not fall under the heading of social security per se in the scope of this term as known in the developed world. But social security provision to a microscopic minority does not mean much in a country of 1,300 million people. In a situation of mass poverty, the developing world needs to redefine the term social security in terms of the requirements of the commoners. Unfortunately, the progress in this area is very slow.

67. On the positive side, however, for the first time in the history of India, a job guarantee legislation[21] has been passed by Indian Parliament on 25 August 2005, which is titled as the National Rural Employment Guarantee Act 2005 (NREGA).[22] This legislation has been renamed as Mahatma Gandhi National Rural Employment Guarantee Act 2005 (MNREGA). MNREGA provides some kind of livelihood security to the poor; it envisages providing at least 100 days of guaranteed wage employment in a financial year to a rural household whose adult member is prepared to volunteer doing unskilled manual work. The Act aims to provide some economic security in India's rural areas. Under MNREGA, 100 days of employment (or unemployment allowance) per household must be provided to able and willing workers, every financial year. It is up to the State Government to decide the amount of unemployment allowance, subject to the stipulation that it should not be less than one-fourth of the minimum wage for the first thirty days, and not less than half of the minimum wage thereafter. This Act aims at improving the purchasing power of the rural people, primarily by providing semi- or un-skilled work to people living in rural India, whether or not they are below the poverty line.

68. The MNREGA is expected to achieve twin objectives of rural development and employment. It stipulates that works must be targeted towards a set of specific rural development activities such as water conservation and harvesting, afforestation, rural connectivity, flood control and protection such as construction and repair of embankments, etc. Digging of new tanks/ponds, percolation tanks and construction of small check dams are also given importance. Workers willing to take employment under the scheme are given work such as land levelling, tree plantation, etc.

---

21. Dr Jean Drèze, a Belgian born economist, at the Delhi School of Economics, University of Delhi, has been a major influence on this project.
22. The new name, Mahatma Gandhi National Rural Employment Guarantee Act, 2005 (MNREGA was given on 2 Oct. 2009, the birthday of Mahatma Gandhi, the Father of the Nation).

69. The MNERGA scheme operates like this: The adult members of rural households submit their name, age and address with a photo to the *Gram Panchayat* (village council). The *Panchayat* is supposed to verify the particulars of the applicant and then register the household concerned. It then issues a job card, which contains the details of the adult member enrolled and his/her photo. A registered person can submit an application for work in writing (for at least fourteen days of continuous work) either to the *panchayat* or to Programme Officer appointed under the scheme. The *panchayat*/programme officer accepts the valid application and issues a dated receipt of application. A letter providing employment is then sent to the applicant and is also displayed at the *panchayat* office. Employment is expected to be provided if possible, within a radius of 5 km. If it is above 5 km, transport allowance and 10% extra living allowance will be paid. New public works can be started, when at least fifty workers become available who cannot be absorbed under existing schemes. If employment under the scheme is not provided within fifteen days of receipt of the application, daily unemployment allowance will be paid to the applicant.

70. Discrimination between men and women is not allowed under the MNREGA. Therefore, men and women have to be paid the same wages. All adults can apply for employment, not just those below the poverty line (BPL). So, this prevents the unnecessary hassles in determining who are BPL families and who are not.

II. Case Law

71. Despite a number of sections in various Acts on the Indian social security system, one can find rules and provisions which are not too clear, or which do not provide precise answers to meet the needs of specific situations. India follows the common law system and not the civil law system that prevails in the continental countries; hence the decided cases of the higher judiciary become the law of the land and must be followed by the concerned subordinate courts in their respective jurisdictions. For example, a large number of decisions have been made by the Supreme Court and various High Courts in construing the meaning of the term 'arising out of and in the course of employment' both under the ECA, and the ESIA. Often, the question of law is determined in the first instance by officials like the Assistant Provident Fund Commissioner or the Medical board as the case may be. Decisions of administrators may be appealed to quasi-judicial forums such as the ESI Court. Cases also go to the higher judiciary consisting of the High Courts and the Supreme Court. Most of the decisions by the Supreme Court have been delivered under its special leave to appeal (SLP) jurisdiction envisaged in Article 136 of the Constitution. Even if a particular decision of a lower Court or a tribunal is not appealable, the Supreme Court has the jurisdiction under this article to hear an appeal in its discretion. Under the SLP jurisdiction, the Court may review awards, orders or decrees on grounds of jurisdictional defects, errors of law apparent on the face of the record or violation of the rules of natural justice.[23] This power is generally exercised in exceptional circumstances to prevent miscarriage of justice.[24] The decisions of the higher judiciary are reported in law reports. These reported decisions offer authoritative interpretation of the law. Such decisions become the law of the land, and interpretations made in them are taken into account by those whose task it is to apply the law.

III. Reports of Commissions

72. Among other sources of influence on social security law, it is important to mention reports of some of the commissions of inquiry set up by the Central Government or any State Government. The Royal Commission on Labour (also known as the Whitley Commission), which submitted its report in 1931, conducted the first major inquiry into conditions of labour. Consequent to this report, the Indian Factories Act was substantially amended in 1934. Similarly, the Labour Investigation Committee which submitted its report in 1946 influenced the legislation on labour welfare, which is also a part of social security system in India. Independent India conducted its major reassessment of the labour scenario through the report of the National Commission on Labour (NCL) in 1969.[25] The Government of India constituted the Second National Commission on Labour (NCL-II),[26] which reviewed the scenario on labour including social security and the protection available to unorganized labour. This Commission was appointed in 1999 which submitted its report in 2002. NCL-II suggested in its very detailed report proposals for an 'umbrella legislation' to cover workers who are not the beneficiaries of the existing labour laws applicable mainly to the 'organized sector'. The United Progressive Alliance (UPA) government appointed another commission in September 2004 titled, the National Commission for Enterprises in the Unorganized Sector (NCEUS), headed by Professor Arjun Sengupta. Based on the recommendations of the NCEUS and the NCL-II, Parliament enacted the Unorganized Workers' Social Security Act, 2008 (UWSSA). It seeks to provide some semblance of labour welfare to especially poor workers in the informal sector. The Act came into force with effect from 16 May 2009. It provides for the formulation of schemes by the Central Government for different sections of unorganized workers in relation to matters such as: life and disability cover; health and maternity benefits; old age protection; and any other benefit as may be determined by the Central Government.

23. I.P. Massey, *Administrative Law*, 4th edn (Lucknow: Eastern Book Company, 1995), 203.
24. *Pritam Singh v. State*, AIR 1950 SC 169.
25. The first NCL was headed by Justice P.B. Gajendragadhkar, a former Chief Justice of India. References to this report can be found in this volume in parts dealing with various aspects of the social security system in India.
26. The second NCL was headed by Mr Ravindra Varma, who was earlier a Union Minister of Labour in the Janata Party Government (1977–1979).

IV. Collective Agreements

73. Collective bargaining is an important source of labour and social security law in the developed world, where the duty of labour and management to bargain is much greater than in India. Collective bargaining is considerably hindered in India by the presence of the compulsory adjudication system, which is in vogue since 1942 when it was first introduced by the British in the form of Rule 81-A of the Defence of India Rules, and was later given a permanent place by the enactment of the IDA. Compulsory adjudication system in India is applicable not just to individual rights disputes but to collective interest disputes as well. Nevertheless, especially multinational companies have made a fairly large-scale use of the existing industrial relations law to effect settlements with their union of employees. Settlements under the IDA can be arrived at through the efforts of the Conciliation Officer (CO)[27] or may be entered into by the parties voluntarily[28], provided a copy is sent to the appropriate Government and the Conciliation Officer concerned. The former is called a conciliated settlement and the latter a voluntary settlement.

74. Over and above the legal entitlements under the social protection provisions, some employers in India have also been providing a variety of benefits to their employees under collective agreements.[29] These benefits are in the nature of provision of medical care, children's education, housing, accident insurance, survivors' benefits and even pension. In some cases, these benefits are provided in substitution of the legal provisions. Many large-sized private employers provide medical insurance facilities to their employees who are not covered by the social security law. Several public sector organizations have their own hospitals and dispensaries to provide medical care to their employees. Many organizations, especially in the public sector provide sickness leave to their employees. Benevolent funds have been set up in many companies, to provide immediate relief to their employees in the event of the death of the breadwinner. These funds are generally of contributory nature to which both employers and employees contribute. Many companies have made provision for employment of dependants on compassionate grounds on the death of the breadwinner. Several organizations, especially banks, insurance companies, public sector undertakings and some multinational companies have evolved their own pension schemes and other retirement benefits.

V. Individual Contract

75. Though it is not quite widespread, it is possible to include in the employment contract provision of some social protection benefits by the employer. Usually, most employment contracts in India state that the employee shall be governed

27. This is also called a 12(3) settlement.
28. This is also known as a 18(1) settlement.
29. For an overview of some such benefits in Asia Brown Boveri Ltd, banks, Gujarat State Fertilizers Co. Ltd, Ingersoll-Rand (India) Ltd, among others, *see* R.K. Surbrahmanya, *Social Security: A Critical Survey* (New Delhi: B.R. Publications, 1998), 53–62.

by the terms and conditions applicable to the employees of the organization. The terms and conditions are provided in the standing orders, which are framed under the Industries Employment (Standing Orders) Act 1946 and are certified by the certifying officer who is a Government official. Most standing orders contain, among others, provision of leave earned (also called privilege leave) by an employee during the course of employment but some even provide for sick leave. Special terms and conditions can be entered into by the employer with particular employees, especially in situations where the employer has a talent retention policy and wishes to attract highly skilled employees as a strategy. But this rarely happens in case of common employees. Employees who are not subjected to the protection of standing orders normally are bound by service rules that may provide similar protection. But the existence of such provisions depends upon the employment policies pursued by the particular employer.

VI. International Standards

76. India is a member of the ILO since its inception. The ILO has had considerable influence on the creation of a comprehensive framework of labour and social security laws in the country. Several conventions and recommendations of the ILO have been implemented through amendments effected in the existing laws. The Universal Declaration of Human Rights (1948) is part of the customary international law. The presence of these rights on international statute books also exerts moral pressure on the State in India to enact laws facilitating these rights. Also, the Indian Government is a signatory to several international instruments which have implications for social security. One of the most recent Conventions in this regard is the United Nations Convention on the Rights of the Child, which provides for safeguarding children's right to social security.

Part I. The Institutions

Introduction

77. Several institutions have been entrusted with the task of administering social security in India. However, an analysis of the institutional framework shows that there does not appear to be a rational coherence between these institutions. At the top is the Central Government, which exercises control on the working of the two key social security laws in the country – the ESI Act and the EPF Act. This control is exercised through several ministries. The basic schemes envisaged under both these Acts work under the overall supervision of the Ministry of Labour of the Central Government which, among others, decides and administers the labour and social security policy in the country. In case the government decides to change its social security policy, the resultant amendments are made in the social security legislation at the initiative of the Central Government. This ministry is headed by the Labour Minister. In fact, presently Parliament has consolidated all labour legislation into four labour codes, one of which is the 'social security code' but none of these four codes have been notified for the purpose of implementation. Thus, the status quo related to multiple labour laws remains in this regard till the four codes are made applicable.

78. Many autonomous public institutions administer social security in the country. The Labour Ministry supervises the working of these public institutions. An important part of social security framework in India is the employers themselves. For, they have been enjoined to provide social security protection to their workers concerned as their unilateral responsibility in the event of certain contingencies. The employers are expected to cooperate with public agencies concerned in providing social security benefits. A novel way in India of involving employers in providing social security to workers especially in the unorganized sector is through the levy of cess on goods produced or exported by them, and then setting up welfare funds for the protection of the workers employed in the covered employments. The beneficiary workers do not contribute to these funds. The funds are administered by the Ministry of Labour, Government of India, through the office of Director General–Labour Welfare (DGLW). These funds are, in a way, poverty-alleviation devices in specified industries where the living conditions of workers are not up to the mark or are quite pathetic. Benefits are provided to the workers concerned out of the welfare funds, by way of social assistance.

Chapter 1. Public Institutions

§1. Central Government and State Government

79. The ESI Act has been created by a central legislation. Even though ESI Corporation is an autonomous institution, the Central Government has considerable control in its functioning. The control is exercised directly as well as through the Ministries of Labour, Health and Finance.

80. The Ministry of Labour plays a key role in reviewing and shaping the country's social security policy. The ministry has a social security wing, which is exclusively looked after by a Joint Secretary. The Ministry of Labour does not interfere directly with the administration of social security. However, the key agency that administers social security law in the country is the ESIC. Its chairman is the Labour Minister and Vice Chairman is the Labour Secretary to the Government of India. Joint Secretary – Social Security Division in the Ministry of Labour is one of the members of the ESI Corporation. The Standing Committee of the ESI Corporation which looks after the working of the ESIC more closely and frequently is headed by the Labour Secretary to the Government of India and the Joint Secretary – Social Security Division is one of its members. The ESIC is headed by the Director General, who is its chief executive.

81. The Ministry of Health – both at the Central and State levels – oversees the working of the medical care system in the country. It decides the health care policy in the country. Besides, the Ministries of Health in the States actually run the administration of the dispensaries and hospitals at the State level – a work that has been devolved on to them by the ESI Corporation.

82. The Central Government approves the investment of money by the ESIC which this Corporation does not require immediately. It also sanctions the raising of loans and the measures for discharging such loans.

83. The Central Government also appoints the Chairman of the ESIC and of the Standing Committee which runs the ESIC. It also constitutes the Medical Benefit Council (MBC) which decides the level of medical care provided by the ESIC to the insured persons (IP). The Government also appoints the Director General (DG) of the ESIC, who is its CEO, and the Financial Commissioner. The Financial Commissioner is concerned with maintaining the Accounts of the Corporation, preparing its budgets, for internal audit of the accounts and recommending investments of funds.

84. Both the Central and State Governments send their representatives as members of the ESIC and the Standing Committee, which are the top decision making bodies for the actual implementation of the ESI Scheme.

85. The Central Government can make alterations in the budget estimates of the ESIC as it considers necessary before according its approval to them. The budget estimates in the finally approved form are placed before Parliament by the administrative ministry concerned.

86. The ESI Act also authorizes the Central Government to supersede the ESIC or its Standing Committee if it is of the opinion that the ESIC or its Standing Committee has persistently made default in performing the duties imposed on any of them under the Act. However, this power has not been exercised so far.

87. The State Governments are obliged to provide to the IP and their families in the State reasonable medical, surgical and obstetric treatment through dispensaries, hospital and diagnostic care centres run by it. However, it may with the approval of the ESIC arrange for their medical treatment at clinics of private medical practitioners on such scales and subject to such terms and conditions as may be agreed upon. The State Government also enters into an agreement with the ESIC with regard to the nature and scale of the medical treatment that should be provided by it to the IP and their families in the state concerned.

88. The Central Government exercises a fairly close control over the administration of the ESI Scheme. The type of benefits provided and the conditions subject to which they may be made available to the employees covered are prescribed by the Central Government through the rules framed under the ESI Act. In relation to creation of posts of the staff of the ESIC and appointment of people to fill these posts is also done by the Central Government.

89. The Central Government nominates the Chairman and the Vice Chairman of the ESIC. The Act does not specify who the Chairman and the Vice Chairman of the ESIC shall be. But there is a practice of appointing the Labour Minister as the Chairman of the ESIC. It appears improper that the Labour Minister is appointed Chairman of the ESIC. The same Labour Minister is the head of the ministry which indirectly administers the corporation and in this capacity can overrule a decision of the ESIC which he presides over. The practice of appointing a minister as Chairman of the ESIC has been disfavoured by the Estimates Committee of Parliament. The Committee also suggested that ministers and government secretaries should not interfere in the day-to-day functioning of the ESIC. But nothing has actually been done. And, the autonomy of the ESIC remains sufficiently diluted; in practice it is merely symbolic. It appears that a Union Minister is appointed as the Chairman presumably on the ground that his presence as the Chairman will help the Central Government to discharge more effectively its accountability to Parliament. It is also felt that it would help in resolving the settlement of controversial issues which often arise in bodies with a tripartite character.

90. The Committees which have reviewed the working of the ESIC have recommended that more powers should be delegated to the ESIC. The 1989 amendment to the Act has conferred more powers to the ESIC but despite them the Central Government's control over the functioning of the Corporation is fairly close. In effect, it has stunted the growth of the Corporation.

§2. Officials of Labour Ministry

91. The Ministry of Labour supervises the activities of the ESIC. Apart from the role exercised by the Labour Minister, other officials of the Labour Ministry, especially the Secretary and the Joint Secretary (Social Security Division) also have a considerable role in the administration of the ESIC. Also, the DG of Labour Welfare is the administrative head of the welfare funds which seek to provide social security by way of social assistance in specified employments.

92. The Labour Secretary is the Chairman of the Standing Committee of the ESIC and Jt. Secretary Labour (Social Security Division) is one of the fifteen other members of the Standing Committee as well as the ESIC. Also, Labour Secretary is the Vice Chairman of the ESIC.

93. The ESI Act provides that the DG of the ESIC is its CEO but he has to obtain prior sanction of the Standing Committee in respect of any contract involving an expenditure exceeding INR 500,000. While delegating any of his powers to any person subordinate to him, he has to obtain the approval of the Standing Committee.

94. The budget estimates of the ESI Corporation are prepared by the Chief Accounts Officer and are submitted by the DG for the approval of the Standing Committee.

95. The annual report of the working and activities of the ESIC are considered by the Standing Committee and are required to be placed for adoption at a meeting of the ESIC.

96. The Standing Committee may after giving the person concerned an opportunity to submit an explanation, disallow any item of account that is contrary to the provisions of the Act, Rules or Regulations. This power is conferred in the interest of propriety and complying with the rules. In actuality, it puts overarching pressure on devising fresh perspectives and approaches by the ESIC top brass.

§3. The Public Institutions

97. In each of the branches of the social security system in India, a public institution is in charge of the administration of the schemes. These institutions work under the supervision of the labour minister. Technically, the institutions (i.e., the ESIC and EPFO) enjoy functional autonomy and separate legal personality. The labour welfare funds are directly administered by the Ministry of Labour through the DG--Welfare Funds, who generally does not enjoy any functional autonomy and works under the direct supervision and control of the Labour Secretary.

98. The key public institutions in the field of social security are as follows:

- the ESI Corporation, which administers the Employees State Insurance Act 1948 (ESI Act);
- the Board of Trustees (BOT) of the Provident Fund organization which administers the Employees Provident Fund and Miscellaneous Provisions Act 1952 (EPF Act); and
- labour welfare organization (LWO) which administers central welfare funds created under various laws especially for unorganized or semi-organized labour.

99. In a sense, all the employers in the country who are subjected to various social security laws can be treated as part of the social security administration. Under the ESI Act and the EPF Act they calculate and collect the employees' contribution and hand them over together with their own contributions to the appropriate authorities. In India payment of unemployment benefit under the I DA in the form of lay-off, retrenchment and closure compensations is the responsibility of the employers concerned. Likewise, the responsibility for payment of gratuity payable under the Payment of Gratuity Act 1972, the payment of maternity benefit payable under the MBA 1961, and payment of employees' compensation under the ECA in case of occupational accidents and diseases is solely that of the employers concerned.

Chapter 2. Constitution and Powers of the Public Institutions

100. We shall now look at the constitution of the social security institutions and the distribution of powers within them and their main responsibilities.

§1. The Constitution of the ESIC and Related Bodies

101. The ESIC is a body corporate which administers the ESI Scheme. It represents tripartite interests. Its own legal personality is distinct from that of the State. However, it is quite closely supervised by the Central Government. The ESIC is headed by a Chairperson, who is appointed by the Central Government. Presently, the Labour Minister is its Chairperson. Apart from the Chairperson, the ESIC consists of a Vice Chairperson to be appointed by the Central Government (presently Labour Secretary) and various members. Presently, there are fifty-two members in all including the Chairperson and Vice Chairperson. The members represent the Central Government, State Governments, employers, employees, medical profession and Parliament. The DG who is the executive head of the ESIC is also an ex officio member.

102. The ESI Act also envisages the constitution of a management to administer the day to day functioning of the ESIC. It is called the Standing Committee. Its members are chosen from the members of the ESIC. It works subject to the control and superintendence of the ESIC. Presently, its Chairperson is the Union Labour Secretary. It has sixteen members including the Chairman. In this case also the DG is the ex officio member. The composition of members of the Standing Committee is of a pattern similar to that of the ESIC.

103. It is provided that the Central Government shall constitute an MBC to advise the ESIC on medical questions and on matters related to the administration of the medical benefit. The DG of Health Services used to be the ex officio chairman of the MBC till recently. But through an enactment of the ESI (Amendment) Act, 2009, the DG (who is normally from the IAS) will be the chairperson of the MBC. Other members include representatives from employers, employees, medical profession, and Central and State Government nominees. The Medical Commissioner of the ESIC is also its (ESIC's) ex officio member. Presently, it has thirty-one members including the Chairperson.

104. The ESIC Act empowers the ESIC to appoint Regional Boards, Local Committees, Regional and Local MBCs in areas it considers necessary.

105. The appointment of Regional Boards is aimed at achieving efficiency by decentralizing the administration. They are also expected to help in speedy disposal of the claims and disputes under the Act. It is provided that a Regional Board may be set up for each State or Union Territory. They perform functions assigned to them by the ESIC and the Standing Committee.

The Chairperson of the Regional Board is nominated by the ESIC in consultation with the State Government. Its members represent the State Government, employers and employees from the State concerned, nominees of the ESIC and the MBC. The Regional Board helps to review, from time to time, the working of the ESIC in the state both on the medical side and the cash benefit side. It is also expected to advise the ESIC and the State Government in relation to measures for improving the working of the scheme. It also helps to promote preventive health measures, safety, personal hygiene and to review abuses of the scheme including false certification, among others.

106. A Local Committee may be set up for such areas as are considered appropriate by the Regional Board. It consists of a chairperson and representatives from employers and employees in the area concerned and nominees of the State Government and the DG of the ESIC.

The Local Committee discusses local problems in regard to the ESIC Scheme. It is expected to refer complaints regarding the working of the scheme, as it considers necessary to the Regional Director concerned. It also advises the ESIC or the Regional Board concerned on matters that are referred to it for advice.

107. The ESI Act empowers the ESIC to appoint Regional and Local MBCs in various areas. The ESIC may delegate to them powers and functions specified in the regulations. However, in actuality Regional or Local Councils have not been set up by the ESIC. This is for the reason that no provision has yet been made in the Regulations with regard to their constitution, powers and functions.

108. Appointment of Principal Officers is envisaged by the ESI Act who are entrusted with the work of actual day-to-day administration of the ESI Scheme. The following are the principal officers of the Corporation:

(a) The DG of the ESIC
(b) Financial Commissioner

These officers are appointed by the Central Government in consultation with the ESIC. The DG is the Chief Executive Officer (CEO) of the ESIC. He is expected to supervise, coordinate and control the work of other principal officers.

The Financial Commissioner has to maintain the accounts of the ESIC, prepare its budget, and arrange for the internal audit of its accounts. He also makes recommendation for investment of the funds of the Corporation. The DG and the Financial Commissioner are the whole-time officers of the ESIC and hold office for a period not exceeding five years, but they can be reappointed.

109. ESIC has come to be recognized as, perhaps, the most important institution of social security in the organized sector in the country, even as workers and trade unions concerned of a large number of organizations have persuaded their management to devise their own scheme of social protection including the provision of medical care. Despite this, the ESIC has become a fairly big organization in terms of its staff, coverage, and facilities being provided. As on 31 March 2020, the ESIC was applicable to 30,966,930 employees, with the number of insured people family units being 31,962,910. The total beneficiaries on this date were 13,24,79,263. The total number of employers covered were 12,36,565. Also, the ESIC had 159 hospitals.

110. The Act was originally applicable to non-seasonal factories using power and employing twenty or more persons, but later on it was made applicable to non-seasonal power-using factories employing ten or more persons and non-power using factories employing twenty or more persons. Under section 1(5) of the ESI Act, the Scheme was extended to shops, hotels, restaurants, cinemas including preview theatre, road motor transport undertakings and newspaper establishment employing twenty or more persons. So far as the coverage of employees is concerned, like most other labour and social security laws, this law also does not cover all employees, but only those getting salary below a certain amount per month are covered. Thus, the Act as on 31 March 2021 covered employees getting a salary of INR 21,000 per month.[30] Parliament passed the Employees' State Insurance (Amendment) Bill, 2009, on 6 May 2010. Among others, the amendment provides the following.

The definition of 'factory' under the ESI Act has now been amended to facilitate coverage of smaller factories. It now covers all factories which employ ten or more persons whether these are run by power or without power. Also, it has also extended social security benefits to those apprentices who are covered by Standing Orders as framed under the Industrial Employment (Standing Orders) Act 1946, and also to those trainees whose training is extended. Further, in the era of globalization, the government is trying to abolish overarching powers of inspectors – a word which is seen quite with suspicion. Therefore, the post of Insurance Inspector is redesignated as Social Security Officer to give them the role of facilitator rather than a controller. In addition, it has added the benefit for workers for the accidents happening while commuting to the place of work and vice versa, which earlier was not covered. The age limit of the dependants has been enhanced from 18 to 25 for the purpose of dependants' benefit. It is likely to benefit large number of workers. Also, as per the power conferred under section 95 of the ESI Act, 1948 the Central Government has extended the applicability of the ESI Scheme to all employees who get a monthly salary up INR 21,000 and work in the covered establishments.

111. Disabled persons working in establishments covered under the ESI Act and getting up to INR 25,000 per month are coverable under the ESI Scheme.

112. Many categories of employees have not so far been covered by the ESI Act. One such class of employees are construction workers. The construction workers working at a construction site have not been covered under the ESI Act, 1948. However, construction workers working within a factory as defined under the ESI Act 1948 are eligible for cover for the limited period when they are working in that factory. But with effect from 1 August 2015, the ESI Act has been made applicable to construction workers working at sites as well.

30. Earlier, the wage-limit for coverage under the ESI Act, was hiked from INR 7,500 to INR 10,000 per month with effect from 1 Oct. 2006.

I. The EPFO

113. The EPFO like the ESIC is non-governmental in character as its activities are not carried on directly by the Central Government, nor by any of its departments. The EPFO's activities are carried on by a BOT constituted under the EPFA.

114. The Central Government has been given the power to appoint the BOT for the EPFO, which is a body corporate having perpetual succession and a common seal.

115. Unlike the ESIC, however, the BOT of the EPFO enjoys much less autonomy; the control of the Central Government in its working is much stronger.

116. The BOT is tripartite in nature and has representation of employers, employees and the Central Government. It is headed by a Chairman appointed by the Central Government.

117. The Central BOT administers the fund vested in it in such manner as may be specified in the EPF Act. Its functions relate to implementing the provisions relating to various schemes envisaged in the EPF Act.

118. The EPF Act empowers the Central Government to constitute a State Board of Trustees (SBOT) for each State in consultation with the Government of that State like the Central BOT, the State BOT is also a body corporate with separate legal personification. A State BOT can exercise such powers and perform such duties as the Central Government might assign to it from time to time. However, State Boards have not actually been set up. In fact there was a proposal to delete section 5-B of the EPF Act which provides for creation of State Boards.[31]

119. Since State BOT envisaged by section 5-B of the EPF Act have not been constituted, the Central Government has constituted Regional Committees for States so as to achieve efficiency in administration by decentralization. A Regional Committee functions under the control of the Central Board.

120. A Regional Committee consists of a Chairman and members representing the State Government, employers, employees and non-official members of the Central BOT ordinarily resident in the State. All members of the regional committee are appointed by the Central Government.

121. The Regional Committees are advisory bodies and advise the Central BOT on matters that the BOT may refer to them from time to time, which usually are related with the administration of the EPF Act in the State. Particularly, they are expected to advise on matters such as recovery of PF contributions from employers, expeditious disposal of prosecution cases, speedy settlement of claims and speedy sanction of advances.

31. Report of the Employees' Provident Fund Review Committee, 1981.

122. The implementation of various schemes under the EPFO requires appointment of several officers. The Central Government appoints a Central Provident Fund Commissioner (CPFC) who is the CEO of the Central BOT. He functions subject to the general control and superintendence of the Board. The Central Government may appoint a Financial Advisor and Chief Accounts Officer to assist the Central PF Commissioner in discharge of his duties. The Central Government may also appoint Additional Provident Fund Commissioners, Deputy Provident Fund Commissioners, Regional Provident Fund Commissioners, Assistant Provident Fund Commissioners and other officers and employees as it may consider necessary for the efficient administration of the scheme.

II. LWO

123. Labour Welfare Funds have been created by the Central Government as well as some State Governments, especially in the unorganized sector. The Central Government has set up welfare funds for mine (iron ore, manganese ore, chrome ore, mica ore, limestone and dolomite) *beedi*, and cinema workers.

124. The Central Ministry of Labour administers the central welfare funds departmentally by creating the LWO. The LWO is headed by the DGLW. Thus, the LWO is not an autonomous body corporate but is part of the Government.

125. The DG of Labour Welfare is assisted by Welfare Commissioner (Headquarters) and nine Regional Welfare Commissioners for administering the welfare funds in various States. The jurisdiction of each welfare commissioner has been specified.

126. The Acts concerned provide for constitution of Advisory Committees for advising the Government in matters related to the administration of the welfare funds.

127. A Central Advisory Committee (CAC), which is of tripartite nature, has been constituted for each welfare fund. The Union Labour Minister is the Chairman of these Committees. Apart from the chairman and the secretary, the CAC has eighteen members, six each from Central Government, employers' organizations and employees' organizations.

Advisory committees have also been constituted for each state. A State tripartite advisory committee is headed by the Labour Minister of the State concerned. These Committees do not enjoy any financial or administrative power. The State Advisory Committee approves the budget under each fund for the respective State.

§2. POWERS AND FUNCTIONS OF PUBLIC INSTITUTIONS

I. The ESI Scheme

128. The budget estimates of the ESIC for every financial year (i.e., 1 April to 31 March) are to be prepared by the Chief Accounts Officer. They are then submitted by the DG to the Standing Committee for approval at a meeting of the Standing Committee to be held before the 1st of February of the preceding year. The Standing Committee shall approve the budget estimates with such changes, as it may consider necessary. The Standing Committee then places the estimates before the ESIC, which after finally adopting the estimates, places them before the Central Government for approval. Finally, they are placed by the administrative ministry (i.e., Ministry of Labour) before Parliament in the month of March preceding the financial year to which the estimates relate. The Standing Committee can have supplementary estimates prepared and submitted to the ESIC if in respect of a financial year further expenditure is likely to be incurred. The procedure relating to the approval of the usual budget estimates applies for the supplementary estimates as well.

129. The annual report on the work and activities of the ESIC is considered by the Standing Committee and placed for adoption at a meeting of the ESIC.

130. The Standing Committee oversees that the funds of the ESIC are spent as per the provisions of the Act, and the rules and regulations. If it finds a violation, it may disallow any item of account which is contrary to these.

131. Apart from the usual functions of the ESIC pertaining to the administration of benefits to the beneficiaries concerned, it is provided that the ESIC may promote measures for the improvement of the health and welfare of IP and for the rehabilitation and re-employment of IP who have been disabled or injured. For this purpose, it may spend from the funds of the ESIC within the limits prescribed by the Central Government.

132. The ESIC is authorized to, with the approval of the State Government, establish and maintain in a State such hospitals, dispensaries and medical services as it may think appropriate for the benefit of IP and their families. It can also enter into an agreement with any local authority, private body or individual related to medical treatment for IP in the area and sharing the cost related to it.

133. The responsibility for providing the medical benefit to IP has been given to the State Governments concerned. However, if the ESIC so desires it may in consultation with the State Government itself undertake this responsibility. The ESIC is providing the medical benefit in Delhi and NOIDA area of the State of Uttar Pradesh directly.

134. The ESIC has drafted regulations for its functioning. They are called ESI (General) Regulations 1950. The Regulations made by the ESIC are required to be published in the official gazette of the Government of India and have the effect as if enacted as an Act. Every regulation made by the ESIC is to be forwarded to the Central Government which has to place its copy before each House of Parliament. The power to amend or annul these regulations vests in Parliament.

135. One of the very important powers of the ESIC is to determine an employer's contribution to the ESIC fund in a certain situation. In the usual circumstances, the employer's establishment itself has to file returns under section 44 of the ESI Act about the compensation payable by it. If the employer does not do so, a determination can be made by the ESIC under section 45A on the basis of the information available to it and also it can make demands on the basis of such a determination. If the employer refuses to comply with the demand made by the ESIC, the matter can come up before the EI Court under section 75.

136. Section 85B of the ESI Act empowers the ESIC to levy and recover damages from an employer who fails to pay the amount due in respect of any contribution or any other amount payable under the Act. The ESIC is also empowered to reduce or wave the damages so recoverable in relation to an establishment which is a sick industrial company for which the Board for Industrial and Financial Reconstruction has sanctioned a scheme for rehabilitation. Since the levy of damages is penal in nature, it has been held that they cannot be imposed in a cursory manner.[32]

137. Powers of the Standing Committee are provided in section 18 of the ESI Act. As per this section, the Committee is empowered to administer the affair of the Corporation under the general superintendence of the ESIC. Also, it can submit to the ESIC matters specified in the regulations for its consideration or submit in its discretion any other matter for the consideration and decision of the ESIC.

138. The MBC constituted under the ESI Act is an advisory body. But it plays a very useful role in establishing or maintenance of the standard of medical care. It advises the ESIC in setting up the Regional and Local MBCs. It also helps in identifying their duties and powers. Another important role of the MBC relates to suggesting the scale and nature of medical benefit provided at hospitals, dispensaries, clinics and other institutions and the nature of medical and staff to be maintained by these. The Council suggests measures needed to be undertaken for the improvement of health and welfare of injured persons and the professional conduct expected of the medical practitioners employed by the ESIC.

139. A regional board is expected to, among others, make suggestions about extension of the ESIC scheme to new areas and other categories of establishments; adopting special measures to meet peculiar conditions in the area; improvement in benefits; provision of indoor medical treatment and measures for the rehabilitation of IP. It is also expected to review from time to time the working of the ESI scheme in the State and promote preventive health measures, safety and personal hygiene.

32. *Beama Manufacturing (P.A.) Ltd v. Regional Director, ESIC* (1990) II LLN 24 (Mad.).

Another important area identified for its role is looking into the grievances and difficulties of the IP and employers. Interestingly, however, no regional boards have been constituted by the ESIC so far.

II. The EPF Organization

140. The EPF organization, as we have noted above, is administered by an autonomous board called the Central Board of Trustees (CBOT). It carries out its work in a manner specified in the EPF scheme. All orders and other instruments are made and executed in the name of the CBOT and controls too are executed in its name. But the Central Government is empowered to issue from time to time directions to State Governments, the CBOT and any other authority.

141. The CBOT is obliged to maintain proper accounts of its income and expenditure in form and manner prescribed by the Central Government. The accounts are audited as other government accounts at the expense of the CBOT.

142. The CBOT has to submit to the Central Government an annual report of its work and activities, which the Government shall cause to be laid before each House of Parliament.

143. The CBOT is consulted by the appropriate Governments for making proposals for granting exemption to an establishment under section 17 of the EPF Act. In such cases, the CBOT is obliged to give its views within a period of three months.

144. As observed earlier, the EPF Act provides for constitution of SBOT, but they have not been constituted so far, and the Regional Committees have been set up for achieving efficiency through decentralization and administration. These Committees function under the control of the Central Board. They are advisory bodies and advise the CBOT in matters referred to them from time to time. Particularly, they make suggestions about progress of recovery of PF contributions and other charges, expeditious disposal of prosecution cases, speedy settlement of claims, annual rendering of accounts to members and speedy sanction of advances.

145. CBOT is empowered to appoint such officers and employees as it may consider necessary for the efficient administration of the schemes under the EPF Act. Pursuant to this, the Chief Provident Fund Commissioner, Additional PF Commissioners, Deputy PF Commissioners, Regional PF Commissioners and Assistant PF Commissioners have been appointed to function as important officers of the EPF organization. These officers have been empowered by section 7A of the Act to decide disputes related to the applicability of the EPF Act and determine the amount due from any employer under any provisions of this Act or schemes framed under it. These powers are of quasi-judicial nature and therefore the establishment concerned has to be given hearing.[33] Thus, they conduct inquiry as they deem necessary to determine the liability of the employer and make order on the basis of the inquiry so conducted. These authorities under the Act have a statutory duty to see that the provisions of the Act are complied with.

146. Section 14B of the EPF Act confers power on the Central PF Commissioner or other officers authorized by the Central Government to recover from the employer damages in certain cases. This is in cases where an employer makes a default in the payment of any contribution to the PF Fund, the Pension Fund or the Insurance Fund. It has been held that the PF Commissioner must take note of several relevant circumstances, before imposing damages for delayed payment. These include the number of defaults, the period of delay, the frequency of defaults and the amount involved.[34] However, the CBOT is empowered to reduce or waive the damages so levied in case of a sick industrial company in respect of which a scheme for rehabilitation has been sanctioned by the Board for Industrial and Financial Reconstruction.

III. Welfare Funds

147. The welfare funds are administered by the DGLW. He is the overall in charge of the LWO and reports to the Labour Secretary, Government of India. He is assisted by a Welfare Commissioner (Headquarters) and Regional Welfare Commissioners posted in different areas. The field formations in the areas concerned work under the supervision of the Welfare Commissioner in each region. The Regional Welfare Commissioner is responsible for administering various schemes covered under the welfare funds in his region. As on 31 March, 2021 there were 17 regional labour welfare commissioners.

---

33. *C. Agarwalla v. Regional Provident Fund Commissioner* (1972) I LLJ 603; *Narsingh Das Agarwala v. Regional Provident Fund Commissioner* (1974) I LLJ 52 (Ori.).
34. *Star of Gujarat Textile Mills Ltd v. Regional PF Commissioner, Ahmedabad*, 1993 LLR 210.

Part II. Contribution and Financing

148. The manner in which a social security scheme obtains and manages the funds required to meet benefit payments including the expenses incurred on the administration of the scheme is an important aspect of social security administration. A social security scheme may form part of the Government's social programme and be funded wholly or partially from the general tax revenues of the Government, quite like the way other components of a social programme are funded. Alternatively, the scheme may be treated as a separate entity which must meet its expenses independently of Government's tax revenues. The finance systems are usually designed with reference to the capacity of the sector covered to finance the scheme. For the masses, social security in India is administered in the form of employment generation schemes, other poverty-alleviation schemes, public health schemes, subsidized health insurance scheme and subsidized availability of essential food and other items. Expenditure on these heads is made from the tax and other revenues of the Central and State Governments.

So far as the social security of employed people is concerned, India still does not have an integrated legal framework on the pattern that one observes in countries in the developed world. Interestingly, the NDA government has been instrumental in combining all social security legislation into a Social Security Code. However, the Code has not yet come into force.

Mainly, social security for the employed is provided through legal imposition of unilateral liability on employers under laws like the ECA, MBA, PGA or through funds constituted from contributions from employers and employees. Governments – Central as well as States – share very little or almost negligible part of the total expenditure made. However, in respect of the social security of its own employees, the entire burden is owned by the Central Government or the State Government concerned as the case may be.

149. The funding of social security is one of the most difficult issues in developing countries such as India. The issues in these countries are not so much related to the efficiency of the system, even as it is much below the expected level. The key concern is the raising of financial resources to provide for the basic minimum needs of people. The problem has been further exacerbated by the adoption of globalization policies by Governments all over the world, which have led to diminution in States' financial resources due to lowering of tariffs and rates of personal and corporate taxation. Also, the huge public sectors have demonstrated dismal records of financial discipline and viability. Thus, it is quite difficult to separate issues in social security from those confronted by the national economy. Several sectors in developing countries make claims for scarce public resources; among these, social security surely does not receive the most favoured treatment from the planners, despite laudable projections made in this regard. In economies that are struggling with poverty-alleviation concerns, productivity considerations overtake the issues of social justice. That is what can be noticed in a developing country like India.

150. The Indian social security system mainly relates to the administration of two distinct funds managed by two different public agencies. One of these is the Employees' State Insurance (ESI) Fund managed by the ESIC constituted under the ESIA. This fund is used for providing protection to the contributors against the contingencies of occupational injuries or death, sickness and maternity. The others are the Provident Fund and the Pension Fund, both of which are managed by the EPFO. These funds cater to the retirement and old age needs of the contributor-members. This part is devoted to discussing the financing of these two sets of funds along with the financing of welfare funds, which is a unique method of providing social assistance to the workers in the unorganized sector in India.

Chapter 1. Financing of the ESI Scheme

151. The ESIS framed under the ESI Act 1948 is the key social insurance scheme in India. It is financed from contributions mainly from the employers and the employees. However, a very small portion of its financial resources come from the Government.

152. Previously, the rates of contribution were provided in the ESI Act itself. Later on, it was thought that it is too cumbersome to provide it that way in the Act. So now, power has been conferred by the ESI Act, whereby the Central Government decides the contribution rates through its power of delegated legislation. Until 31 December 1996 the employers' contribution was equal to 4% of the wages payable to an employee. The employee's contribution, on the other hand, was equal to 1.5%. These rates have been revised many times. The current rates of contribution (revised with effect from 1 July 2019) payable by the employer and the employee are 3.25% and 0.75% of the employee's monthly wages respectively. Employees whose average daily wages are below a specified amount are exempted from making the contribution. Initially, those whose daily wages were below INR 1 were exempted from paying any contribution, though they enjoyed all the benefits of the ESI Scheme. Presently, this exemption limit stands hiked to INR 100 per day. However, employers have to contribute their own share in respect of these employees as well. An employer is liable to pay his contribution in respect of every employee and deduct employees' contribution from wages bill and shall pay these contributions at the above specified rates to the ESIC within twenty-one days of the last day of the calendar month in which the contributions fall due. The employer deposits its contribution as well as the contribution of the employees to the ESI Fund in the designated branches of the State Bank of India (SBI). The State Governments contribute only a portion of the expenditure on the provision of medical care, whose share presently is one-eighth (12.5%) of the medical expenditure of the ESIC.

153. The ESIC has prescribed a ceiling on the shareable expenditure on medical care. All capital expenditure on the construction of ESI buildings including their maintenance is borne exclusively by the ESIC.

154. Interest on its investments is another significant source of income for the ESIC scheme. All contributions received under the ESI Act and all other money belonging to the fund which are not immediately required for defraying expenditure on day-to-day requirements are invested in the manner prescribed.

155. The question of arrears on account of default by the employers of covered establishments is a serious problem that the ESIC faces. The Corporation takes legal and penal action under the provisions of the ESI Act and the Indian Penal Code (IPC) for recovery of ESI dues. It has set up its own recovery machinery in all the States. Despite this, however, the problem remains.

Chapter 2. Financing of Provident Funds and Pensions

156. Provident funds and pensions are considered as major parts of the social security system in India. The main law in this regard is the EPFA. Presently, three schemes are in operation under this legislation: the EPFS; the EDLIS; and the EPS. The three schemes are administered by a tripartite body called the CBOT.

§1. Contributions

157. The normal rate of contribution payable under the EPF Act by the employees and the employers has been revised from time to time. Presently, the rate of contribution is 12% on the aggregate wages except in respect of the following category of establishments where the rate is 10% on the aggregate wages on which contribution is payable:

(i) any establishment in which less than twenty persons are employed;
(ii) Any sick industrial company as defined in clause (O) of subsection (I) of section 3 of the Sick Industrial Companies (Special Provisions) Act 1985 (SICA) and which has been declared as such by the BFIR established under section 4 of the SICA.
(iii) Any establishment which has at the end of any financial year accumulated losses equal to or exceeding its entire net worth, that is the sum total of paid up capital and free reserves, and has also suffered cash losses in such financial year.

The employees are free to contribute to the provident fund at any higher rate without any ceiling subject to the condition that the employers will not have any obligation to make a matching contribution in excess of the statutory rates.

An interesting development in the EPF contribution has been announced by the NDA government. It had designed the Pradhan Mantri Rojgar Protsahan Yojana (PMRPY) Plan Scheme so as to incentivize employers for generation of new employment. Under this scheme the Government of India will be paying the full employer's contribution towards EPF and EPS both w.e.f. 1 April 2018 (earlier benefit was applicable for the employer's contribution towards EPS only) for the new employment. The employer is now incentivized for increasing the employment base of workers in the establishment. It is also estimated that a large number of workers will find jobs in such establishments. A direct benefit is that these workers will have access to social security benefits of the organized sector.

158. The cost of administration of the EPF scheme is met from contributions from employers, which presently is 1.10% of wages from unexempted establishments. In case of exempted establishments, the employers are required to pay inspection charges at the rate of 0.18% of wages of which contribution to provident fund is payable.

159. The EDLIS came into force from 1 August 1976. All the employees who are members of the EPF are required to become members of this scheme as well. However, exemption to any establishment can be granted by the CPFC from the EDLIS subject to conditions. No contribution is payable by the employee, for availing the insurance cover under this scheme. Only the employers are required to pay contributions to the EDLIS Fund at the rate of 0.5% of pay, i.e., basic wages, dearness allowance, cash value of food concession and retaining allowance, if any. Also, the employers of all covered establishments are required to pay administrative charges to the Insurance Fund for meeting the expenses in administering the EDLIS. The rate of administrative charges is 0.01% of basic wage, dearness allowance including cash value of food concession and retaining allowance, if any. In case of exempted establishments the employers are required to pay inspection charges at the rate of 0.005% of basic wages, dearness allowance, cash value of food concession, and retaining allowance of employees concerned. The employee and the Government do not contribute to the EDLIS.

160. So far as the EPS is concerned, it derives its financial resource (as was the case with its predecessor scheme, i.e., the Employees' Family Pension Scheme 1971) by partial diversion from the provident fund contribution. From and out of the contributions payable by the employer in each month under the EPF Act and the rules framed under it, contribution representing 8.33% of the employees' pay has to be remitted by the employer to the pension fund within fifteen days of the close of every month by a separate bank draft on account of pension fund contribution. The Central Government also contributes to the Pension Fund at the rate of 1.16% of the employee's pay. Neither the employer nor the employee is required to make any additional contribution. In fact, no part of the employees' contribution to the provident fund is transferred to the pension fund. The pension scheme is funded exclusively from the contributions from the employers and the Central Government. Also, all accumulations of the ceased Family Pension Fund have been merged in the Pension Fund. In case the wages of an employee exceeds INR 15,000 per month, the contribution payable to the pension fund by the employer and Central Government in respect of such employee shall be limited only to INR 15,000 per month.

161. While the EPF Act has given power to the Central Government to enhance the rate of PF contribution, it does not prescribe any criteria to be adopted while exercising this discretion. It simply says that the Central Government may do so subject to such inquiry as it may deem fit to make. However, no systematic efforts have been made by the Central Government towards organizing a systematic inquiry into the conditions of industries/classes of establishments to determine their paying capacity, in respect of obligations under the EPF Act. The Government issues notification merely on the recommendation of the CPFC.

I. Arrears of EPF Contribution

162. The EPF organization faces a serious problem of arrears in payment of contributions. The EPF organization recovers outstanding dues from the defaulting employers, under section 8 of the EPF Act. It also initiates prosecution against the defaulting employers, under section 14 of the EPF Act. The organization also prosecutes employers who deduct employees' share of contribution but do not remit the same to the EPF Fund. This is regarded as a criminal offence of the nature of breach of trust. Such prosecutions are launched under sections 406 and 409 of the Indian Penal Code. During 2018–2019 the arrears under all the schemes as on the 31 March 2019 were of the order of INR 8,922.25 crores. Any amount due from an employer under the EPF Act, 1952 whether in respect of employers' or employees' contribution is deemed to be the first charge on the assets of the establishment.[35]

§2. Investments

163. The SBI, the largest public sector commercial bank in India, has been collecting contributions and administrative charges that are envisaged in the three schemes framed under the EPF Act. The arrangement at present provides for a float period of three days and then five days for transfer of funds to the linked branch from local base branch and outstation base branch respectively. Therefore, there is a time gap for the availability of funds for investment by EPFO. This problem is now being overcome by e-transfer in one of the regional offices of EPFO. This is likely to be extended across all over the country so that funds are immediately available for investment.

164. The total contributions collected in the three schemes under the EPF Act during 2018–2019 was as under:

(1) Total contribution collected under the Employee Provident Fund was INR 120,109.04 crores.
(2) Total contribution collected in the Employee Pension Fund was INR 46,661.64 crores.
(3) Total contribution collected in the Deposit-Linked Insurance Fund was INR 3,434.77 crores.

165. EPFO has introduced competition in fund management, by resorting to appointment of Multiple Fund Managers. Funds were allocated among the chosen fund managers in the inverse ratio of their financial bids so that the lowest bidder got the highest quantum to manage. This is likely to lead to more professional management; better monitoring due to comparative analysis of the performance of the fund managers; and reducing the idling of funds. In view of the importance of this work, a leading credit rating has been appointed as the consultant to facilitate smooth and effective management of the new system.

---

35. *Union Bank of India v. Asstt. Provident Fund Commissioner & Recovery Officer* [2005 LLR 1018 (Ker.)] EPF contribution payable is first charge.

166. The funds that are invested by CBOT of the EPF during a financial year are the net contributions received to the Fund after adjusting the payments made in respect of advances, loans, withdrawals and final settlements.

167. So far as investment of corpus is concerned, the EPFO invests mainly in public sector financial institutions, and is not taking the risk of entering the private corporate sector. This is keeping in view Indian cultural realities about the need to be guided by security considerations in protecting old age funds of the lower and middle class employees.

Chapter 3. Financing of Welfare Funds

168. Welfare funds are a peculiar method of providing social security in India. This is especially so in the unorganized sector. Workers in the unorganized sector in general suffer from low earnings, lack of stability and durability of employment including its migratory nature. It is difficult to extend to them the benefits of a contribution-oriented or employer-liability-oriented social security scheme. The concept of welfare fund has been evolved to extend a measure of social assistance to workers in the unorganized sector.

169. The scheme of welfare funds is largely applicable to those workers who are outside the framework of the specific employer and employee relationship. The resources under this scheme are raised by the Government on a non-contributory basis. Welfare services are delivered without any linkage to contribution made in respect of the individual worker.

170. Welfare funds are financed out of the proceeds of cess levied under respective Cess/Funds Acts on manufactured *beedis*, feature films, export of mica, consumption of limestone and dolomite and consumption and export of iron ore, manganese ore and chrome ore.

171. Welfare funds follow a sectoral approach. These funds are in addition to a large number of various other poverty-alleviation and employment generation programmes, which follow a regional approach and for which most of these workers are eligible. The concerned welfare legislation enables the Central Government to meet the expenditure related to the intended welfare measures and facilities. Towards these ends, various welfare schemes have been formulated and are under operation in the fields of education, health and housing. Presently, welfare funds under the following Acts are operational:

The Mica Mines Labour Welfare Fund Act, 1946;
The Limestone and Dolomite Mines Labour Welfare Fund Act, 1972;
The Iron Ore, Manganese Ore and Chrome Ore Mines Labour Welfare Fund Act, 1976;
The Beedi Workers' Welfare Fund Act, 1976; and
The Cine Workers' Welfare Fund Act, 1981.

172. The cess is collected by different departments of Government in different employments. In case of *beedi* and limestone establishments, it is collected by the Excise Department of the Government of India along with the excise duty. For cine establishments it is collected by the Central Board of Film Certification. In case of mica it is collected by the Customs Department of the Central Government on exports made. The cess collected initially goes to the Consolidated Fund of India. From there it is transferred to the Ministry of Labour to be administered by the DGLW.

173. Two new legislations involving welfare fund for building and other construction workers have also been brought on the statute book. These are the Building and Other Construction Workers (Regulation of Employment and Conditions of Service) Act 1996 (BOCWA); and the Building and Other Construction Workers Welfare Cess Act 1996 (BOCWWCA). The BOCWA, *inter alia*, provides for creation of a welfare fund at the State level to be financed by the contributions made by beneficiaries, levy of cess on all construction works at rates between 1% and 2% of the construction cost incurred by an employer, and non-mandatory grants/loans by the Central/State Governments. The fund remained non-operationalized for a very long time, even as its corpus has increased to INR 37,482 crores.[36] A case has been pending before the Supreme Court of India seeking a direction to the Government to act.

36. The Secretary for Ministry of Labour & Employment, Government of India recently told the SC that the total cess collection has increased to INR 37,482 crore and that the total utilization has increased to INR 9,491 crore as of 30 Jun. 2017.

Chapter 4. Financing of MNREGA Scheme

174. Under the MNREGA, the Central Government meets the cost of the payment of wage, three-fourths of material cost and some percentage of administrative cost. State Governments are obliged to meet the cost of unemployment allowance, one-fourth of material cost and administrative cost of State council. Since the State Governments pay the unemployment allowance, this has the effect of incentivizing them to offer employment to beneficiary workers. In any case, however, it is up to the State Government to decide the amount of unemployment allowance, subject to the stipulation that it is not to be less than one-fourth of the minimum wage for the first thirty days, and not less than half the minimum wage thereafter. In the 2021–2022 budget of the Government of India, the Minister of Finance made the highest allocation ever to MNREGA scheme where he provided 73,000 crores for it.

Part III. Health Care

175. Health care is widely regarded as a very important branch of social security anywhere, for health is a concern for people in all sections of society and all age groups. No doubt, there has been a significant increase in public infrastructure in the country over the years. The doctor-to-patient ratio in India is only 6 for every 10,000 people. This is far low compared to that in nearly all developed countries, e.g., Australia (1 for every 249), the UK (5 for every 1,665) and the US (9 for every 548). On an average the global ratio stands at 15 doctors for every 10,000 people.

176. Cumulatively 30% of the total health expenditure in the country is incurred by the public sector, the rest 70% is borne by consumers. Household health expenditures include out of pocket expenditures (95%) and insurance (5%). Out of pocket expenditures – the payments made directly by individuals at the point of services which are not covered under any financial protection scheme – dominate. The highest percentage of out-of-pocket health expenditure (52%) is made towards medicines. Based on the level of health care required, there are three types of health care providing institutions in India. They include: primary care (made available at primary health centres), secondary care (that is provided at district hospitals), and tertiary care (care available at specialized hospitals like All India Institute of medical Sciences). PHCs symbolize the first level of contact between health care professionals and people. Primary health care infrastructure in rural areas can be divided into a three tier system: Sub-Centres (SCs), Primary Health Centres (PHCs), and Community Health Centres (CHCs). A similar set up is maintained in urban areas.

Private health care in the country consists of profit hospitals/nursing homes; charitable hospitals and institutes; and private practitioners. Public health care structure is different for rural and urban areas. The rural health care structure consists of Community health centres (CHC); primary health centres (PHC); and health sub-centres (HSCs). The urban structure consists of tertiary care hospitals; district hospitals and urban health centres.

177. India has nearly six lakh villages; and as noted earlier, more than 70% of the population still lives in villages. Providing health care needs for this section of the population in the country is a real challenge, if India wants to improve its human development index. India is being talked about as a medical tourism destination for people from other countries, due to the cheaper rates of medical treatment in the country compared to the developed world. But the poverty incidence in the country is so high as to make the advanced health care system unavailable to the masses. Health care, therefore, in a country like India has to be a welfare state responsibility.

The present system mainly caters to the rich, upper middle and the organized working class; there too, especially in relation to the working of the ESIC that provides medical facilities to the industrial employees, much is wanting in the standard of the care available.

Fortunately, the NDA government has framed a health insurance scheme called Ayushman Bharat Yojana which is aimed at making the poor people in the country eligible for cashless treatment in all government hospitals and also select private hospitals. It provides a hospitalization cover of INR 5 lakh per family per year to about estimated 10.7 crore families that belong to poor and vulnerable sections of population. This insurance coverage envisages hospitalization at the secondary and tertiary health care levels.

Chapter 1. Basic Structure of Health Care System

§1. Structure of Rural Health Care System

178. Medical care in India to the masses is largely provided, or is supposed to be provided, by the Central and State Governments and local bodies through hospitals and health care centres, where they are expected to make available free treatment to people. However, it is important to admit at the very outset that public has extremely low trust in the capability and working of these health centres, and people look for better options. These health centres are known as primary health centres (PHC) and their HSCs. They are believed to be the main vehicle for delivering rural health care in the country. It is the duty of the State Governments to establish and maintain these PHCs. PHCs are the first contact between the village community and the medical officer. The PHC is supposed to act as a referral unit. Usually, there are about 4 to 6 beds for patients in a PHC. The staff that looks after a PHC include a Medical Officer, Block Extension Educator, a female Health Assistant, a compounder, a driver and a laboratory technician. In all fourteen paramedical and other staff support a medical officer. Among others, their main activities involve curative, preventive, primitive and family welfare services. They are expected to fulfil the objectives of the Minimum Needs Programme (MNP) and Basic Minimum Services Programme (BMSP) of the Central Government. Each PHC is intended to cover a population of one lakh that is roughly spread over about 100 villages. Each PHC is also provided with a jeep and other requisite facilities so as to enable it to carry out small surgeries. As on the 31 March, 2019, there were 160,713 Sub-Centres (SCs), 30,045 Primary Health. Centres (PHCs) and 5,685 Community Health Centres (CHCs).

179. Normally, a PHC has six HSCs to attend to the basic health care needs of the population. HSC is the first contact point between the community and the primary health care system. Each HSC has a female health worker/ANM (Auxiliary Nurse Midwife) and one male health worker. Also, it has one female health assistant (who is known as, lady health visitor or LHV) and one male health assistant who oversees the supervision of six HSCs. The HSCs are provided with basic drugs for minor ailments, so as to meet the essential health needs of the population.

180. CHCs are in higher rung of medical hierarchy. A CHC is manned by four medical specialists, which includes a surgeon, physician, gynaecologist, and a paediatrician. They are supported by twenty-one paramedical and other staff. The norm is that it will have thirty indoor beds with an operation theatre (OT), X-ray arrangement, a labour room and laboratory facilities for basic obstetric care, apart from specialist consultants. A CHC works as a referral centre for four PHCs. It also provides specialist consultations.

§2. Efforts Towards Improving the Rural Health Care System

181. Knowing well the enormity of the problem, the Central Government is making efforts at improving the health care delivery. It is planning to operationalize all CHCs as twenty-four hours first referral units (FRUs). A standard set of basic drugs and equipment is enlisted at CHCs level. Attempts are being made to enhance the quality of health care. The health ministry has insisted that every CHC prominently displays the charter of patients' rights at the entrance of the CHC.

182. Despite claims of improvement in the health sector, the country faces an acute shortage of health centres. Nearly, a third of the existing health infrastructure operates from rented buildings. There is a usual problem of hygiene and maintenance. Rampant absenteeism of doctors and staff is a serious problem.

183. The National Health Mission is India's flagship health sector programme, which underscores the Health for All vision a reality. Its aim is to revitalize rural and urban health sectors. It comprises National Rural Health Mission and the National Urban Health Mission. The Central Government allocated to National Health Mission INR 32,995 crores for 2019–2020. The priority focus of NHM is Reproductive and Child Health services. The successful implementation of Janani Suraksha Yojana (JSY) and Accredited Social Health Activist (ASHA) programmes had a significant impact on people's behaviour and brought pregnant women in large numbers to public health institutions. India has deployed more than one million Accredited Social Health Care (ASHA) workers who are acting as transformational change agents. The NHM has also empowered people through Village Health and Sanitation Committees to formulate village health plans and exercise supervisory oversight of ASHA workers.

184. As on 4 July 2019, India had 10.57 lakh doctors registered under different state medical councils. But it is estimated that around 9.26 lakh doctors could be actually available for active service. Of these, as per the data of the National Health Profile 2019, only about 10% are employed in the public health sector. The country needs about 5 lakh more doctors so as to meet the WHO standards. Every year about 80,055 students enrol for the MBBS programme.

§3. Health Care System for the Organized Sector

185. ESIC created under the ESI Act, the principal social security law in the country, also provides medical care to the IP and their family members who are employed in factories and establishments. Unlike the PHCs which are a social welfare measure, the ESIS is a social insurance scheme based on contributions from the employer and the employees concerned. Other schemes envisaging provision of medical care include the Central Government Health Service (CGHS) run by the Central Government for its employees and their family members; similar schemes run by the State Governments for their employees and their family members; schemes evolved by large public sector employers such as Steel Authority of India

Ltd (SAIL), Coal India Ltd (CIL), among others; Health Insurance schemes of the General Insurance Corporation (GIC), which is a public sector insurance company and provision of health care facilities by private hospitals and medical practitioners. Despite these, the provision of health care facilities in India is highly inadequate and by and large inefficient. It is difficult to think of solving health problems in a country of India's size, population, resources and complexity through a social insurance system. It has to be understood in the context of the general health policy of the country. In this part, we shall discuss the availability of cash benefit in sickness situations as well as medical care provisions, through the social insurance mechanism. We shall also discuss issues related to improving the existing formal sector's medical benefit as well as the possibility of developing this as part of a comprehensive social insurance scheme for working people in general.

Chapter 2. Sickness Insurance for Industrial Workers

186. This Chapter will examine the nature and conditions for availing the sickness benefit, the rate of sickness benefit and administration of the plan.

§1. Eligibility and Amount of Sickness Benefit

187. Sickness benefit is one of the most important benefits payable by the ESI Corporation in the event of an IP becoming sick. Sickness usually involves inability to earn. This cash benefit seeks to restore the earnings, though only in part, lost by the IP due to his sickness. The authority certifying the award of the sickness benefit should be satisfied that the IP concerned is sick and his medical condition requires abstention from work. Thus, a medical certificate to this effect is required to be submitted from a qualified medical practitioner. The certificate should indicate both the conditions for availing the sickness benefit – that the IP is sick and that his medical condition requires abstention from work.

188. In order to be eligible, the claimant must be covered by the ESI scheme. The payment of sickness benefit in India is thus of the social insurance type. Those who work in government offices, public sector or quasi-government organizations also avail of this benefit in a different form. They do not get it as a social insurance benefit. It can, however, be an employee welfare device. The beneficiaries are usually entitled to twenty half-pay medical leaves in a year, which can be commuted into ten full-pay leaves. Many progressive industrial establishments also provide for availing of medical leave by their employees, on the pattern prevailing in quasi-government organizations. In fact, some people who are covered by the ESI Act get the sickness benefit as well as medical leave on full or half pay depending upon the collective agreement or service conditions regulating such employees. State Government employees are also provided in most cases medical leave facilities on the pattern of the Central Government employees.

189. The ESI Rules provide that a person shall be qualified to claim sickness benefit for any sickness occurring in any benefit period, if the contributions in respect of him were payable for not less than seventy-eight days in the corresponding contribution period.[37] The financial year has been divided into two six-month periods in the ESI regulations for the purpose of knowing the contribution period and the benefit period. The two contribution periods in a financial year consisting of six-months each are (i) from 1 April to 30 September; and (ii) from 1 October to 31 March. The two six-month benefit periods corresponding for these contribution periods are (i) 1 January to 30 June in the year following, and (ii) 1 July to 31 December in the year following. For contributions made to the ESI scheme in the

37. *See* Rule 55 of the Employees' State Insurance (Central) Rules, 1950 as amended by G.S.R. 185 dated 1 Sep. 1998. Prior to this amendment, Rule 55 provided that to avail sickness benefit an IP must have paid contribution for half the number of days in the contribution period, which means 50% of six months, i.e., three months.

contribution period, sickness benefit can be availed in the benefit period. In case a person becomes a member of the scheme on say the first day in the contribution period, he will have to wait for a maximum of nine months for being eligible for receiving the sickness benefit. Thus, there is a minimum time limit, a period during which the person concerned must have been insured for becoming eligible to claim sickness benefit. Under the present conditions, IP usually take seven to nine months to qualify for getting sickness benefit, after they start making contribution to the ESI scheme. However, once they qualify they continue to remain eligible until they work for at least three months in the contribution period.

190. The purpose of providing qualifying conditions is to prevent abuse. In a way, the qualifying period constitutes a trial period during which the insured person must establish that he belongs to the group for which the sickness benefit has been provided for. The provision of qualifying condition proves harsh for *badli* (replacement) and casual workers. In India, a large number of workers fall in this category. Even as they pay their contribution to the ESI scheme, they are not able to avail of the sickness and maternity benefit due to the qualifying conditions on one hand and the non-availability of the work to them on a regular basis on the other. Since this category of workers mostly work on intermittent intervals, they often fail to qualify due to technical rules of eligibility for not having worked for the requisite number of days in the corresponding contribution period.

The ESIS Review Committee 1982 recommended that separate schemes be drawn up for such workers providing for medical, maternity and work-injury benefits only, but no sickness benefit. However, it suggested that no contribution should be charged from such workers. But this recommendation of the Committee has not been implemented.

191. The payment of sickness benefit depends upon the wage group to which the IP belongs. It is paid only to the IP and not to family members. The rate of the sickness benefit is 70% of the average daily wage up to 91 days in two consecutive benefit periods.

192. Wages have been defined in section 2(23) of the ESI Act to mean 'all remuneration paid or payable in cash to an employee if the terms of the contract of employment, express or implied, were fulfilled and includes any payment to an employee in respect of any period of authorized leave, lockout, strike which is not illegal or lay off and other additional remuneration if any, paid at intervals not exceeding two months, but does not include the following:

(i) any contribution paid by the employer to any pension fund or provident fund, or under the ESI Act;
(ii) any traveling allowance or the value of any traveling concessions;
(iii) any sum paid to the person employed to defray special expenses entailed on him by the nature of his employment; or
(iv) any gratuity payable on discharge.

193. The statutory formula for deriving average daily wage divides the monthly wages by 26 instead of 30; that is why, the standard benefit comes to be a little higher in all cases. The table providing for SBR can be reproduced in Table 2

*Table 2 Revised Sickness Benefit Rates**

	Average Daily Wages Are	*Standard Benefit Rate (in INR)*
1.	Below INR 28	14 or full average daily wage whichever is less
2.	INR 28 and above but below INR 32	16
3.	INR 32 and above but below INR 36	18
4.	INR 36 and above but below INR 40	20
5.	INR 40 and above but below INR 48	24
6.	INR 48 and above but below INR 56	28
7.	INR 56 and above but below INR 60	30
8.	INR 60 and above but below INR 64	32
9.	INR 64 and above but below INR 72	36
10.	INR 72 and above but below INR 76	38
11.	INR 76 and above but below INR 80	40
12.	INR 80 and above but below INR 88	44
13.	INR 88 and above but below INR 96	48
14.	INR 96 and above but below INR 106	53
15.	INR 106 and above but below INR 116	58
16.	INR 116 and above but below INR 126	63
17.	INR 126 and above but below INR 136	68
18.	INR 136 and above but below INR 146	73
19.	INR 146 and above but below INR 156	78
20.	INR 156 and above but below INR 166	83
21.	INR 166 and above but below INR 176	88
22.	INR 176 and above but below INR 186	93
23.	INR 186 and above but below INR 196	98
24.	INR 196 and above but below INR 206	103
25.	INR 206 and above but below INR 216	108
26.	INR 216 and above but below INR 226	113
27.	INR 226 and above but below INR 236	118
28.	INR 236 and above but below INR 250	125
29.	INR 250 and above but below INR 260	130

	Average Daily Wages Are	*Standard Benefit Rate (in INR)*
30.	INR 260 and above but below INR 270	135
31.	INR 270 and above but below INR 280	140
32.	INR 280 and above but below INR 290	145
33.	INR 290 and above but below INR 300	150
34.	INR 300 and above but below INR 310	155
35.	INR 310 and above but below INR 320	160
36.	INR 320 and above but below INR 330	165
37.	INR 330 and above but below INR 340	170
38.	INR 340 and above but below INR 350	175
39.	INR 350 and above but below INR 360	180
40.	INR 360 and above but below INR 370	185
41.	INR 370 and above but below INR 380	190
42.	INR 380 and above	195

*The latest Standard Benefit Rates fixed by the Central Government under Rule 54 of Employees' State Insurance (Central Rules) 1950.

§2. Duration of Protection

194. The sickness benefit is payable to the IP, for the period of certified sickness when he is unable to work, in the form of periodical payments. This benefit can be availed of for a maximum period of ninety-one days, in two consecutive benefit periods, i.e., one year.[38]

195. IPs suffering from long-term diseases were experiencing great hardship on expiry of ninety-one days Sickness benefit. Often they, though not fit for duty, felt pressed for a Final certificate. Hence, a provision for paying Sickness Benefit for an extended period – called Extended Sickness Benefit (ESB) – of up to two years in an ESB period of three years. An IP suffering from certain long-term diseases is entitled to ESB, only after exhausting Sickness Benefit to which he may be eligible. A common list of these long-term diseases for which ESB is payable is reviewed by the ESIC from time to time. The latest list includes thirty-four diseases which have been put in eleven groups as per International Classification of diseases and the names of many existing diseases have been changed. These diseases include certain specified Infectious Diseases, Neoplasms, Endocrine, Nutritional and Metabolic

38. This is in consonance with the ILO convention of 1952 which fixed the duration of sickness benefit for developing countries at thirteen weeks.

Disorders, certain specified disorders of Nervous System, certain Disease of Eye, Diseases of Cardiovascular System, certain Chest Diseases, certain diseases of the Digestive System, certain Orthopaedic Diseases, psychoses, etc. In addition to the above list, DG/Medical Commissioner are authorized to sanction ESB for a maximum period up to 730 days in cases of rare but treatable diseases or under special circumstances, such as, adverse reaction to drugs which have not been included in the above list, depending on the merits of each case, on the recommendations of the authorized officers running the medical scheme.

196. To be entitled to the ESB, an IP should have been in continuous employment for two years or more at the beginning of a spell of sickness in which the disease is diagnosed and should also satisfy other contributory conditions. ESB shall be payable for a period of 124 days initially and may be extended up to 309 days in chronic suitable cases by Regional Deputy Medical Commissioner/Medical Referee/Administrative Medical Officer/Chief Executive of the ESI Scheme in the State or his nominee on the report of the specialist(s).

197. The ESI scheme also provides for enhanced sickness benefit at twice the ordinary sickness benefit rate (i.e., about full-day wages) to IP for undergoing sterilization operation for family planning. It is payable for a period of seven days for undergoing vasectomy and fourteen days for undergoing tubectomy operation. This period can be further extended in case there are post-operative complications, etc. This benefit is not subject to the stipulation of two days of waiting period and is in addition to ninety-one days' sickness benefit that an IP can avail during a year.

§3. Drawing Benefits and Wages Concurrently

198. In principle, an IP cannot carry on any salaried activity or work for remuneration, while he is in receipt of the daily sickness or maternity allowance. Still, it may be seen that some IPs return to work during the compensation period because merely receiving the SBR, which is roughly 70% of the wages, is not sufficient to cover the loss of earnings involved.

Will an IP be entitled to sickness benefit in such a situation? Section 63 of the ESI Act prohibits entitlement to sickness or temporary disablement benefit (TDB) on any day on which he works or remains on leave or on a holiday in respect of which he receives wages or on any day on which he remains on strike.

§4. Drawing Benefits under Any Other Law

199. Section 47 of the ESI Act debars an IP from claiming benefits under any other Act similar to those provided under the ESI Act. This section is couched in general terms and prohibits entitlement to all benefits of similar nature. In a decided case[39] however, the Supreme Court has held that medical benefit enjoyed by an IP under the contract of service or standing orders[40] would not be affected by the extension of the ESI scheme. Hence, the employees cannot take away any superior benefit which they are obliged to give to their employees under the employment contract or standing orders.

In another leading case,[41] the Supreme Court took a similar view, where a dispute arose between the employer and its employees regarding sick leave. The matter was referred to the labour tribunal for adjudication. The tribunal granted seven days' sick leave to the employees with full pay and dearness allowance with facility of accumulation. The employer challenged the tribunal's award before the Supreme Court. The Supreme Court was asked to decide whether the benefits admissible under the ESI Act in the matter of granting of sick leave are such as to justify the employees' demand for sick leave. It was held that the benefits granted by the tribunal are not similar to those provided by the ESI Act. The court said that it was so because 'the Act in fact does not deal with the question of sick leave'.

§5. The Waiting Period

200. Most social security schemes pay sickness benefit only if the incapacity caused by sickness extends beyond a waiting period, which is usually two or three days. The provision of the waiting period is permissible even under the ILO conventions. It also helps in saving expenses because brief illness involves a large number of cases. The cost of administering sickness benefit in such a large number of cases will be very high. It is presumed that people should be prepared for short contingencies of sickness as something natural, and no appreciable hardship is involved in loss of wages for a few days. Sickness benefit under the ESI Act cannot be given for the first two days of sickness in the case of a spell of sickness following, at an interval of not more than fifteen days, the spell of sickness for which sickness benefit was last paid.

§6. Tackling Higher Incidence of Sickness Benefit

201. There have been variations in the incidence of sickness benefit days per employee per annum among the States. The ESIC analyses the relevant statistics received at the headquarter office every month and the abnormal trends in any local

39. *Basant Kumar Sarkar v. Eagle Rolling Mills Ltd*, AIR 1964 SC 1260.
40. Standing orders are rules of workplace working certified by a government officer (called Certifying Officer) under the Industries Employment (Standing Orders) Act 1946. These rules in a way are an extension of the contract of employment. All employers covered by the Standing Orders Act have to get standing orders certified as per the requirements of the Act. The standing orders once certified can be altered by the certifying officer on request from the employer or workers or jointly both. In case of difference of opinion, the certifying officer adjudicates on these orders on the basis of justness and fairness.
41. *Alembic Glass Industries v. Workmen*, AIR 1976 SC 2091.

office are taken up with the Regional Directors and Administrative Medical Officers concerned, with a view to take appropriate remedial measures to control lax certification.

202. It is provided[42] that where the incidence of sickness benefit payment to IP in any state exceeds the all-India average, the amount of such excess shall be shared between the ESIC and the State Government in such proportion as they may fix by agreement. The Corporation may, however, waive the recovery of the whole or any part of the share to be borne by the State Government. Recoveries under this provision have reportedly been made from some states. This has helped in bringing down the incidence of sickness benefit.

203. Incidence of sickness may be excessive in an establishment due to the neglect of the owner/occupier to observe prescribed health regulations or due to unsanitary conditions of any lodgings of the IP attributable to the occupier. It is provided[43] that in such cases the ESIC may recover excess expenditure incurred by it as sickness benefit. This provision has however not been used by the ESIC so far to make such recoveries.

§7. Misuse of Sickness Benefit

204. The ESIC has come across cases of misuse of sickness benefit facility by the IP. It has discovered cases of false medical certificates having been submitted by the IP. On such discoveries, the Corporation has been requesting the Labour Secretaries of the State Governments concerned to control laxity in medical certification and to take suitable action in such cases. In such cases the Regional Directors have been advised to liaise with the State Governments as well as Directors (Medical), ESI schemes of the states concerned to initiate steps to control lax certification. The measures taken by the ESIC in this regard include the following:

(1) Withdrawal of power of certification of the Insurance Medical Officers (IMOs) in the affected areas and setting up of a panel of doctors for issuance of medical certificates by the State Government.
(2) Restriction on the powers of the IMOs to issue medical certificate initially for seven days only and thereafter for the next seven days on the recommendation of the specialist. Further certificates may be issued only if the patient was admitted to hospital.
(3) Identification of doctors responsible for lax/excessive certification and to forward their names to the State Government for taking suitable action against them.

42. Section 69, the ESI Act 1948.
43. Section 69(1), the ESI Act 1948.

(4) Withdrawal of power of the local office managers to condone delay in submission of medical certificates under Regulation 64 of the ESI (General) Regulations 1950 and acceptance of documents other than Certificates as alternative evidence under Regulation 53 of the aforesaid regulations of the affected centres.
(5) Initiation of incapacity references by the local office manager weekly instead of fortnightly intervals.
(6) Supplying the list of those IP, who had availed sickness benefit for fifty days or more by the local office manager to the IMOs so that they may be vigilant and alert, while issuing further medical certificates to such IP.
(7) Setting up of investigation teams at two levels for the areas affected by the high incidence of certification with a view to suggesting various measures for controlling lax certification.
(8) Seeking the help and involvement of the labour unions/employee representatives to curb lax certification.

Chapter 3. Providing Medical Care under ESI Scheme

205. In this Chapter, we shall describe and analyse the medical care system of the ESI scheme, and its working towards realization of the goals projected.

206. Since health is a major concern for all age groups including those belonging to industrial workers, provision of medical care or medical benefit as it is popularly known in India, is a major concern of the social security system in India. In general, medical care is provided by several agencies. The biggest infrastructure of medical care in the country is owned and managed by the Central and State Governments and local bodies. They have hospitals, dispensaries and primary health centres (PHCs) all over the country where medical care is provided by them free to all citizens. Any one can avail these facilities without a means test. However, the quality of the care provided by this network and the administrative efficiency of this public sub-system is highly suspect. One is naturally tempted to look for alternative methods of receiving medical care.

There are several other bodies that provide medical care. They include the ESIS run by the ESI Corporation; the CGHS Scheme and similar schemes run by the State Governments for their employees; schemes provided for their employees by some large public sector employers like CIL, SAIL; Health Insurance Schemes of public sector Insurance companies; and private sector employers like the Tata Steel Ltd; and medical care purchasable from private hospitals and doctors, among others.

207. The ESI Scheme created under the ESI Act is the main social insurance scheme in the country. The medical benefit under this Act has been described as the kingpin of the entire ESI scheme, for it is the only benefit in the scheme which protects both the IP and their family members. Also, most of the cash benefits available to a worker are in some way linked to the medical treatment and its certification. Entitlement to medical benefit for the IP is provided in section 56 of the ESI Act. It provides that IPs or (where such medical benefit is extended to his family) a member of his family whose condition requires medical treatment and attendance shall be entitled to derive medical benefit. The benefit can be given in the form of outpatient treatment and attendance in a hospital or dispensary, clinic or other institution or by visit to the home of the IP or treatment as in-patient in a hospital or other institution. The quality and scale of medical care will be such as is prescribed in the Employees' State Insurance (General) Regulations 1950.

208. The ESIS provides full medical care in the form of medical attendance, treatment, drugs and injections, specialist consultation and hospitalization to IP and also to members of their families where the facility for Specialist consultation and hospitalization has been extended to the families. For the families, this benefit has been divided into two categories as under: full medical care, which consists of hospitalization facilities and includes specialist services, drugs and dressings and diets as required for in-patients; and expanded medical care, which consists of consultation with the specialists and supply of special medicines and drugs as may be prescribed by them in addition to the out-patient care. This also includes facilities for special laboratory tests and X-Ray examinations.

209. Apart from the curative services provided through hospitals and dispensaries, the ESIC also provides the facilities such as immunization, family welfare services, and supply of special aids. The ESIC has embarked upon a massive programme of immunization of young children of IP. Under this programme, preventive inoculation and vaccines are given against diseases like diphtheria, pertussis, polio, tetanus, measles, mumps, rubella, tuberculosis, etc. Along with the immunization programme, the ESIC has been undertaking provision of family Welfare Services to the beneficiaries of the Scheme. It has also extended additional cash incentive to IP, to promote acceptance of sterilization method by providing sickness cash benefit equal to full wage for a period of seven days for vasectomy and fourteen days for tubectomy. The period for which cash benefit is admissible is extended beyond the above limits, in the event of any complications after Family Planning operations. IP and members of their families are provided artificial limbs, hearing aids, and artificial appliances like spinal supports, cervical collars, walking callipers, crutches, wheel chairs and cardiac pace makers as a part of medical care under the Scheme.

210. Medical benefit is available to an IP or his family members from the date of joining the scheme. Unlike the case of sickness and maternity benefits, there are no contribution conditions for availing this benefit. While IPs are provided full medical care, the family members are provided different types of medical care, which ranges from out-patient care to full medical care. As per the latest Annual Report of the ESIC (2019–2020), as on 31 March 2020 the IP family units covered that were being provided full medical care were 3.41 crores. The total number of core beneficiaries on the same date was 13.25 crores.

211. By an amendment to section 56 of the ESI Act in 1991, the availability of medical benefit has been extended to permanently disabled IP who cease to be in insurable employment on account of permanent disablement. The benefit is also available to the spouses of such IP; it is payable until the date on which he would have vacated the employment on reaching the age of superannuation, if he had not sustained such permanent disablement. Under this category, the persons covered have to pay a nominal contribution per month. This contribution is payable at a time for one year in advance. The medical benefit has also been extended to an IP who has retired from service on attaining the age of superannuation and to his spouse. The payment stipulation in this category of cases is also the same, as in case of disabled IPs. The condition in this case is that the person should have superannuated after having been in insurable employment for not less than five years. But persons whose wages exceed the wage limit prescribed for coverage or who leave employment or do not contribute for the prescribed period are not entitled to take benefit of this provision.[44]

44. *See* s. 56, Employees' State Insurance Act 1948 and Rule 61, Employee State Insurance (Central) Rules, 1950.

§1. Medical Infrastructure of ESIC and Forms of Medical Benefit

212. Medical benefit under the ESI scheme is provided in the form of outpatient treatment and attendance in a hospital or dispensary or clinic. Three types of medical care are envisaged in the ESI scheme. These are medical care, expanded medical care, and full medical care. All persons insured under the scheme are entitled to full medical care. Sometimes, appropriate facilities do not exist in the hospitals and dispensaries set up by the ESIC. In such cases, required facilities are indented from hospitals belonging to government or other institutions. In case of family members of the IP, specialist treatment is made available only to the extent it is available in hospitals and dispensaries set up by the ESIC or in government hospitals where beds are reserved for beneficiaries under the ESI scheme.

213. Under the ESI scheme, medical attendance to and treatment of the IPs and their family members are being provided by the State Governments. There is an agreement to this effect between the ESIC and State Governments. In Delhi and neighbouring Noida area of U.P. State, the ESIC itself has undertaken the responsibility of medical treatment. It is provided, that the ESIC may itself undertake the responsibility for providing medical benefit to IP, in a State in consultation with the State Government concerned.

214. For medical service delivery, the ESIC has since its inception created a vast network of infrastructural facilities across the country. These consist of ESI hospitals, dispensaries, diagnostic centres, etc. Besides, the ESIC empanels private medical practitioners at certain centres, for providing out-patient care to the ESI beneficiaries. This is in those cases where the density of worker population is very high and it is difficult to find space to construct hospitals and dispensaries. The expenditure incurred on the provision of medical benefit is shared by the ESIC and the respective State Government, in the ratio of 7:1 within the prescribed per capita ceiling.

215. By the end of March 2020, the ESIC had commissioned 20,050 beds in 159 ESI hospitals. For out-patient services, 1,807 ESI service dispensaries have been commissioned by the above date. The ESIC had also empanelled 1,287 private medical practitioners (IMPs) for providing medical care to ESI Beneficiaries[45]. Besides the 159 ESI hospitals, there was a tie-up arrangement for super-speciality treatment with more than 1,000 private and government hospitals.

216. A fairly comprehensive degree of medical care is provided in the above hospitals and dispensaries run under the ESI scheme in the form of medical attendance, medical treatment, provision of drugs and injections, provision of specialist consultation and hospitalization where necessary. Besides this, there is provision of home visits, in case of need, by the ESI doctors for IP as well as family members. IP are provided artificial limbs, hearing aids, dentures, spectacles, cervical collars, walking callipers, wheel chairs, cardiac pace makers, etc. as part of their medical

45. ESIC, 'Annual Report 2019–2020, New Delhi, p. 44.

treatment. The ESI scheme has also been providing for immunization of young children of IP against diphtheria, small pox, polio, tetanus, measles and tuberculosis. The judiciary[46] has been concerned in making the medical practitioners of the ESIC accountable to the members. In view of this it has held, that the Consumer Protection Act, 1985 (CPA) is applicable to dispensaries and hospitals run by the ESIC. So the doctors and hospitals can be held responsible for the consequences of their negligence towards consumers. The adjudicatory mechanism set by this consumer protection legislation is more expeditious, and will instil a greater sense of responsibility among the doctors.

Three types of medical care are provided and they are out-patient care, specialist service and hospital services. The total expenditure incurred on provision of Medical Care, during 2019–2020, was about 8,989.12 crores, which includes the one-eighth share of the State Government, as well as, the money spent by them over and above the per capita ceiling and expenditure on Medical Hospitals and Super Speciality Treatments.

I. Out-Patient Care

217. Two systems are simultaneously in use for providing out-patient care to the IP and their families. These are the service system and the panel system.

A. Service System

218. In case of service system, ESI dispensaries have been provided exclusively for the beneficiaries of the ESIS. These dispensaries employ full-time doctors and staff. They belong to the State Medical Service. Their jobs are transferable between ESI dispensaries and the Government dispensaries and hospitals. The doctors are paid non-practicing allowance (NPA) as in case of government hospitals. They are not allowed to engage themselves in private practice. However, it is important to understand that doctors and other staff are highly reluctant to accept postings under the ESI scheme. This is despite the fact that ESIC grants special ESI allowance to medical officers in its dispensaries. In order to make their jobs more attractive some State Governments have constituted separate ESI cadres.

219. Under the service system of the ESIS scheme, full-time dispensaries have been established in areas where the number of insurable employees' family units is 1,000 or more. These dispensaries are staffed and equipped to provide services such as minor surgery, routine laboratory tests, distribution of medicines, etc. A mini-dispensary is set up in areas where this number is between 500 and 1,000.

A mini-dispensary has a minimum of one medical officer, one staff nurse, one pharmacist and one clerk. Wherever appropriate, dispensaries belonging to Government or local bodies or primary health centres (PHCs) can also be used to serve the ESI beneficiaries. This is so done in areas which do not have sufficient number of

46. *Kishore Lal v. Chairman, Employees' State Corporation* [2007 (6) SCALE 660 (SC)].

IP to justify opening a full-time dispensary. In such cases, the doctors and staff people are remunerated on the basis of the number of IP family units attached to them. Sometimes, the beneficiaries are scattered over a fairly large area. In such cases mobile dispensaries are being used to provide medical care.

220. As on 31 March 2020, 1,502 ESI service dispensaries and 308 ISM units have been commissioned for out-patient services. Also, 1,287 private medical practitioners (IMPs) have been empanelled who provide primary medical care to ESI beneficiaries. B. Panel System

221. Panel system is in use in places where it is difficult to open ESI dispensaries, due to lack of space. Under this system, an allocation committee appoints a panel of medical practitioners to provide medical care to the ESI beneficiaries.

222. A panel doctor is required to have his own consulting room and dispensary and has to comply with certain minimum standards, which are verified by authorized inspectors before a doctor is empanelled. The IP is free to choose a panel doctor of his choice, for registering himself under the ESIS scheme. The panel agreement stipulates the range of services to be provided, clinic hours, domiciliary visits, among others. By way of remuneration, the panel doctors are paid a capitation fee. This fee is revised from time to time.

223. Apart from ordinary medicines, a panel doctor is supposed to provide domiciliary as well as ambulatory care. Medicines other than these can be obtained by the panel doctors from approved panel chemists or ESI medical stores. In case a panel doctor requires a diagnostic aid, he refers the patient to one of the diagnostic centres which are directly set up by the ESIC. If he feels it necessary, the patient may be referred to a specialist for advice and for prescribing costlier medicines. In a few cases, the ESI Corporation also utilizes the employers' dispensaries. For this purpose, a capitation fee is payable to the employer.

II. Specialist Service

224. ESIS provides specialist care to its beneficiaries in all branches of medicine and surgery. Such care is provided in the out-patient department of an ESI hospital or at separate specialist/diagnostic centres that have been set up for this purpose. Diagnostic centres have been set up in different industrial centres.

225. All centres do not have doctors in all areas of specialization. In some cases specialists are provided on a centre-wise basis. These include medicine, surgery, tuberculosis, obstetrics and gynaecology, pathology, paediatrics, eye, ENT, skin and sexually transmitted diseases, radiology, orthopaedics and physiotherapy. Some specialists are appointed on a zonal basis. Such specialists are appointed in the area of psychiatry, leprosy, dentistry, cardiology, neurology, urology and plastic surgery. State level specialists are provided in case of cardiac surgery, malignant diseases, neuro-surgery and thoracic surgery.

226. More than 300 specialist centres are currently functioning under the scheme. Specialists working in them are working either as full-time salaried employees or on part-time basis depending upon the number of hours of their service per week. Full-time specialists are paid non-practicing allowance, and are not allowed to undertake private practice.

227. The ESIS also envisages treatment of cases requiring super-specialty treatment where the facility required is not available at ESI hospitals. In such cases there is an understanding that the State Government concerned shall refer such cases to institutes of eminence within or outside the state. In such cases payments are made directly to the institute concerned.

III. Hospital Services

228. The vast network of infrastructural facilities created by the ESI Corporation, among others, includes ESI hospitals. These hospitals, as also the annexes to Government or public hospitals built for the benefit of ESI beneficiaries, provide hospitalization facilities. In some areas, it is not feasible to justify a separate ESI hospital. In such a case, hospitalization for ESI beneficiaries is provided through reservation of beds in existing or Government hospitals. For this purpose, the ESIC bears the cost of these reserved beds at fixed per diem rate. Till March 2020, ESIC had built 159 hospitals, and 1,502 dispensaries and diagnostic centres.

229. ESIC has set up five zonal occupational disease centres at New Delhi, Chennai, Kolkata, Mumbai and Indore. These centres provide facilities for early detection and diagnosis of occupational diseases of ESI beneficiaries of neighbouring states in the respective zones.

230. The ESIC provides finances for hospital construction from its capital construction fund. This fund has been created by transferring a certain percentage of income of the ESI Corporation.

231. Almost all hospitals run under the ESI scheme, including smaller hospitals are provided with services of specialists in medicine, obstetrics and gynaecology. Hospitals with 500 or more beds are also staffed with specialists in paediatrics, orthopaedics, ENT, anaesthesia, eye, radiology, pathology, skin diseases, chest diseases, dentistry and psychiatry. Sometimes, beneficiaries require highly sophisticated super-specialty treatment. In the area of heart surgery, cancer treatment, kidney transplant, etc. the beneficiaries are referred to specialized government and other institutions in the country at the cost of the scheme.

232. Mostly, the treatment to patients is provided in ESI hospitals. However, in emergencies, treatment can be taken in other hospitals – run privately or by government. In such cases, ESI reimburses the cost of the treatment to the beneficiaries. The ESI (amendment) Act 2009 has now enabled the ESIC to appoint consultants and specialists on contract basis for better delivery of super-specialty services.

233. It has been noted that the quality of services provided in the ESI hospitals is higher than that in hospitals run by Government or others where per diem payment is made by ESIC for reserved bed for care of beneficiaries.

234. Ambulance services are also provided to patients for specialist consultation, investigation or admission if the patient is unable to travel by other modes of conveyance. In areas which do not have sufficient number of family units so as to be provided with ambulance services, the beneficiaries are paid conveyance charges by the ESI Corporation at prescribed rates.

235. Drugs and medicines are provided to the beneficiaries free of cost. In case a particular medicine is not available in the hospital, the patients are allowed to buy the medicine from the market and claim reimbursement. While certain drugs can be prescribed by doctors working in ESI dispensaries and hospitals as well as panel medical practitioners, others can be prescribed only by a specialist.

236. The beneficiaries are also provided with artificial aids and appliances that are essential for their treatment and rehabilitation.

§2. Budget Limitations and Control

237. Medical benefit is the singular head of expenditure which takes away maximum resources of the ESI Corporation. The quality of the services and the level of medical care in case of an organization like the ESIC depend upon effective administration including budgetary planning and control.

238. One of the key administrative mechanisms for deciding the quality of medical care to be provided by the ESI scheme is the MBC. The MBC is a statutory body in which various interest groups including State Governments are represented. The MBC specifies the type of service to be provided to the beneficiaries, scale of medical benefit, the standard norms and yardsticks for establishing hospitals and dispensaries and staffing them, provision of specialist and super-specialty care, etc. The MBC plays a crucial role in budgetary planning and control.

239. The ESIC follows an approach of uniformity, providing the level of medical care in all States. To this effect, the Corporation has prescribed ceilings on *per capita* expenditure on medical care. This amount is shareable between the ESIC and the State Governments. These ceilings are reviewed and revised from time to time. The fixation of ceiling helps exercise budgetary control as well as maintain a qualitative and quantitative uniformity in the provision of medical care under the scheme.

240. The norms for staffing the dispensaries also act as some kind of control measures. The number of persons employed in them depends upon the number of family units attached with each dispensary. But since the incidence of sickness differs from area to area, it would be perhaps better to link the number of staff members with the numbers of medical attendance in a dispensary.

241. The actual provision of medical care through dispensaries and hospitals has been entrusted by the ESIC to the State Governments. The responsibilities for the day-to-day supervision and quality control of medical care under the scheme, in turn, are entrusted by the State Government to the Government Health Service department. In the city of Delhi and the adjoining NOIDA area, the ESIC administers the provision of medical care directly.

242. Thus, it is clear that there is a dual control structure on the working of the medical care Administration of the ESIS. The State Governments' health service department as well as the ESIC exercise supervision on the quality and level of medical benefits.

243. The set-up of medical supervision in the States is headed by the Director of Medical Services. The ESIC has also constituted tripartite regional Boards and local committees at the State levels. These boards and committees have representation from workers, employees and the State Governments. The Local Committees conduct periodical reviews and inspections. They also investigate various complaints regarding the functioning of the medical care scheme.

244. At the level of the ESIC, the administrative set up is headed by the DG of the Corporation. He is assisted by the Medical Commissioner of the ESIC, in organizing visits to the ESI medical institutions and for conducting inspection about the way the statutory responsibility of the medical care administration is being performed by the concerned staff. The Medical Commissioners' staff for this purpose consists of a number of inspectors who are called Medical Referees who carry out periodical inspection of the dispensaries, clinics and other medical institutions. These medical referees are qualified medical officers based in each state. Also, senior medical personnel are appointed to the positions of Regional Deputy Medical Commissioners on a zonal basis. The ESIC has a General-Purpose Subcommittee too which periodically visits medical institutions in different states for conducting reviews and in-depth inspection of the institution concerned. This subcommittee comprises medical experts and representatives of workers and employers on the ESIC. It conducts reviews of manpower requirements and availability of drugs, medicines and other facilities and suggests remedial measures to improve the functioning of the medical benefit scheme.

Chapter 4. Health Insurance for People BPL

245. One of the experiments by the Central Government (through its Ministry of Labour) towards reaching effective health care to the poor, especially those below the poverty line (BPL), is the Rashtriya Swasthya Bima Yojna[47] (RSBY) which was announced by the then Prime Minister Dr Manmohan Singh on 15 August 2007 and was formally launched on 1 October 2007. This scheme was devised especially in view of the living conditions of BPL families, who find it very difficult to cope with health hazards. This issue is more difficult for the poor as they are not able to meet their needs of nutrition as per prescribed standards.

§1. Background of the RSBY

246. Fighting with health problems often leads the poorer people into a debt trap as they find themselves in a situation of permanent threat to their income earning capacity. They tend to ignore the need of treatment due to lack of resources, fearing wage loss. Often, they wait till the last moment when it is too late and in several cases it leads to disastrous consequences. Many times, they are forced to sell their assets and property or cut other important spending like children's education. Health insurance is expected to help them avoid some of these tragic consequences. A well designed and implemented system of health insurance is necessary for such classes of people so as to provide them effective health care. In the past, Governments have tried to provide a health insurance cover to selected beneficiaries either at the State level or National level. However, most of these schemes did not prove to be effective for various reasons. They mostly involved assistance by public agencies. Often there were issues with either the design or implementation of these schemes or with both. With this background in view, RSBY was designed to meet some of the health needs of the BPL families. The scheme is a health insurance scheme linking public and private sector hospitals to the needs of the BPL families through state support.

§2. Basic Structure of the Scheme

247. RSBY envisaged smart card based cashless health insurance cover of INR 30,000 per year to a covered BPL family of five, for meeting hospitalization expenses in return of a contribution of a nominal fee per annum by the family, which covers up to five members of the family. It takes care of most of the illnesses of the members covered including maternity benefit and also covering new born for the remaining policy period. Perhaps, the most interesting aspect of the scheme is that the pre-existing diseases are also covered. The scheme covers transportation cost too of INR 100 per visit with an overall limit of INR 1,000 per year. There is no age limit for people being covered. Hence, senior citizens are also covered.

47. This name of the scheme is in Hindi language. It means: National Health Insurance Scheme.

248. The scheme was launched by the Ministry of Labour and Employment, Government of India. The objective of RSBY is to provide protection to BPL households from financial liabilities arising out of health shocks that involve hospitalization. Government even fixed the package rates for the hospitals for a large number of interventions. Pre-existing conditions are covered from day one. The five members of the family covered include the head of the household, spouse and up to three dependants. Beneficiaries need to pay only INR 30 as registration fee while Central and State Governments pay the premium to the insurer selected by the State Government on the basis of a competitive bidding.

249. The hallmark of the RSBY is an attempt to conceptualize the scheme on the basis of the beneficiary's requirements. The scheme is not a charity scheme, but is a business model for all stakeholders with the objective and hope that it would be taken seriously and not like other government schemes that often fall into background. It also provides a freedom to the target group to choose between private and public hospitals. The beneficiary can choose from almost 1,000 private and government hospitals. The poor beneficiary now has a choice to leave a bad hospital and go to a better one. There are no needs for pre-approvals, which are often not available for the powerless. They often find it almost impossible to move a bureaucratic system. Since the poor are generally migratory they can use the smart card wherever they go. In all, there are inbuilt incentives in the scheme for all stakeholders. It has a good potential of expansion and sustainability. A biometric enabled smart card is issued to each beneficiary family, which includes their fingerprints and photographs. The smart card is valid throughout the country. A Unique ID is given to each RSBY beneficiary as well as the empanelled hospital. In case the BPL family migrates, there is a provision of splitting the card at the district kiosk. Interestingly, the total premium money by the beneficiary will continue to remain INR 30.

An elaborate backend data management system has been put in place for tracing the transactions across the country. This helps facilitate periodic analytical reports. All the covered hospitals under the scheme are empanelled under the scheme and are IT enabled; they are connected to the server at the district level. This is likely to help in conducting research about the working of the scheme. A beneficiary of RSBY gets cashless benefit in any of the empanelled hospitals. They send online claims to the insurer who get paid electronically. Each implementing state selects a private or non-governmental insurer based on a competitive bidding process, and the insurer is tasked with enrolling eligible beneficiaries, creating a provider network, and handling administrative functions.

§3. Benefits under the Scheme

250. The scheme covers for hospitalization expenses of INR 30,000 per family per annum on a family floater basis. Family can be of maximum five members including husband, wife, and three dependants. It includes 727 pre-defined surgical packages including Maternity and Newborn Care. It covers Day Care Surgeries.

Perhaps, the most interesting part is that all pre-existing diseases are covered from day one. Also envisaged are coverage of pre- and post-hospitalization expenses and limited transportation cost.

§4. Built-In Incentives for Stakeholders

251. The scheme is built on incentives for all stakeholders. The insurer is paid premium for each household enrolled for the scheme. This provides motivation to the insurer to enrol as many members as possible from the eligible list of households. This is expected to result in coverage of larger number of people in the beneficiary categories. The hospitals concerned are expected to take into view the needs of the beneficiaries more seriously, as a very large number of people have been empowered by the scheme, which involves a huge sum of money. Hospitals are paid on the basis of per beneficiary treated, so they are not likely to neglect them, which has been the case with the treatment in government hospitals. Since public hospitals too will get the money from the insurer (as the beneficiaries are insured) the money can be used for their own purposes. Thus, it will foster a competitive spirit among public and private hospitals in improving the quality of service that they provide. Many intermediaries such as non-governmental organizations (NGOs) and micro-financial institutions (MFIs) have the incentive in helping the BPL families. Such intermediaries are also paid for the assistance rendered. This will enhance their interest and seriousness in the project.

§5. Sources of Funding

252. The main liability is of the Central Government, which is 75% of the premium amount. The State Government contributes 25% of the premium. This is on per family basis. Also, in case there is an increase in the premium that would be borne by the State Government. State Governments also have to meet the administrative expenses required for the scheme not included in the premium cost. By this gesture, the government discharges its duty to BPL citizens, by assisting them in providing better quality health care. The beneficiary contributes INR 30 per family per year. Both Public and Private health care providers can be empanelled. The enrolment is done at the village level and the Smart Card too is provided there. The cost of the Smart Card is borne by the Central Government.

§6. Process of Getting the Benefits

253. The beneficiary can use his/her smart card in hospital empanelled, under the scheme across India at the time of the need. They have to show the smart card at the hospital concerned. Undoubtedly, this adds to the attractiveness of the scheme, particularly, when a poor family migrates from one place to the other. Biometric verification of the beneficiary is done before the patient is admitted for hospitalization. When the patient is discharged from the hospital, the amount is deducted from the smart card. The beneficiary will receive INR 100 as the transport allowance.

The process for the hospitals is as follows: The first step is to get the hospital empanelled in the RSBY scheme. Then the hospital has to install necessary hardware and software and get its staff trained in technology. The hospital will have to provide cashless treatment to the beneficiary who possesses the RSBY smart card. After that, the hospital will send electronic/paperless claim to the insurer. The payment for the treatment will also be received by the hospital online wherever possible.

§7. Working of RSBY and Challenges

254. Some surveys conducted on the quality of implementation of the scheme revealed that access to hospitalization facilities for the common people has been improving. The scheme has certainly reduced people's out of pocket expenditure (OOPE) on health. The use of smart card has helped inculcate awareness and competencies of handling IT-enabled services by semi-literate people. They also reduced incidence of frauds, errors and leakages. Portability of the cards across the country is certainly an attractive feature of the scheme, which also has inbuilt capacity to create a healthy competition among the service providers.

255. Communicating the scheme to all target groups and convincing them about its benefits has not been an easy task. But perhaps, the most daunting challenge before the government has been to extend the benefits of this scheme to other poorer people working in the informal sector who are above the poverty line (APL) and do not enjoy the status of BPL families. Interestingly, the scheme has been extended to building and other construction workers who are registered with the Welfare Boards constituted under Building & Other Construction Workers Act, 1996. The health care infrastructure in the country is also highly inadequate, so as to cater to the needs of such a large segment of the population. The quality of services available especially in government hospitals is also much to be desired. The government also does not have a track record of efficacious implementation of such welfare schemes. Another serious issue is of availability of hospitals in rural areas; doctors too are not willing to work in these areas due to lack of facilities that they can enjoy in cities and towns.

Chapter 5. Ayushman Bharat Yojna: National Health Protection Mission (AB-NHPM)

256. So far as common people are concerned, the working of the health care sector needs much to be desired. The RSBY scheme was meant for BPL families and had a very low coverage of health risks. For the middle and higher income groups, health industry is counted as the fastest growing. But those out of this class are facing formidable problems in the area of health protection.

Very recently the Central Government has launched an ambitious medical scheme at the national level. This was *called: 'Ayushman Bharat Yojana (ABY): National Health Protection Scheme*'. ABY was launched on the basis of the data revealed by the 71st Round of National Sample Survey Organization (NSSO). Among others, it found that 85.9% of rural households and 82% of urban households had no access to health care insurance. The Central Government intends to eventually merge the RSBY in the recently launched ABY.

257. ABY aims at ensuring complete and efficient health care services to the people covered. It claims to provide poor people affordable medical facilities in the form of health insurance. The scheme was announced on the Independence Day and launched on 25 September 2018. It is targeted at some 10.74 crore poor and vulnerable families every year identified as per the Socio-Economic Caste Census (SECC). So the focus has moved from BPL families to poor and vulnerable ones. Families targeted are both from rural as well as urban areas. The government claims that ABY will be helpful in setting up a fresh health framework in the rural areas including the hinterland; and that it would contribute towards enhancing the quality of life of especially the poor and deprived sections.

258. **Who is covered under ABY:** According to the SECC survey 2011, there were in total 24.49 crore households out of which 17.97 crores were rural households and 6.51 crores were urban households. The scheme makes the following categories of people eligible for ABY:

In Rural areas

1. Households living in only one room with kucha walls and kucha roof.
2. Households with no adult member between age 16 and 59
3. Female-headed households with no adult male member between age 16 and 59
4. Households having at least one disabled member and no able-bodied adult member
5. SC/ST households
6. Landless households deriving major part of their income from manual casual labour
7. Households without shelter
8. Destitute/living on alms
9. Manual scavenger families

10. Primitive tribal groups
11. Legally released bonded labour

In Urban areas:

The following occupational categories of workers are automatically included in the list

1. Rag picker
2. Beggar
3. Domestic worker
4. Street vendor/ Cobbler/hawker / Other service provider working on streets
5. Construction worker/ Plumber/ Mason/ Labour/ Painter/ Welder/ Security guard/ Coolie and another head-load worker
6. Sweeper/ Sanitation worker / Mali (Gardener)
7. Home-based worker/ Artisan/ Handicrafts worker / Tailor
8. Transport worker/ Driver/ Conductor/ Helper to drivers and conductors/ Cart puller/ Rickshaw puller
9. Shop worker/ Assistant/ Peon in small establishment/ Helper/Delivery assistant / Attendant/ Waiter
10. Electrician/ Mechanic/ Assembler/ Repair worker
11. Washer-man/ Chowkidar

259. ABY provides health insurance coverage of INR 5 lakhs to each of the target group family (called beneficiaries) every year. The medical benefits provided under this scheme will be based on the government's deprivation norms. The intended benefit is in the form of secondary and tertiary care hospitalization. The scheme has been launched by the central health ministry. It has about 1,354 medical packages, which among others include surgical procedures and medical treatments that involve expenses related to medicines, transport, and diagnostics.

260. ABY amalgamates the two existing Central Government schemes, which are Senior Citizen Health Insurance Scheme (SCHIS) and the RSBY. The two stated objectives of ABY are: one, setting up of health and wellness centres all over India to provide extensive primary medical services to the poor, vulnerable families; and two, granting health insurance coverage to about 40% of the population deprived of basic health care services.

261. The components of ABY are twofold: first, it includes setting up of 1.5 lakh 'Health and Wellness Centres' (HWCs) all over the country with a view to bringing basic health care facilities within the reach of the people. HWCs are expected to provide Comprehensive Primary Health Care (CPHC), including child care, maternal care, treating of non-communicable diseases, free medications, and diagnostic facilities. The first such HWC was launched by Prime Minister Narendra Modi on 14 April 2018 in Bijapur in Karnataka state. Second, the scheme includes National

Health Protection Mission (NHPM), which involves health insurance coverage to be given to poor and deprived families. HWCs are expected to spread the awareness about the Ayushman (longeval) Bharat.

262. ABY is applicable all over the country. But the state of Odisha has declined the idea of applying this scheme for its people. Some states like Punjab, Karnataka, Kerala, and Delhi have still to come on board. The beneficiary families can avail of cashless health benefits from any public or private empanelled hospital in the country.

263. The payment rates for different treatments are to be decided by the government in advance so as to help control the costs.

264. The beneficiary family members are required to carry Aadhaar card or other prescribed identity proofs for availing the benefits at the empanelled hospitals.

265. National Health Agency (NHA): The Central Government has established the National Health Agency (NHA) for effective implementation of the scheme. It is a self-governing entity that was established on 11 May 2018. It will help in the formulation of the policies and guidelines, management, implementation, and rolling out of the scheme. It will also facilitate coordinating with the State Governments, and supervision and maintenance of ABY all over India. NHA will work as a link between the central and the State Governments, the insurance agencies, and the outside world.

266. The states implementing ABY have to set up a State Health Agency (SHA), which will receive the funds transferred under the scheme by the Central Government.

267. The scheme also envisages that the Central Government and the Niti Aayog (policy commission) will create a modular IT platform for assisting paperless, cashless transactions.

268. ABY provides for the following benefits:

- Coverage to each family by way of insurance for INR 5 lakhs for each family for secondary and tertiary care procedures.
- Beneficiaries include all family members irrespective of the family size, age, or gender.
- Priority is given to female children, women, and senior citizens.
- The scheme essentially covers eligible families present in the database of SECC (socio-economic caste census).
- Free of cost medical treatment for all eligible families.
- No extra money can be charged by empanelled hospitals for beneficiaries' treatment.
- Health care facilities are cashless and paperless.

- Medical packages for beneficiaries include medicine, diagnostics cost, surgery and other treatments.
- Beneficiaries can avail of services under the ABY all over India.

269. Burden of Expenses under the scheme: The beneficiaries of this scheme are not required to pay anything from their pockets. Since this is a medical insurance scheme, all premium expenses payable are borne by the government. They would be shared by the Central and the State Government concerned. The central Ministry of Finance has specified the ratio in which the two sets of government would share the expenses. It has been provided that the expenditure will be based on the actual expenditure or the maximum premium, whichever is less, in a fixed ratio.

Chapter 6. Health Care Provided Through Labour Welfare Schemes

270. As noted earlier, the country has devised a unique method of social assistance through its LWO that functions under the Ministry of Labour. But this is mainly for workers employed in five sets of industries and members of their family, i.e., iron ore mines, limestone and dolomite mines, mica mines, *beedi*, and cinema. Basic health care under this scheme is extended through eleven hospitals and 244 static-cum-mobile dispensaries all over the country that have been built by the LWO, out of the cess collected by it from the employers concerned.

271. Since the residential colonies of miners/beedi workers are located at different places it is not always possible for LWO to set up Hospitals/Dispensaries in each residential locality. One solution to this problem is to run mobile medical units to meet the health needs of the workers and their families at their doorstop.

272. The headquarters of the mobile van is usually located at a suitable place. Often it is attached to some hospital or dispensary. The van makes trips as per programme laid down by the Welfare Commissioner of the region concerned. The Welfare Commissioner decides the medicines and equipment to be provided in the mobile van, in consultation with District Medical Authorities of State Government or Medical Officer of the LWO. Serious cases are transferred to hospital to which the mobile unit is attached.

The non-recurring expenditure on the mobile medical unit comprises the cost of a jeep and cost of the furniture and equipment. The recurring expenditure will comprise the cost of medicines, registration charges of the vehicle and expenses on petrol, rent for garage, and where necessary, pay and allowances of the staff. The staff of the mobile unit consists of one Medical Officer; one Nurse; one Compounder/Pharmacist; one driver; and one Dresser/Attendant.

273. In addition, there is provision for reimbursement of medical expenditure for the treatment of some serious diseases like cancer, heart, kidney transplant; minor diseases like hernia, appendectomy, ulcer, gynaecological diseases, and prostate diseases; purchase of spectacles, etc. There is provision for medical assistance for tuberculosis, mental diseases, leprosy, and serious accidents. Availability of these treatments at such hospitals exclusively meant for the vulnerable workers in these industries is bound to be a big relief, as the medical facilities in common public hospitals are much below the expected standards. Provision of artificial limbs has also been added.

Chapter 7. Towards Efficacious Medical Care Administration

274. There are two sets of issues that require attention for developing a comprehensive provision of medical care to wider sections of population in a country of India's size. These are making the existing medical care arrangements more efficient; and, developing a viable structure of health care organization so as to form part of a comprehensive health policy for all people living in the country.

275. It is also, too well known that the working of the ESI Scheme is far below the expectations of the beneficiaries. The problem is not just related to the availability of facilities in the ESI dispensaries and hospitals. But, the real issue is the satisfaction level of the beneficiaries of the ESIS, who mince no words in demonstrating their dissatisfaction with the services provided. The existing arrangement leaves much to be desired. Several establishments have sought exemption from the scheme. They have before them the example of those establishments who are running their own scheme better than the ESI scheme. Even trade unions have agitated against the working of the ESI scheme. Many of them feel that ESIC should be closed down.[48] There are cases where workers have gone to the higher judiciary to seek direction to the Central Government to consider exemption of their establishment from the ESI Scheme and the courts have granted the relief.[49] It is due to these workers' protests that the extension of the scheme to new sectors of employment like mines and plantations is stagnating. But, certainly attempts are being made to improve the quality of medical facilities in ESI hospitals and dispensaries; but systemic problems can be resolved only to a limited extent.

276. Workers have also strongly opposed the inclusion of casual and contract workers, under the contributory schemes. While this class of workers are required to contribute to the ESIS, they are not able to avail some of the benefits under the scheme because of their unstable employment conditions. Their conditions are of intermittent and discontinuous nature.

277. Difficulties experienced in the working of the scheme are also relatable with its control and coordination in various states. Complexity is created by the lack of proper coordination between the control of the scheme by health and labour departments of the governments as also with their relationship with the ESI Corporation.

278. One suggestion which has been made for overcoming the administrative malaise relates to the disintegration of the cash benefits and the medical benefits under the ESI scheme. Suggestions have been made to the effect, that ESIC should be concerned only with the administration of cash benefits including the benefits payable as unemployment compensation under the *Rajiv Gandhi Shramik Kalyan*

48. R.K.A. Subrahmanya, 'Extension of Social Insurance Scheme in the Formal Sector', in *Social Security for All Indians,* ed. Wouter van Ginneken (Delhi: Oxford University Press, 1998), 56.
49. *Natural Jute Manufacturing Corporation National Employees' Union and Others v. Union of India and Others* (1995) I LLJ 1098 (Cal.).

Yojana (RGSKY) of the ESIC. Presently, the unemployment compensation as envisaged under Chapters V-A and V-B of the IDA in three forms[50] is the unilateral responsibility of the employers concerned. The National Labour Law Association (NLLA) has suggested the formation of a National Social Security Authority of India (NSSAI) for administering all cash benefits. After a long wait, however, the Social Security Code 2020 has been enacted which integrates various social security legislations, but it is still waiting implementation.

A National Health Insurance Agency (NHIA) is required to be created for insuring medical care. This agency should mainly confine its activities to social health insurance for regular employees of the non-government sector. It can provide medical care not just through hospitals and clinics in the public sector, but can explore the possibility of involving private and voluntary sector. Until the latter are made a part of the health care scheme, it is difficult to expect miraculous results from reorganization. Rather, even the role of private medical practitioners may also be explored in this regard, so as to increase its acceptability among the beneficiaries. It is also important that the possibility of joint ventures with private insurers should be explored.

We are now living in a globalized world where freedom of choice is becoming more important than state-imposed unitary mechanisms. People are moving away from state-monopoly products and services to the larger number of options being offered by the private sector or through PPP (public-private partnership). Experience has proved that a system has to have inbuilt incentives for efficient functioning. Over-bureaucratization tends to take away initiative and super-imposes procedural rationalities which reinforce red-tapism. Mere creation of hospitals, dispensaries, diagnostic centres and infrastructure does not deliver the goods by themselves.

279. Certain broad guidelines[51] may be noted for exploring alternative choices. Three sets of broad parameters are suggested to guide the proposed changes. First, change in the administration must create a choice for the beneficiaries so that there is an in-built pressure on alternative agencies to perform as per the exigencies of competitive requirements. Second, emphasis should also be laid on preventive and educative medicine so that efforts are made towards improving health rather than just treating sickness. For example, there may be requirements of periodical medical check-ups; communications may be issued by a central agency (ESIC in this case) advising people covered on health matters through multiple efforts. Third, it has been suggested that the role of the ESIS should be based on assumptions that seek to encourage group practice on the model of health maintenance organization. The ESIS may take upon itself the role of reimbursing medical expenditure as per the pre-determined rates for services received at a large number of approved medical organizations. The idea underlying these broad points for fresh thinking is to

---

50. These three forms are lay-off compensation, retrenchment compensation, and closure compensation.
51. These broad guidelines are based on views expressed by the following: R.K.A. Subrahmanya, *Social Security – A Critical Survey* (New Delhi: B.R. Publishing Corporation, 1998), 150–151; S. Guhan, 'Towards a Comprehensive Social Security Policy', in *Social Security For All Indians*, ed. Wouter van Ginneken (Delhi: Oxford University Press, 1998).

break away from the existing archaic model of medical care administration in India, which has been rejected by its customers due to its inefficiency and the corruption involved. These administrative changes are likely to lead to attitudinal changes for those involved in providing medical care. Something similar is perhaps the idea underlying the Ayushman Bharat Scheme meant for common people where people are free to get medical treatment from private or public hospitals.

§1. Extending the Coverage of Health Care

280. It is important to note that only about 10% to 15% of the population in India is covered by the formal social security scheme. This is despite the recently launched Ayushman Bharat Scheme by the NDA government in 2018, which claims to provide health insurance cover to 10 crore family members.

In the matter of provision of health care facilities we do have a vast network of government hospitals, dispensaries and primary health centres (PHCs) which are supposed to provide health care to public in general, but as noted above the working of this infrastructural network is quite dismal. Despite that, it is important to underscore that in a country of India's size, improving the working of PHCs has to be one of the top priorities. Only they can help reach health care to masses of people all over the country. But, there has hardly been any radical change in the approach to managing the public health care system. As per the most recent poverty estimates of UNDP the incidence of multidimensional poverty index of different countries has been estimated. It says that for 2015–2016, the below-poverty people in India are 27.5%. So the social insurance approach to managing the health care system cannot be expected to produce miraculous results from that point of view. It is for this reason, that health insurance does not enjoy a prominent place in the Indian health care policy. A considerable part of the income is spent by people on health expenditure. This is so also in the case of poor people.

281. The real problem in the public system for health care for the masses is the shortage of doctors who can serve in rural areas; which pushes poor people to avail expensive private medical services, which they find it difficult to afford. As per the budget of 2017-18, the government spending on health is just 1.3% of the GDP, which is highly inadequate. Unless health for masses becomes a national priority, it is difficult to find solution to this menacing problem. The government has several priority areas in poverty alleviation; health care is just one of them. The problem is undoubtedly enormous. It is compounded by corruption in public systems and the usual inertia in people employed in them.

282. It is believed that 80% of the medical staff is serving just 20% of the people, that too those who mainly live in cities and towns. In both PHCs and CHCs there is a requirement of 50,685 nurses and midwives but only 29,776 are in position. In PHCs and CHCs there is acute shortage of specialized doctors, nurses and midwives. There is also the issue of governance and eradication of corruption. But recently, the government's improvement models reflect reliance on public-private partnership. Serious thinking is required in this direction so far as provision of social security through improvement in the public health system is concerned.

283. Can the problem be resolved merely by providing more doctors in rural areas or by devising a scheme like the ABY. The key question is, what structural arrangements are devised so that people are made to pay for their medical care by way of social protection. A large part of the workforce in India is self-employed and is not covered by any social insurance scheme for health care. They make use of only the private hospitals and doctors, due to unavailability of alternatives. The real challenge for the ESIC is, to so devise the ESIS as to cater to the needs of people in general. That was the vision that ESIC had set before itself. Intriguingly, even the people presently covered want to opt out of the ESI Scheme because they feel that its medical care (which they perceive to be its *raison d'être*) is as bad as that of the public health care system which is free. Therefore, they feel disinclined to pay for it through contributions. The propensity to pay for health care is related with the availability of quality health care. Therefore, any discourse on extending the coverage of the health insurance system has to be linked to improvement of its quality.

284. So as to keep pace with the current thinking in health care administration at the global level, there is a strong need for exploring diversified delivery patterns of health care services. More and more public and private facilities are developing with which health insurance institutions are entering into arrangements. Thus, more than one method is being made available which eventually helps in improving the efficacy of these programmes. It also makes them attractive to people in general. This flexibility in approach to provision of health care has to be the key assumption in any future discussion on this subject. A central agency like the ESIC (or National Health Insurance Agency, as it may be called after reforms) has to therefore, innovate and devise new mechanisms to cater to all sections of public.

285. The real challenge in health care administration is towards developing health insurance as complementary to public health services, which should aim to eventually supplant the latter. If the insurance scheme can be made attractive, persons belonging to the self-employed category and those in the higher income groups would feel attracted towards such a scheme.

286. At this juncture, it is also important to consider whether we can make health insurance optional. The long range goal has to be towards making it optional. In this regard, there is no necessity of putting a wage ceiling for coverage of a scheme like ESIS which presently is INR 21,000 per month. But this issue is not to be treated simplistically. It is deeply intertwined with several inter-connected complexities, which are both systemic and attitudinal.

287. The first step towards reforms for larger coverage so as to reach health insurance to all working people and not just to wage earners is to separate the administration of disbursement of cash benefits and the availability of medical benefit. This will lead to the setting up of another national agency, which could be described as NHIA. Those employers who have their own arrangement of provision of medical care may continue to provide the existing facilities.

288. Present restrictions on wage ceiling and those related to the number of persons employed for coverage should also be removed. This thinking is being debated in the corridors of powers but without any action.

289. While the current notion of health care insurance is oriented to some degree of privatization, it may not quite succeed in rural areas. This will involve heavy burden on poor people since charges are likely to go up substantially even for health insurance. This necessitates mobilizing voluntary efforts in organizing the health care programmes.[52]

290. As India is being watched globally as an emerging economy, the country needs to act fast on improving the health status of people, longevity of life, and skill levels, so as to take full advantage of the global economic developments. It is important that conditions are created so that there is demand for health care insurance from the workers. Such a demand has presently died down, because of the dismal working of the public institutions in general and the working of the ESIC in particular. A lot of eyes are set on the working and effectiveness of NHPM. It is too early to say, how the scheme works among the poorest of the poor. It does appear promising especially in view of enhancing the insurance limit for the family as also involving the private hospitals to meet their needs. But the government must devise a very effective system of communicating the NHPM scheme to the target groups, which seems to be much wanting. There is general apathy to the poor and the powerless, which will be a big challenge for the enforcers of the scheme. More in-built incentives would be needed to overcome these hurdles. This is an uphill task given the fact that the whole might of the Government is oriented towards success of the economic reforms; and the government wants to develop the quality of skills in the country and the need for greater contentment among people in general.

So far as working of the medical scheme in PHCs and CHCs is concerned, one of the most difficult issues to tackle is fighting corruption among bureaucracy and public institutions. Apart from this, more thinking is required towards making health a national priority. Amartya Sen, the Harvard professor and Nobel Laureate in Economics for 1998, rightly argues that investment in health, among others, can eventually lead to a competitive advantage in a globalizing world.

291. Government Initiatives like NHPM and ABY are expected to work towards better health care for the poor. These schemes are, in a way, a public–private partnership, as private insurance companies will be competing with those in the public sector to get more business. There is no point harping on preaching to improve the

52. One very good example of this can be seen in ACCORD (Action for Community Organization, Rehabilitation and Development), an organization providing medical care to tribals in Gudalur, Tamil Nadu State, for more than a decade. *See* the paper: K.V. Eswara Prasad, 'Health Insurance for Tribals: ACCORD's Experience in Gudalur, Tamil Nadu', in *Social Security for All Indians,* ed. Wouter van Ginneken (Delhi: Oxford University Press, 1998.

functioning of the public hospitals. There is a need for systemic restructuring whereby people and institutions are incentivized to perform better, and unnecessary bureaucracy is cut down. India has to find ways to discover new ways of public-private partnership, in health care administration. Efforts may be made towards addressing geographic accessibility through PPP and harnessing local resources. Also, efficient dissemination of health care related information is required. As the working of the NHPM unfolds itself, it will surely be helpful for a better health care administration.

Part IV. Family Allowances

292. Despite being a founder member of the ILO, India has not been able to achieve for its population several basic labour standards, including the provision for payment of family allowance. Convention No. 102[53] and Recommendation No. 67[54] of the ILO envisage assistance to residents by way of family benefit. But such a provision has been made neither under the ESI scheme nor by way of imposition of any unilateral liability on the employer nor through any social assistance scheme.[55]

293. The Central as well as most State Governments in India, however, provide some symbolic assistance by way of educational assistance for children of their employees. For the Central Government employees, this assistance is provided under the Central Civil Services (Educational Assistance) Order 1983. The assistance envisaged under this order relates to reimbursement of tuition fee, subsidy for purchase of books and children's educational allowance. The amount of assistance provided under this order varies from time to time as suggested by different Pay Commissions. Most State Governments also provide children's educational allowance on the Central Government's pattern. Overall, however, the amount payable is not quite substantial.

294. The Indian Government on the recommendations made by the Sixth as also Seventh Central Pay Commission has adopted the following policy on children's education allowance payable to government employees.[56] The allowance is now called 'Children Education Allowance Scheme'. It can now be availed by Government servants up to a maximum of two children. Reimbursement as indicated above

53. Convention No. 102 of the ILO relates to Minimum Standards of Social Security. It requires that every member should secure to the persons who satisfy the prescribed condition the provision of family benefit for the maintenance of children. It is provided that this benefit should be in the form of a periodical payment or a provision in the form of food, clothing, housing, holidays or domestic help or a combination of these benefits, whether in cash or kind.
54. Recommendation No. 67 of the ILO relates to Income Security. It envisages that society should normally cooperate with parents through general measures of assistance designed to secure the well-being of dependent children.
55. Family allowance programmes may be universal or be related to employment. Under the universal programmes, allowances are paid to all families having certain specified number of children. Such allowances are deemed to be payable under the usual obligations of a welfare state towards its subjects including children or by way of a social assistance. The payment of family allowance can also be linked to payment of contribution by wage-earning classes under a social insurance scheme.
56. These orders are effective from 1 Sep. 2008.

will be applicable for expenditure on the education of school going children only, i.e., for children from classes nursery to twelfth standard. Henceforth, the reimbursement of Children Education Allowance shall have no nexus with the performance of the child in his class. The Items for which reimbursements can be claimed under this scheme are tuition fee, admission fee, laboratory fee, special fee charged for agriculture, electronics, music or any other subject, fee charged for practical work under the programme of work experience, fee paid for the use of any aid or appliance by the child, library fee, games/sports fee and fee for extra-curricular activities. This also includes reimbursement for purchase of one set of text books and notebooks, two sets of school uniforms and one set of school shoes which can be claimed for a child, in a year.

295. Some progressive employers also provide for children's educational allowance to their employees in the public as well as private sector, either unilaterally or under collective agreements.

296. The Central Government as well as some State Governments administer several welfare funds to provide social security protection to specific categories of workers especially those in the unorganized sector. For example, such welfare funds exist for, among others, mine, *beedi*, cinema, and construction workers. The various welfare funds so created provide for provision and improvement of educational facilities, provision and improvement of nutrition and provision of family welfare.

297. The provision of family allowance is related with the problem of child labour. The incidence of child labour especially in developing countries is high. The number of children not attending schools in India is also very high. While the problem of child labour and non-school-going children is related with poverty in general, it has a social security dimension as well. Provision of family allowance for maintenance of children may encourage parents to withdraw their labour from work. If children allowance is linked to sending them to school, it may also help tackling the problem of illiteracy in the country. Therefore, there is an urgent need for State action in this regard. Some schemes for providing financial incentives to the SCs and STs families already exist as measures for alleviation of poverty among the SCs and STs. Keeping in view the magnitude of the problem and the state of financial health of the Government, however, the possibility of introducing a general scheme of family benefit appears to be merely a distant dream.

Part V. Incapacity to Work

298. There can be several situations in which a person may find himself or herself incapable of working. This may happen in case of an industrial accident, disability due to sickness, physical invalidity, maternity or limitations imposed by old age. Separate parts in a volume, such as this, can be devoted to discussing the entitlement to social security benefits in these contexts.[57]

299. In India, concepts such as incapacity or invalidity protection are not quite popular. However, terms like employees' compensation or protection against industrial accidents are well known. Even invalidity pension was unknown until very recently, when it was introduced for the first time by the EPS framed under the EPFA. This part mainly deals with incapacity compensation relating to funeral, maternity and invalidity.

57. *See*, for example, Part VI for employees' compensation in case of incapacity due to industrial accidents and occupational diseases, Part III for incapacity due to sickness, i.e., sickness benefit, and Part VIII for pension payable in case of old age.

Chapter 1. Reimbursement of Funeral Expenses

300. The ESI Act originally provided for the payment of funeral benefit to meet the expenses incurred by the relatives of the deceased in an IP's funeral. Later on, however, it has been retitled as reimbursement of funeral expenses. The reimbursement is made under the employees' social insurance scheme framed under the ESI Act. It can be paid in case only of the death of the IP and not a pensioner. The ECA did not provide for reimbursement of expenditure on funeral even in cases of death caused by an employment injury. There was an amendment in it in 1995 whereby a new subsection (4) of section 4 was inducted to provide for it. However, under the ECA the employer pays for funeral expenditure of only such workmen whose death results from employment injury.

301. The amount of reimbursement to defray funeral expenses on death of an IP under the ESI Act is limited to the extent of INR 15,000. Under the ECA also, the funeral expenses payable by the employer is INR 5,000.[58] The amount is paid under both the laws to either the eldest surviving member of the family or to the person who has actually incurred expenditure on the funeral.

302. The ESI Act has provided that the death of the IP shall be immediately reported to the local office of the deceased IP. In case the death takes place at the employer's premises then the employer shall make such a report to the local office. If the death takes place anywhere else then the duty to report it to the local office is on the person entitled and intending to claim the funeral expenses. However, it can be any other person present at the time of death. The IMO attending the IP at the time of death or the one who examines the body after death or other institution where the person died shall issue free of charge a death certificate in Form 17 to the person entitled and intending to claim reimbursement of funeral expenses. The ESIC may, however, accept any other evidence in lieu of the death certificate by the IMO, if in its opinion the circumstances of any particular case so justify.

58. Earlier the sum payable under this head was INR 1,000. This was increased to INR 2,500 by the Workmen's Compensation (Amendment) Act, 2000. But as per the latest version of this Act s. 4 (4) of the ECA envisages that If the injury of the employee results in his death, the employer shall, in addition to the compensation payable, deposit with the Commissioner a sum of not less than INR 5,000 for payment of the same to the eldest surviving dependant of the employee towards the expenditure of the funeral of such employee or where the employee did not have a dependant or was not living with his dependant at the time of his death to the person who actually incurred such expenditure.

Interestingly, the amended section also has the effect of not going to Parliament for any further alteration in this amount in the future. Now, the revision can be effected by the Central Government itself which may, by notification in the Official Gazette, from time to time, enhance the amount specified in this subsection by issuing a notification.

303. A claim for reimbursement of funeral expenses is to be submitted to the appropriate local office of the ESIC in Form 25A by the claimant entitled under the Act. Such a claim shall be paid not later than fifteen days after the claim was made. Under the ECA, the funeral expenditure is deposited by the employer with the Compensation Commissioner along with the compensation for death payable by him.

Chapter 2. Maternity Benefit

304. One of the earliest conventions that the ILO adopted was the Maternity Protection Convention 1919.[59] This Convention aimed to enable the woman worker to care for herself and her baby during the period immediately before and after confinement. India being a founder member of the ILO, is one of the first countries to enact maternity benefit laws in consonance with this convention.

305. Maternity benefit in India is available to different women employees through various schemes. The most progressive of these is a social insurance scheme envisaged under the ESI Act, 1948. Under this scheme for entitlement to maternity benefit, contributions have to be paid by the employees concerned at common rate. Like the ECA envisaging unilateral liability of the employer for injuries and death of the worker concerned, the MBA 1960 also envisages the employer's unilateral liability for women workers for their maternity needs. Also, a maternity benefit scheme has been framed by the Central Government, which envisages provision of maternity benefit as social assistance subject to means test. Some State Governments have also drawn their own maternity assistance schemes.

§1. Maternity Benefit under Social Insurance and as Employer's Liability

306. The MBA applies to every establishment being a factory, mine, plantation, establishments belonging to Government and establishments wherein persons are employed for exhibition of equestrian, acrobatic and other performance. By an amendment, the MBA has been extended to every shop or establishment in which ten or more persons are employed or were employed on any day in the preceding twelve months. Section 2(1) of the Act also provides that a State Government concerned may extend the application of the Act to any other establishment or class of establishments with the approval of the Central Government. Such establishments could be industrial, commercial, agricultural or otherwise. Also, extension by the State Government under this section requires not less than two months' notice. Several State Governments have extended the coverage of the MBA under this section. Interestingly, unlike many other labour and social security laws, there is no wage limit for the application of the MBA; all women employees employed in an establishment covered under it are protected. The Supreme Court has observed that maternity benefit is payable even to daily wager women.[60] Of course, this is subject to meeting other conditions.

---

59. The convention envisages provision of abstention from work by the pregnant worker for a period of at least twelve weeks, starting six weeks before the expected date of confinement, but in any event continuing for six weeks after the actual date of confinement. It is also provided that she should be provided medical care by a doctor or midwife; cash payment for maintenance during this time; assurance of reinstatement in her job after confinement and arrangements for nursing the baby.
60. *Municipal Corporation of Delhi v. Female Workers (Muster roll)*, AIR 2000 SC 1274 (SC).

307. The application of the ESIA, which also envisages provision of maternity benefit, has been noted in Part III. This law covers employees getting monthly salary not exceeding INR 21,000 per month. The MBA is not applicable to those employees who are covered by the ESI Act. However, an employee who is excluded by the ESI Act, due to her exceeding the coverage limit gets covered by the MBA, if this Act is otherwise applicable to the establishment in which she is employed.

308. Under the MBA, a woman employee is entitled to maternity benefit up to a period of twenty six weeks, for which no more than eight weeks shall precede the date of her expected delivery. But the maximum period of maternity benefit entitled to a woman having two or more than two surviving children shall be twelve weeks of which not more than six weeks shall precede the date of her expected delivery. In case the woman dies during this period the maternity benefit is payable for the entire period on behalf of the child. If the child also does not survive, the maternity benefit is payable only until the date of the death of the child. Similar provisions are provided by the ESI Act.

309. There are two other situations under which maternity benefit is payable under both the Acts. They are miscarriage and sickness arising out of pregnancy or confinement. In case of miscarriage, the woman is entitled to maternity benefit up to six weeks following the date of miscarriage. In case of illness arising out of pregnancy or confinement, the woman would be entitled to additional benefit up to one month.

310. In order to be eligible to receive the maternity benefit under the MBA, the woman employee concerned should have worked in an establishment of the employer from whom she claims the benefit, for a period of not less than eighty days in twelve months preceding the date of her expected delivery. For calculating this period of eighty days,[61] holidays with wages declared under any law and the days on which an employee is laid off have also to be taken into account. The ESI Act also requires payment of contribution by the employee concerned for at least eighty days, so as to be eligible for the maternity benefit.

311. Under the MBA, the rate of cash benefit payable is equal to the average daily wage[62] of the employee. However, under the ESI Act the benefit is payable at twice the SBR. The SBR[63] works out to be in some cases a little more and in other cases a little less, than the average wage.

61. The Maternity Benefit Convention of the ILO does not prescribe any eligibility period for becoming entitled to maternity benefit. It expects national laws to prescribe the minimum period of work by the worker for becoming eligible. This requirement keeps away women employees who may join employment with an employer just for getting the maternity benefit.
62. Under the MBA, average daily wage for this purpose is to be computed on the basis of wages payable to the woman employee, for the days on which she has worked during the period of three calendar months immediately preceding the date from which she absents herself on account of maternity or minimum wages fixed or revised under the Minimum Wages Act or INR 10 whichever is the highest.
63. For the table providing revised SBR for various slabs of wages, *see* Part III.

312. The MBA envisages, that no employer shall knowingly employ a woman in any establishment during the six weeks immediately following the date of delivery or miscarriage and that no woman should work during this period. Also, it is provided that the employer should not require a pregnant woman to do any work of arduous nature, during a period of ten weeks immediately before the date of her expected delivery. However, the ESI Act does not provide for any such provision.

313. Under the ESI Act, a woman is entitled to medical benefits in the nature of pre-natal confinement and post-natal care. However, no such protection has been provided for, directly under the MBA. Instead, this law envisages a medical bonus, if the employer does not provide for such care. This Act says, that every woman entitled to maternity benefit under the Act is entitled to receive a medical bonus of INR 3,500, if no pre-natal confinement and post-natal care is provided for by the employer free of charge. Some State Governments provide for a higher sum of money, as medical bonus.

314. Under the MBA, every woman who returns to duty after delivery of a child shall be allowed in the course of her daily work two breaks for nursing the child, until the child attains the age of fifteen months. The employer shall not make any deductions from her wages, for providing these breaks. However, the ESI Act does not make any such provision. The MBA has been amended to make a provision of a crèche by every establishment having fifty or more employees. It also says that the employer shall allow the woman concerned four visits a day to the crèche within a distance of 500 meters from the main entrance of the establishment, which shall also include the interval for rest allowed to her. MBA also envisages that every establishment shall intimate in writing and electronically to every woman at the time of her initial appointment regarding every benefit available under the Act.

315. Both the Acts prohibit dismissal of a woman on account of maternity condition. They also ensure that the conditions of her service shall not be varied to her disadvantage, during her absence when she is on maternity leave. Further, similar protection is provided against termination of her service while on maternity leave, except that she can be dismissed for gross misconduct. In this case, however, she is entitled to submit an appeal to the designated authority.[64]

316. The MBA provides a two-weeks' leave with wages at the rate of maternity benefit to women workers who undergo tubectomy operations. The ESI scheme provides enhanced sickness benefit at double the ordinary SBR (i.e., almost full average daily wages) for undergoing tubectomy operation. The period can be extended in case of post-operative complications.

317. The MBA has been amended to provide for six weeks' leave with wages, in case of medical termination of pregnancy (MTP). However, there is no such provision in the ESI scheme.

---

64. The Central Government has appointed the Chief Inspector of Mines and the Chief Labour Commissioner (Central) as competent authorities for this purpose.

§2. Maternity Benefit for Government Employees

318. Maternity benefit in the form of maternity leave is also available to women employees of Government for 180 days.[65] This is available twice in the entire career of a woman employee. The limit of two children is provided as a device to promote family planning. In case of miscarriage, women employees are entitled to maternity leave for a period not exceeding forty-five days. Some States like Kerala and Haryana already provided maternity leave for six months.[66] Government employees are also entitled to pre-natal care, confinement as well as post-natal care. They are also entitled to leave, in case of sickness arising out of pregnancy or confinement.

§3. Social Assistance Schemes

319. The Central Government introduced a National Maternity Benefit Scheme (NMBS), which was modified in 1995 to be *Janani Suraksha Yojana (JSY)* in 2005. The Central and State Governments have several schemes that target specific groups of the population recognized as being more vulnerable, such as the poor, the aged and women, among others. The main schemes for women are the JSY and the Integrated Child Development Services (ICDS); the latter has a component of supplementary nutrition for pregnant women, lactating mothers and adolescent girls. Under this scheme, women below the poverty line (BPL) are provided financial assistance for maternity protection. The scheme is presently implemented by the central health ministry. Under the NMBS, pregnant women from BPL families were entitled to cash assistance of INR 500 for up to two births, 8 to 12 weeks before delivery. The objectives of the JSY are reducing maternal and infant mortality. The NMBs' focus was the provision of maternity benefits. The guidelines for the implementation of the JSY say, 'While the NMBS is linked to provision of a better diet for pregnant women from BPL families, the JSY integrates the cash assistance with antenatal care during the pregnancy period, institutional care during delivery and immediate post-delivery period in a health centre by establishing a system of coordinated care by field level health worker.' The scheme links the cash assistance to antenatal check-ups and an institutional delivery.

The JSY's assistance has been raised to INR 1,600, which will be paid to all pregnant eligible BPL women irrespective of place of delivery. For getting the benefit, it is not mandatory to have antenatal check-ups. The BPL criterion has been removed for institutional deliveries. In low-performing states the number of births for which assistance is provided under the NMBS has been removed.

---

65. This was done on the recommendation of the Sixth Pay Commission for Central Government employees. These recommendations were implemented with effect from 1 Jan. 2006. Before this, the period for maternity leave was 135 days.
66. R.K.A. Subrahmanya, *Social Security – A Critical Survey* (New Delhi: B.R. Publishing Corporation, 1998), 172.

320. The Central Government administers many Labour Welfare Funds, including for *beedi* workers. The Beedi Workers' Welfare Fund provides for a cash assistance to a woman employed in a *beedi*-manufacturing establishment, by way of maternity assistance. However, such assistance can be claimed only twice in one's lifetime. These schemes do not provide for any protection related to conditions of service, employment or any medical benefit.

Chapter 3. Invalidity Pension

321. There has been no provision for any invalidity pension in the country except in case of invalidity resulting from employment injury, under the Employees' Compensation Act (ECA) or the ESI Act. Under both these laws, the invalidity compensation envisaged results from an employment injury. But there has been no protection against invalidity resulting from an injury or otherwise outside the employment injury.

322. So as to be in consonance with the Recommendation No. 67 concerning income security (1944)[67] and the Minimum Standards of Social Security Convention No. 102,[68] the ESIS Review Committee (1966) suggested introduction of invalidity pension. The Committee recommended that it would be better to tag the invalidity pension with the old age pension, when the latter is introduced in the country. The Central Government did introduce the EPS, under the EPF Act with effect from 16 November 1995. Interestingly, this scheme, among others, provides for an invalidity pension as per the recommendations of the ESIS Review Committee.

323. The scheme applies to EPF members who are permanently incapacitated, due to any bodily or mental injury in the course of service. The scheme thus, envisages a permanent disability pension.

§1. Conditions of Entitlement

324. In order to be eligible for invalidity or permanent disability pension under the EPS, the following conditions are required to be fulfilled:

(i) the claimant must be a member of the EPS;
(ii) the claimant must become permanently and totally disabled during the employment;
(iii) the pension is payable, even if the claimant has not rendered the pensionable service entitling him/her to receive pension.[69] However, she/he should have made at least one month's contribution to the Pension Fund; and

67. This Recommendation suggests payment of invalidity benefit for inability to engage in any substantially gainful work by reason of a chronic condition due to disease or injury, or by reason of the loss of a member or function. The recommendation distinguishes such invalidity from invalidity caused by employment injury.
68. This Convention provides that Invalidity Benefit covers the inability to engage in any gainful activity, to the extent prescribed, which inability is likely to be permanent or persists after the exhaustion of sickness benefit. The Convention suggests that the benefit should be a periodical payment equal to not less than 40% of the previous earnings of the wage of an ordinary adult male worker. It also permits a qualifying period of fifteen years of contribution or employment which may be reduced to five years.
69. The entitlement to pension and its rate is provided in para. 12 of the EPS.

(iv) the claimant has undergone medical examination as prescribed by the Central Board to determine, whether or not he or she is permanently and totally unfit for the employment which he or she was doing at the time of such disablement.

§2. Rate of Benefit

325. As per the EPS the amount of invalidity pension is determined on the basis of the same formula[70] as is applicable to superannuation or retirement pension. However, in case of invalidity benefit there is no eligibility clause of a minimum of ten years of service. The invalidity pension is admissible under sub-paragraph (2) to (5) of paragraph 12.

326. The monthly member's pension in case of invalidity shall be payable from the date following the date of permanent total disablement. The member will get it for the lifetime.

§3. Comment

327. So far as the eligibility criteria for invalidity are concerned, the invalidity pension under the EPS is more favourable than that envisaged by the ILO Convention. However, pension under the EPS may not assure a benefit of 'not less than 40% of the previous earnings in all cases'.

328. The Economic Administration Reforms Committee, in 1984 had recommended that a comprehensive accident insurance scheme should be introduced for all persons who are in the age group of 15 to 55, which should provide for compensation in case of death as well as loss of limbs. On the basis of this recommendation, the General Insurance Corporation (GIC) has introduced a scheme which is called Personal Accident Insurance Social Security Scheme (PASS). However, PASS provides only for compensation in case of death and not of incapacity. There is urgent need for introduction of a scheme, to protect invalidity. To begin with, an insurance scheme may be launched. Later on, India will have to work towards evolving a social assistance scheme to cover invalidity so that the scheme is extended to the general population, including the poor.

70. For knowing details of the formula, *see* Part VIII titled 'Provident Funds and Pensions'.

Part VI. Compensation for Employment Accidents and Occupational Diseases

329. Providing social protection to workers against employment accidents and occupational diseases has not yet become common for the working class in general. But, for the workforce employed in industry, one of the earliest attempts in India towards developing at least a minimal degree of state protection has been in this area. The law to this effect was passed in 1923; it was titled the Workman's Compensation Act 1923 (WCA). This legislation continues to be on the statute book until today, though its name has recently been changed to Employees Compensation Act 1923 (ECA).[71] This first social security law is also treated as, perhaps, the oldest piece of labour legislation in India. The law of social security is mostly treated as a part of labour law in the country by the academics, professional practitioners and employers, alike. In fact, there are almost no or very few books on social security law in India, as such. The ECA also has, perhaps, the widest application in terms of coverage of workers, as this legislation covers many employments in the unorganized sector as well. In fact, this Act even applies to some parts of agricultural operations. The Act seeks to provide a speedy and cheap forum[72] to the employee for claiming compensation and gives wide powers to the commissioner to adjudicate claims and implement its intended objectives.

330. Strictly speaking, the ECA, may not be regarded as a social security law because it creates a unilateral liability of the employers concerned to pay compensation to the worker or his/her dependants (in case of death), for employment accidents and occupational diseases. Technically speaking, it may neither fall in the category of social insurance nor any social assistance. It is based on the dictum – 'Let the cost of the product bear the blood of the worker.' The compensation payable by the employer is not related to the negligence of the employer or its/his agents, but involves a kind of strict liability as it is so almost all over the globe. The scheme of ECA is not even a branch of law of tort. In a way, it manifests features of social insurance as well as tort. As in case of tort but unlike social insurance, this law is premised on employer's unilateral liability. As in the case of social insurance

71. The Workmen's Compensation (Amendment) Act, 2009 received the assent of the President of India on 22 Dec. 2009.
72. Commissioner under the ECA enjoys administrative, adjudicatory and advisory powers to facilitate speedy disposal of claims under this Act.

but unlike tort, the right to compensation and amount of compensation are based on a social theory of safeguarding employee[73] against employment contingencies related to accidents. Employers' unilateral liability is the most negative feature of this law which has made its implementation difficult. For, the employers try to avoid their liability by any means – lawful or unlawful. That is why, a large number of accident cases do not come to the knowledge of the enforcement authority, which is designated as 'Commissioner' under the Act. Overall, its enforcement can be said to be only poor. Some academics, therefore say that this is a dying law as it was intended to be completely replaced by a more progressive social insurance piece of legislation so that the intended protection can be effectively implemented. However, that goal does not appear to be in sight, given the state of general labour law implementation in the country and the vast number of employees who are not yet covered under this piece of legislation. But at the same time, it should be said that attempts are being made to extend its coverage and enhance the nature of protection provided by it.[1]

331. The ECA provides for payment of compensation for employment-related injuries, which result in temporary or permanent disablement or death of the workman. Also covered under this Act is incapacity due to occupational disease of certain types. Compensation is payable as a lump sum and not by way of a monthly pension, as should be the case. This becomes another serious limitation of the Act, because many semi-literate employees squander away the compensation money by indulging in unnecessary expenditure. Interestingly, there is no wage ceiling for entitlement to obtain the benefit under the Act, though there is a notional ceiling on monthly wages for the purpose of calculating the compensation amount. But, the compensation is payable only to those who are employed in specified employments and usually are not employed in clerical or managerial capacity. But in many though not all employments, even persons employed in clerical capacity are also included. Thus, a fairly wide section of workforce remains uncovered. But some states like Delhi have extended the coverage to persons employed in all types of employments. Also, it should be noted that, the ECA provides no preventive measure against accidents and injuries. Further, those covered by this legislation are not entitled to any cash benefit such as sickness compensation nor any medical benefit. And, if the injury somehow cannot be said to have a causal connection (a legal fiction) with the employment, no compensation is payable. The burden of proof for establishing such a causal connection is on the employee and is quite heavy. In many situations, the employee's case fails due to his/her inability to bring evidence to prove his case.

332. The existence of the ECA, which even though envisages a unilateral liability of the employee, does prove to be of considerable help to the employee who is given an opportunity to secure the benefit under the Act. It has been rightly observed, that the provision for compensation is not the only benefit flowing from

73. Earlier, it contained the term workman. But, after the latest amendment to this Act which received the assent of the President of India on 22 Dec. 2009, the term workman in this piece of legislation has been replaced by the term, 'employee' in all its contents.

a law like the ECA, but its presence on the statute book in a way helps fostering prevention of accidents, giving employees greater freedom from anxiety, and in rendering industrial work more attractive.[74] However, the mechanism is quite inadequate. Even as the compensation payable under the Act may prove quite burdensome especially for small employers, the arrangement is not sufficient for the victim's recovery and rehabilitation. No emphasis is laid on the prevention of occupational risk that is faced by the workers, which in fact should be the key concern of a law dealing with occupational accidents. The Factories Act 1948 was amended after the Bhopal Gas Disaster,[75] so as to make available to factory workers a preventive safety mechanism against occupational hazards. This was, no doubt, one of the worst industrial accidents in human history. But it happened in one of the locations of the Union Carbide situated in Bhopal, in India and not in Virginia, USA where this multinational company is running a similar plant. This fact shows that lackadaisical of the employers are in ensuring safety against the hazards of industrial operations, in developing countries. Industrial health and safety in these countries appear to be low on the agenda of the State as well as on that of the employers. Employees' carelessness to their own safety in a country like India is partly attributable to their lack of education and general sense of low awareness. The post-Bhopal Factories Act provides protection against only some of the dangers. And, these safeguards apply only to those workers who are employed in establishments that can be termed as factories. A large part of the working class covered by the ECA consists of non-factory employees. Overall, therefore, the ECA is incompatible with prevention of accidents. But, since industrial hazards cannot be entirely wished away, the compensation mechanism envisaged under the Act remains a useful tool of social protection.

333. After independence, the Central Government in India did succeed in enacting a social insurance law called the Employees State Insurance Act 1948 (ESI Act), which partly overcomes the limitations of the ECA. The ESI Act, among others, provides for cash as well as medical benefits. Apart from other cash benefits, it provides for life-long periodical (not lump sum like in case of ECA) payments of compensation to employees, in case of permanent disablement resulting from employment injuries as also to the widow of the deceased in case of death and in some cases to other dependants. The passage of the ESI Act has shifted the responsibility of the industrial accidents from the employer to a social insurance agency. But this Act has a limited coverage. It does not apply to all employments that are covered under the ECA. It covers only factories under the Factories Act and other notified establishments. Also, employees getting wages above INR 21,000 per month go out of protection. When an employee goes out of the protection of the ESI Act, he or she is covered by the ECA, if he is otherwise eligible for coverage under the ECA. In many cases, s/he does not come under the protection umbrella of the

74. *Report of the Royal Commission on Labour in India* (New Delhi: Agricole Publishing Company, 1931), 298.
75. On 3 Dec. 1984, Union Carbide's pesticide plant in Bhopal, India, was the scene of one of the worst industrial disasters in the world. The accident involved leakage of more than 40 tonnes of poisonous gas which spread to a populated area. It resulted in the killing of 5,324 people; a large number were injured.

ECA especially if s/he works in a clerical or administrative capacity. Interestingly, the ESI Act covers all types of employees provided their wages are below the specified limit.

334. In this part, we shall analyse the framework of social protection against employment accidents and occupational diseases as provided in the ECA and the ESIA. We shall also analyse the extent to which the latter piece of legislation is an improvement over the former.

Chapter 1. Compensation for Employment Accidents

335. We shall now examine the persons protected by the ECA, the nature of the protection, the extent of and conditions for employer's liability, scope of the term 'arising out of and in the course of employment' and the events to be considered in this regard.

§1. The Workers Covered

336. We shall first attempt to understand the persons protected by the ECA and then distinguish them from those who are left out. The Act also empowers the State Government concerned to extend the coverage of the Act, by including additional employments.

I. Definition of Employee

337. The ECA provides protection to those employed people who come within the definition of 'employee' as defined in section 2(1)(n) read with Schedule II of the Act. A combined reading of section 2 (1) (n) and Schedule II of the ECA shows that those who are employed in clerical or administrative positions in a factory are generally not covered by the provisions of the Act.[76] It has however been held that merely designating a person as supervisor[77] would not take away from him the status of a workman or employee, if he is actually doing manual work. Also, it has been held that the definition of workman under the WCA (now renamed as ECA) was wide enough and does not contemplate that there should be a letter of appointment to establish the relationship of employer and employee.[78] Previously, the definition was restricted to those persons whose average monthly wage was below INR 1,000 but by an amendment in 1984 the wage ceiling has been removed.

The definition covers workers employed in certain employments, apart from manufacturing process carried on in factories in general. Among others, persons covered include railway servants except those who are permanently employed in any administrative district or sub-divisional office of a railway. To determine whether a person other than a railway servant is a workman or not, a reference has to be made to Schedule II, which lists the employments to which the ECA applies. About fifty employments[79] are listed in Schedule II.

---

76. *Director, Printing and Stationery & Publication v. Brahmanand Dhall*, 1997 Lab. IC 2808 (Ori.).
77. *Managing Director, J & K PCC v. Commissioner for Workmen's Compensation & Others* (1991) I LLJ 65(J&K).
78. *United India Assurance Co. Ltd Hyderabad v. K Anjaneyulu* 2007 LLR 1075 (AP).
79. The WCA was amended in 1995 to provide, among others, for addition of sixteen hazardous employments to the then existing employments in Schedule II. It was again amended in 2009 which renamed the Act as Employees Compensation Act 1923 (ECA). The amended Act received the assent of the President of India on 22 Dec. 2009.

338. Schedule II, among others, includes persons employed in a factory (as defined in the Factories Act 1948) or any work incidental to it; employed in manufacture of explosives, mining operations; employed as the master or as a seaman of any ship or in specified related operations; employed in maintenance or construction of buildings, embankments and roads; employed as railway guard or inspector; employed in plantations of tea, coffee, etc.; employed in training or keeping wild animals; employed as a driver or in farming by tractor or in a circus. Some of the employments which were added through amendment in 1995 include mechanized harvesting and threshing operations, spraying/dusting of insecticides in agricultural operations, horticultural operations, forestry, bee-keeping, fish catching in sea, handling of horses, mules, bulls, newspaper establishments, etc. This amendment also empowered the Central Government to add to Schedule II any employment which is of hazardous nature. Earlier, addition of employments to Schedule II could be done by notification only by the State Governments. As per this power, the Central Government in November 1997 added divers. Later on, cooks employed in hotels and restaurants were also added.

339. It is the claimant who has to prove that she/he is an employee within the meaning of the section. But, if the employer claims that the claimant falls in an excluded category, then it is the employer who has to prove the contention. For example, the employer has to establish that the claimant was employed as a casual[80] workman or that he was not employed in the employer's trade or business. Even a person employed on daily wages basis can be a workman.[81]

340. By and large, the Indian judiciary has given liberal construction to most labour and social security laws, especially till the beginning of globalization. This is due to the coverage of most such matters in the Directive Principles of State Policy in the Constitution, which are based on the philosophy of a protectionist Welfare State. The wider protection envisaged is discernible in the interpretation of the term workman also. In a decided case[82] the question was whether a licensed railway porter was a workman under the WCA.

Even though a licensed porter is not included in Schedule II of the Act, the Kerala High Court held that a porter is a workman. It said that since the porters were performing a statutory duty and were performing work under the overall control and supervision of the railways, they were workmen for the purpose of the WCA. The Court observed that whether or not a person is a workman (now employee) depends upon the fact and circumstances of each case. The fact that payment is made at piece rate or by a third person under an arrangement with the employer will not affect the relationship.

80. *Raj Rani v. Firm Nar Singh Das*, AIR 1964 Punj. 315. But Act 46 of 2000, which amended the former version of this Act has dropped the words 'other than a person whose employment is of casual nature and who is employed otherwise than for the purposes of the employer's trade or business'. Thus, the Act is now applicable to casual employees also.
81. *Gorelal v. Dropadibai and Others*, AIR 1968 M.P. 24; *Asstt. Director of Fisheries v. Mathumeentachiva*, AIR 1963 Mad. 9.
82. *Narayanan v. Southern Railway* (1980) I LLJ 395 (Ker.).

II. Persons Excluded

341. In order to hold a person as an employee, it is necessary to prove that there exists a 'contract of employment' whether express or implied. In other words, a person is not a workman if there is a 'contract for employment'. In that case the person may be said to be an independent contractor. Mere use of the word wages does not necessarily constitute a relationship of contract of employment. Courts have held that the relationship of employer and employee is established, if the employer has some degree of control and could regulate the action of the employee during the time he is engaged in doing his work.[83] An independent employee, in pursuit of an independent business, undertakes to do specific work for other person without submitting himself to the other's control about the details of work. In a decided case[84] an employee E of company A was summoned by another company B after he had come home finishing his duty at the company A. He was called to undertake some repair of a machine at B's factory for INR 25 as remuneration. While working at B's factory, he received injuries and died. It was held that E was not a workman but only an independent contractor as he had no contract of service with company B.

342. The operation of the Act has been excluded in case of members of the armed forces of the Union.

343. The WCA did not protect a person whose employment is 'of casual nature and who has been employed otherwise than for the purpose of employer's trade or business'. Courts had read the entire clause conjunctively, and held that to take a person out of the definition both conditions must be fulfilled.[85] The term casual had been held to be not a term of precision, but merely a colloquial term. To know whether a work was of casual nature, one had to look at the nature and not duration of service. Courts underscored the need for a liberal construction of this term.[86]

For excluding a person from the meaning of the term workman, two things had to be proved one, that his employment was of casual nature; and two, that his employment was otherwise than in the employer's trade or business.[87] In one case[88] a person was engaged by the owner of a house for painting on daily wages. He was injured while doing work. It was held that the plaintiff was not entitled to any compensation because the owner of the house was not carrying on any business of repairing. It was merely an odd job for which he employed a person as casual labour. Trade and business had, however, been given a wide connotation. The activities of the Public Works Department, though not trade, amount to business.[89] But

83. *K.R. Reddiar Gold Merchant and Jeweller v. His Workers* (1956) II LLJ 139.
84. *Ganesh Foundry Works v. Bhagwati and Others* (1985) I LLJ 95 (P&H).
85. *Mahmood v. Balwant Singh*, 1980 Lab. IC 300; *Vijay Ram v. Chandu Prakash*, 1981 Lab. IC 359.
86. *Raj Rani v. Firm Narsing Dass*, AIR 1964 Punj. 315; *Sitharama v. Ayyaswami*, AIR 1956 Mad. 212; *Patel Engineering v. Commissioner for Compensation*, 1978 Lab. IC 1279.
87. *Sitharama v. Ayyaswami*, AIR 1956 Mad. 212; *Amri Naran v. Suken Employees Coop. Society Ltd*, 1987 Lab. IC 1197 (Guj.); *Kochappan v. Krishnan* (1987) II LLJ 174.
88. *Gopal Das Nandey v. Adladi Bibee* (1976) II LLJ 96 (Cal.).
89. *Bai Mani v. Executive Engineer* (1986) II LLJ 426 (Guj.).

now after the Act has been amended in 2009, all this controversy is of historical importance, and casual employees are also included.

III. Extending the Coverage of Protection

344. Though the legislature mainly wanted to cover the employees employed in employments stated in Schedule II of the Act, they were aware of the need for extending the coverage of the Act as and when felt so by the political executive. Therefore, such an extension power has been conferred by section 2(3) of the ECA on the State Governments. For this, the Government has to give a notification in the official gazette, and the notice should be of not less than three months. Thus, a State Government may add to Schedule II any class of persons employed in any occupation which it is satisfied is a hazardous occupation. However, while giving such a notification the Government may stipulate that the extension of the Act shall apply to specified injuries only. By an amendment to the Act in 1997, even the Central Government has been authorized to add to Schedule II.

345. Earlier, the Act was applicable to workmen working in scheduled employments on monthly wages not exceeding INR 1,000 per month. But, the 1984 amendment to the Act did away with this limit altogether. However, a notional ceiling was imposed at INR 1,000 per month only for calculation of the compensation. That means, for the purpose of calculating the compensation payable in respect of disablement or death of a person covered it was presumed that his wages were not more than INR 1,000 per month. Later on, this notional ceiling for the purpose of computation of compensation was raised to INR 2,000 per month by the 1995 amendment to the WCA, and was further raised to INR 4,000 by the Workmen's Compensation (Amendment) Act 2000 (Act 46 of 2,000). The Workmen's Compensation (Amendment) Act of 2009 has now conferred the power of revising the notional ceiling for the purpose of calculation of compensation on the Central Government. The ECA need not require amendment by Parliament on this issue any more. The Central Government can revise this amount by a notification. In 2020, the ceiling of wages for calculation of compensation is at INR 15,000 per month.

§2. Employer's Liability

346. So far as occupational accidents are concerned, the ECA provides for employer's unilateral liability only in certain cases; but in others there is provision for providing the protection through social insurance of occupational accidents. The latter category of cases comes under the ESI Act 1948. Under the ESI Act, the employer's liability is to pay contributions to the ESI Fund, which takes care of several contingencies including occupational accidents. In this chapter, we will be concerned with the employer's liability under the ECA. The employer's liability envisaged under the ECA is a departure from the traditional form of employer's liability emanating from the law of torts.

I. The Traditional Concept of Employer's Liability

347. Before the WCA was enacted, the employer's liability for injuries to workman (now employee under the changed name the ECA) was based on negligence or fault of the employer, i.e., it was a liability only if it came under the law of torts. The heirs of a workman could make a claim for compensation against the employer under the Fatal Accidents Act 1855, in case the accident resulted from any wrongful act, neglect or default of the employer. The claim could also be made on the person who caused the death. Proof of the employer's fault was the basis of his liability. The worker had to prove that the employer was responsible for the injuries suffered. Thus, in most industrial accidents the employee could hardly get damages because of the heavy burden of proof of negligence on his/her part. The principle governing compensation was dependent on the suffering caused to the employee or the expenses incurred by him on his treatment. Contributory negligence was a ground for reducing the amount of compensation receivable.

II. Employer's Liability under ECA

348. The ECA (formerly WCA) has created a new type of liability, which is not based on any fault on the part of the employer or his agents. The provisions of this law are not a mere amendment to the existing law, but symbolize a totally new law rooted in humanitarian considerations of industry's working.

The ECA delineates the employer's liability under section 3(1). It envisages that if personal injury is caused to a workman by accident arising out of and in the course of his employment, his employer shall be liable to pay compensation in accordance with Chapter II of the Act. For knowing the employer's liability three terms need to be elaborated, namely (a) personal injury; (b) accident; and (c) arising out of and in the course of employment.

§3. Determinants of Employer's Liability

I. Personal Injury

349. The ECA has not defined the term injury. Ordinarily, injury refers to a physical injury. But personal injury under the ECA actually means much more than that. It includes a mental injury or strain or nervous shock. In one case,[90] an electrician had to go frequently to a heating room, from a cooling plant. Consequently, he contracted pneumonia which resulted in his death. It was held, that the injury in the present case was due to his going frequently from the heating room to the cooling plant, as it was his indispensable duty to do so. In another case,[91] the death of a worker from a heat stroke has also been held to be personal injury, entitling the dependants to compensation.

90. *Indian News Chronicle v. Mrs Lazarus*, AIR 1961 Punj. 102.
91. *Mrs Santan Fernandez v. B.P.* (India) Ltd, 58 Bom. L.R. 149.

II. Accident

350. The word accident has also not been defined in the ECA. But it includes any mishap, or untoward event not expected or designed. Its meaning is discernible from decisions of several cases. In one case,[92] the Gujarat High Court explained that accident is 'some unexpected event happening without design even though there may be negligence on the part of the workman. It ... means a mishap or an untoward event not expected or designed ... . It includes not only occurrences such as collisions, tripping over floor obstacles, falls of roof, but also less obvious ones causing injury, e.g., strain which causes rupture, exposure to a draught causing chill, exertion in a stokehold causing apoplexy, and shock causing neurasthenia'. Whether a particular event is an accident has to be seen both, from the viewpoint of the person who causes it and the viewpoint of the person who suffers it. In a case, a series of small events may produce an injury which can be said to constitute an accident. The terms 'injury' and 'accident' imply existence of some external factor to cause death, apart from internal ailment of the body. Even murder of a worker, when on duty was held to be an accident arising out of and in the course of employment.[93] But murders of different types came to be distinguished by the Supreme Court.[94] It was held that the difference between a murder which is not an accident and a murder which is an accident under the Act would depend on the proximity of the cause of such murder. If the dominant intention of the act of felony is to kill any particular person, when such killing is not an accidental murder but is a murder simpliciter then it will not be an accident. But, if the course of murder or act of murder was originally not intended and the same was caused in furtherance of any other felonious act, then such murder is an accidental murder.

III. Arising Out of and in the Course of Employment

351. In order to hold the employer liable, it is important that the accident which caused the injury to the worker resulted from an accident which not only arose in the course of employment, but also arose out of employment. This expression is the key to section 3. The term has been subjected to considerable judicial controversy. Courts have expressed that the words 'arising out of and in the course of employment' used in the ECA have to be construed, keeping in view the beneficial nature of the enactment. So, when the cleaner of a lorry went to a restaurant to get food on the instructions of the driver and met with an accident and died, it was held to be a case of accident arising out of and in the course of employment.[95]

---

92. *Bai Shakri v. New Manekchowk Mills Co.*, AIR 1961 Guj. 34.
93. *Oriental Insurance Co. Ltd v. Rachna Devi* 2005 LLR 55 (Punj & Har).
94. *Rita Devi v. New India Assurance Co. Ltd* 2000 (5) SCC 113.
95. *New India Assurance Co. Ltd, Secunderabad v. Smt. Padmavathi* 2005 LLR 869 (AP).

352. The word employment referred to in this term has not to be defined in a narrow manner by reference only to the duties of the employee but the character, conditions, incidents and special risks involved will help in determining employment.

A. Course of Employment

353. Courts have held that the term 'course of employment' emphasizes the time and place where the accidental injury was caused, and the word 'out of employment' emphasizes that there must be a causal connection between the employment and accidental injury. The term 'in the course of employment' refers to work that the employee is employed to do and which is incidental to it. Ordinarily, course of employment begins as soon as a person reaches his place of work where he is supposed to be doing his work. Thus, when an employee is in transit to do some work on behalf of his employer, but out of the ordinary place of work he will be said to be in the course of employment and will be entitled to compensation. In a decided case,[96] the deceased employee was sent out to a nearby tea shop to fetch two glasses of tea and again to return the empty glasses. While he was coming back to his Mill after returning the glasses, he received stab wounds on the road and died. It was held that the accident arose in the course of workman's employment. Similarly, in another case,[97] the job of an employee was to repair railway clocks at various stations. While he was in transit, he was stabbed in a railway compartment. It was held that the accident arose in the course of employment and also out of employment. The term in the course of employment covers the whole of the time during which the workman is carrying out his duties or doing work incidental to his contract of service.

354. In another interesting case,[98] an employee employed by Stevedores was injured as a result of assault by ship's crew, while attempting to drink water. The water arrangement was not being made by Stevedores and the employee was supposed to have taken water from the ship itself. It was held that the accident arose in the course of employment. The Court said that the injury received within reasonable limits of time and space will be regarded as employment injury. Thus, accident occurring while satisfying thirst or satisfying bodily needs in the use of food, drink and tobacco will be regarded as employment injury. It is necessary that the employee must show that at the time of accident he was engaged in employer's business or in furthering that business and not doing something that can be said to be for his own benefit. Work in the course of employment is, therefore, not confined to the period of actual labour nor just to the acts required by the workman's employment. But, it is important to ask, as to how far a servant can go outside the appointed sphere. Courts have allowed reasonable extension of the limits of time and space.

96. *Varkeyachan v. Thomman*, 1979 Lab. IC 986 (Ker.).
97. *The General Manager, G.I.P. Railway v. Jamlabai* (Unreported case) decided on 20 Jun. 1949.
98. *P.E. Davis & Co. v. Kesto Routa*, AIR 1968 Cal. 129.

B. Out of Employment

355. Looking at a large number of decisions on the expression 'arising out of employment' delivered by the higher judiciary in India, it appears that this phrase tends to defy articulation. It is often difficult to articulate the test for its determination. Nevertheless, it is settled that this term suggests a causal connection between the employment and accidental injury. The cause between the two should be proximate and not any remote. In a well-known decision, *Mackinnon Mackenzie & Co. Private Ltd v. I.M. Issak,*[99] the SC observed that the words 'arising out of employment' means that the injury has resulted from some risk incidental to the duties of service, which unless engaged in the duty owing to the master, it is reasonable to believe that the workman would not otherwise have suffered. The Court emphasized the causal relationship between the accident and the employment.

356. In *Mackenzie*, the Supreme Court approved the test laid down in a famous British case, *Lancashire and Yorkshire Railway Co. v. Highley.*[100] The test in this case was – 'was it part of the injured person's employment to hazard, to suffer or to do that which caused his injury? If yes, the injury arose out of his employment, if not it did not'.

In *Mackenzie*, a seaman was last seen on the ship at about 3 a.m. and was found missing at 6.15 a.m. on the same day. His dead body could not be found, after a search was conducted. It was held that there was no natural evidence to infer that the death was caused by an accident which arose out of his employment. The Supreme Court held that the burden of proof rested upon the workman (his widow in this case) to show that the accident arose out of employment, though it was not necessary to do so by direct evidence. The same could be inferred from the facts.

357. Despite the above decision, several cases came before the higher judiciary where application of the *Lancashire* test as approved in *Mackenzie* has posed problems. In a decision[101] of the Bombay High Court, difficulty was felt in inferring a causal connection. There, a bomb was placed in the premises of a workshop by some unknown persons, which exploded and injured a workman. The Court said that there may be circumstances attending the employment which would go to show that the workman received personal injury as a result of the accident arising out of his employment. The rule is, Court said, if a particular accident would not have happened to a workman had he not been employed to work in a particular place and condition, it would be accident arising out of the employment.

In a somewhat similar situation occurring in another case,[102] a boy was employed by a company in a tea shop and it was a part of his duty to bring tea from the shop which was situated outside the factory gate and to serve it to various persons working in the factory. One day while the boy was coming out of the factory after serving tea to the workers, he passed through a violent mob which was fired by the

---

99. (1970) 2. Lab. IC 1413 (SC).
100. 1917 AC 352.
101. *Trustees, Port of Bombay v. Yamunabai*, AIR 1952 Bom. 382.
102. *National Iron and Steel Co. Ltd v. Manorama*, AIR 1953 Cal. 143.

police. A bullet hit the boy resulting in his death. It was held by the Calcutta High Court that the accident arose out of and in the course of employment. The Court said that the death occurred because of the risk to which he was exposed, by the nature of his employment.

358. A difficulty arises if during the period of employment, the workman does something which is not a part of his service. Courts have held that for awarding compensation, it should be work naturally connected with the class of work that he is supposed to do and the injury must result from it. This question came to be considered in another case.[103] An employee was employed in a lorry belonging to his employer carrying material from the quarry site. His duty was to load and unload the material. While the lorry was moving, he attempted to hit a rabbit which was passing on the road; in the process he fell down and died. The Court held that no compensation was payable because hitting a rabbit which ran across the truck was not a part of the workman's service for which he was employed. Thus, in a way, the court applied the 'added peril' doctrine to deny the benefit to the workman. In another interesting case,[104] during the course of employment, an employee went to take tea on the ground floor. There he came to know that while cleaning the seepage water one hospital employee and another worker had fallen into the well. Out of instinct with a view to rescue them he broke the security cordon and jumped into the well, and died. It was held by the Madras High Court the deceased had out of his own volition, gone and attended to the rescuing work in the seepage well which he was not called upon by the employer to do and it was a kind of work with which the deceased was not at all concerned with. Applying the principle of added peril, the court exonerated the employer of any liability to pay compensation to the claimants.

359. There have, however, been cases of added peril which have been protected by the Courts to be arising out of employment. In *R.B. Moondra & Co.* v. *Mst. Bhanwari*,[105] the deceased workman was a driver of a truck that was used for carrying petrol in a tank. On the previous day, he had reported to his employer that the tank was leaking and so water was put in it for detecting the leakage. The next morning, the employer asked the driver to enter the tank to see from where it leaked. He entered the tank which had no petrol in it and for detecting the leakage he lighted a match stick to see pores, if any. Consequently, the truck caught fire and the driver died. The employer pleaded that he had added peril by negligently and carelessly lighting the matchstick, and had not been asked by him to do so. The Court held the accident to be one arising out of employment and negatived the application of added peril, in this case. It said, if the act leading to the accident was one within the sphere of employment or incidental to it or in the interest of the employer, then the accident would be said to arise out and in the course of employment. A somewhat similar situation occurred in another case,[106] where the mechanic employed to

103. *Smt. Koduri v. Polongi Atchamma* (1969) Lab. 1C 1415 (Andh. Pra.).
104. *K. Rathinam v. Apollo Enterprises represented by its Pratap C. Reddy* 2001 LLR 1126 (Mad.).
105. AIR 1970 Raj. 111.
106. *M/S J.D. & Co. Mills v. ESI Corporation*, AIR 1963 A.P. 210.

disconnect the crushing machine from the rest of the moving machinery was absent from the site. An unskilled workman noticed that the crushing machine was running without any business. His duty was merely to feed the oil mill by pouring groundnut seeds into the crushing machine. He kicked off the moving pulley to stop the running of the crushing machine. Consequently, he got caught between the pulley and the belt and died instantaneously. The Andhra Pradesh High Court held that whatever the workman did was in the interest of the employer and was intended to save the machine to get damaged.

360. Several instances occur while an employee faces risks seemingly unconnected with the employment. In such cases, the facts need to be analysed minutely, depending upon the facts and circumstances of the case. Courts have stretched the concept of employer's duty to protect the interest of the workers. In case of assault on a workman by co-workers or by strangers while they are working, or where the workman is exposed to a natural calamity like an earthquake, flood or snakebite, etc., employers owe a common law duty to their servants to take reasonable care for their safety. This includes, safety of the premises and the plant where the workers work. It also extends to the method of work and the actual conduct of work. The employers must take reasonable steps to protect the worker from unreasonable risks.

In a decided case,[107] a jeep driver of a bank took an officer of the bank to a village in connection with recovery proceedings conducted by the bank. He parked the jeep in the rest house and went to the market where he was assaulted by some unknown persons in the crowd and was found dead. It was held that the risk incurred by the driver in going to the market was incidental to his employment, to take the jeep to the village. So this protection will, extend when the workman is asked by his supervisor to bring lunch for him from his home, or is asked to do the work beyond duty hours[108] or is told to go out of the workplace (including a public road) to do some work connected with the employment or incidental to it.

1. Injuries by Risk Personal to the Claimant

361. An important question to ask is – will every death or injury during the working hours be deemed to arise out of employment? This question has been considered in a number of cases. It has been held[109] that if a workman dies as a natural result of the disease from which he is suffering, it cannot be inferred that his death was caused by employment. In one such case,[110] the deceased was employed in the

107. *Salamabegum v. District Branch Manager, Maharashtra State Cooperative Land Development Bank Beed & Another* (1990) I LLJ 112 (Bom.).

108. *Raj Dulari v. Superintending Engineer PSEB & Another* (1989) II LLJ 132 (P&H.).

109. *Smt. Laxmibai v. Port Trust, Bombay* (1954) I LLJ 614 (Bom.). Also *see Ramlal Jawaharlal v. Smt. Leela Bai* (1972) II LLJ 589 (Raj.); *Gujarat State Road Transport Corpn. v. Bai Jiviben Arjan* (1981) I Lab. IC 86 (Guj.).

110. *Bai Shakri v. New Maneck Chowk Mills Co. Ltd* (1961) I LLJ 585 (Guj.). Also *see Shakuntala Chandrakant Shreshti v. Prabhakar Maruti Garvali & Another* 2007 LLR 285 (SC), where the Supreme Court negatived claim in similar circumstances as stress of work could not be proved.

weaving department of a mill. His duty commenced from 3 p.m. Before commencing his duty, he went to a sister department to see a friend. There, he suffered a heart attack at 3.20 p.m. and was admitted to a hospital for a month. Then he left his employment and died after some time. It was held, that this case did not fall in the category of accident causing employment injury. The Court did admit that it was not necessary that the workman must be actually working at the time of the accident. It was also said that in cases where the balance of evidence shows a greater probability that the work contributed to the causing of personal injury, it would be enough for the worker to succeed. In another case,[111] the deceased was a goods train driver. One day, when he was on duty he collapsed and died while talking to the guard at a wayside station. He took rest at intermediate stations. The Court held, the fact that the workman died a natural death, because of a disease from which he was suffering and that the death resulting on account of normal wear and tear of his employment will not entitle him to receive compensation. In such cases, it was necessary not just to show that he died because of the heart disease (as reported in this case) from which he was suffering, but also because of some contributing cause relatable to his employment or his duties that he was performing. But, when a bus driver died of heart attack after driving a bus for twelve hours and complaining of chest pain, it was held that it was not necessary for the dependants to prove that the deceased was engaged in some exceptional work of a particular kind which had caused excess strain on the deceased so as to result in his death, it could be said that there was a proximate nexus between the death and employment.[112]

2. Injuries by Mixed Risks

362. The Supreme Court has held[113] that if the employment is a contributory cause or accelerated the death of a worker suffering from a natural disease, then the employer would be held liable. Therefore, if personal risk coupled with employment produced injury, the injury is considered to arise out of employment. In a case,[114] a factory worker who was suffering from heart disease profusely sweated when he was coming out of the factory and died after four hours. It was held that the stress and strain of work in the factory must be taken to be an accelerating factor for his death and the employer was held liable. In another related case,[115] a senior cook employed with Western Railway was working on the cooking gas in the cooking room of a running train. He inhaled excessive gas and was admitted to a hospital. However, eventually he died. It was held that working on the cooking stove could not be the immediate cause of death, but hard work on a cooking stove could lead to strain and accelerated the death. His death therefore was held to be

111. *Kamla Bai v. Divisional Superintendent, Central Railway, Nagpur* (1971) I LLJ 603 (Bom.).
112. *Divisional Controller, NEKRTC, Bellary v. Marembee & Others* 2004 LLR 33.
113. *Mackinnon Mackenzie & Co. v. Ritta Fernandes* (1969) II LLJ 812 (SC).
114. *Director (T&M) D.N.K. Project v. Smt. D. Buchitalli* (1989) LLJ 259 (Orissa).
115. *Divisional Personnel Officer, Western Rly. Jaipur & Another v. Ashiya Begum* (1993) II LLJ 795 (Raj.).

resulting out of employment. In yet another case,[116] the door keeper in a cinema theatre was working for 14 to 15 hours per day. He was suffering from tuberculosis. While on duty, he suffered a heart attack and died. The Gujarat High Court held, that there was a nexus between the heart attack and the employment of the deceased. It was observed that the work accelerated the death due to the heart attack.

3. Towards Reaching a Test of Employer's Liability

363. From the decisions analysed above, certain principles can be drawn which help to know whether or not the accident arose out of employment. Interestingly, the full bench of the Assam High Court[117] summarized as follows the cases falling in the category of those where the injury arose out of employment:

(1) the employee was in fact employed on or performing the duties of his employment at the time of the accident;
(2) the accident occurred at or about the place where he was performing these duties or where the performance of these duties required him to be present; and
(3) the immediate act which led to or resulted in the accident had some form of causal relation with the performance of these duties and such causal connection could be held to exist, if the immediate act which led to the accident is not so remote from the sphere of his duties or the performance thereof, as to be regarded as something foreign to them.

While applying these general tests, one has also to keep in view that in actuality most cases reflect peculiarities. Therefore, each case should be decided on its own merits subject to these broad tests. It is discernible from the above decisions that in some cases the Courts have diluted the 'added peril doctrine', to provide relief to the workman concerned in case the negligent act committed by the workman actually was meant to benefit the employer. Whatever may be the facts of a case, the principle still stands, that the burden of proof that the accident 'arose out of and in the course of employment' is on the workman and in case of death on his dependants.

C. Notional Extension of Employer's Premises

364. The time and place where the accident takes place are very important for knowing whether an accident has resulted in the course of and out of employment. Under ordinary circumstances, a person's employment begins when he reaches the place of work and ends when he has left the workplace. The time taken in reaching the workplace from home and that in coming back from the workplace to home is

116. *Devibehn Dudhabhai v. Manager, Liberty Talkies & Another* (1994) II LLJ 1207 (Guj.).
117. *Assam Railway & Trading Co. v. Saraswati Devi*, AIR 1963 Ass. 127. Also *see*: *Kondisetti Anjaih v. T. Lakshmaiah*, AIR 1961 AP 15; *Satyanarayana v. Narayana Swami*, AIR 1961 AP 18.

usually not included in the course of employment. However, it is now settled that there may be a reasonable extension of time and place of employment. For this, it is necessary that there is a nexus between the time and the place of the accident and the employment. It has been held that, if in going to or coming back from his or her work the employee has to use an access which forms part of the employer's premises, or which the worker is entitled to traverse because he is going to or coming back from his work, the workman will be deemed to be on the master's business while s/he is using that access.[118] The concept of 'duty' will be deemed to apply to the extended premises. This is known as the doctrine of 'notional extension of employer's premises'.

In some cases, the doctrine is considered as the implied term in the employment contract, in others it is treated as the proved or practical necessity.[119] Thus, in a case the deceased watchman was returning home after his night duty when he developed chest pain and the resultant cardiac arrest. Applying the theory of notional extension of time to the facts and circumstances of the case, it was held that the deceased had died due to an accident arising out of and in the course of his employment.[120] The doctrine of notional extension became well settled, in some well-known British cases. In one[121] of these, the Railway Company made an agreement with a colliery company in which the workman worked, to run a special train for the colliery workers between the colliery and the place of residence of the workers. Each workman was provided with a pass and the amount of fair was deducted from his wages. A worker was injured while traveling in the train. Though the workman had a right to travel by the special train, but there was no obligation to do so as there were alternative means of travel. It was held that the accident did not arise out of employment, as there was no obligation to travel by the special train as per the contract of service. The Court also said that, if the features of the locality are such that the means of transit offered by the employer would have been the only means of transit to transport the workman to his place of work, then an obligation on the employer to provide such a means could be implied.

365. The doctrine of notional extension has been applied in several cases in India. Thus, in case the journey after or before work is made in a truck, bus, car or other vehicle provided by the employer, an injury during that journey is incurred in the course of employment. The rationale for this extension is that, the employer itself or himself broadened the range of employment and the consequent risks. In such cases, it will be presumed that the employer sends 'the employee home in a small ambulatory portion of the premises'.[122]

In a case,[123] the railway workshop in which the workman worked was situated at about a mile, from the Lucknow railway station. The workman used to travel by a

118. *Per Lord Macmillan in Northumbrian Shipping Co. Ltd v. Mccullum* (1932), 48 Times L.R. 568 at 572.
119. *Richards v. Morris* (1915) 1 KB 222; *Varadarajulu Naidu v. M. Boyan*, AIR 1954 Mad. 1113; *G.M, BEST Undertakings v. Mrs. Agnes*, AIR 1964 SC 193.
120. *United India Assurance Co. Ltd v. Smt. Shushila* 2004 LLR 425 (Kar.).
121. *St. Helens Colliery Co. Ltd v. Hewlston*, 1924 AC 59.
122. S.C. Srivastava, *Social Security and Labour Laws* (Lucknow: Eastern Book Company, 1985), 82.
123. *Works Manager, Carriage and Wagon Shop E.I.R. v. Mahabir*, AIR 1954 All. 132.

workman's special train from a nearby town to Lucknow railway station. The train was provided by the railways. After getting down at the Lucknow railway station, workers usually reached the workshop after crossing the railway lines in preference to the alternative sub-way and over-bridge routes. A workman, after finishing his duties at the workshop, was returning to the railway station to catch the train by crossing the railway lines. He was run over by a shunting engine and received injuries. The employer was held liable, by applying the notional extension doctrine.

366. With the passage of time, courts in India have widened the scope of the notional extension doctrine, by applying it even to cases where there is no obligation to travel by the means of transport provided by the employer. This is so, if it can be established that it was in the interest of efficiency that the workman should avail the service provided by the employer. This was so held by the Supreme Court in a decided case.[124] In this case, the employer was a public transport undertaking running bus service in the city of Bombay. The employer (BEST) offered to its employees the facility of traveling by buses provided by the BEST from home to bus depots and back. This was a welfare measure to ensure that the employees reach the bus depot on time and go back. The service was free and the employees could use it as of right, though there was no compulsion to do so and there were alternative means available to them. A driver was traveling, while going home from his depot. He was injured in an accident in the course of the travel. The accident was held to be in course of employment.

367. It should be noted that, despite some liberal interpretations of the notional extension doctrine, the judiciary has fortified the protection by clarifying that when a workman (now employee) is on a public road or public place or public transport, he is there as any other member of the public and will be treated to be in the course of employment. It was so held in a case,[125] where the workman employed in a salt works used to return home after finishing his work by a public path, then through a sandy area in the open public and finally across a creek with a ferry boat. While crossing the creek in the ferry boat, which capsized due to bad weather, he was drowned. The Supreme Court held that the notional extension could not be applied at the point where the boat capsized. It said the proximity of the place of accident to the place of work is irrelevant for the purpose. It was also observed that the facts and circumstances of each case will have to be examined very carefully in order to determine whether the accident can be said to arise out of employment of the workman, keeping in view at all times the theory of notional extension.

368. In some cases where there is sufficient proximity both in time and place with the workman's employment, the notional extension concept has been applied. Thus in a case,[126] the employer company had two separate gates for going and coming for convenient egress and ingress of employees. A workman was standing outside the gate, just five minutes before the start of his shift. He was knocked down

---

124. *B.E.S.T. Undertakings v. Mrs Agnes*, AIR 1964 SC 193.
125. *Saurashtra Salt Manufacturing Co. v. Bai Velu Raja*, AIR 1958 SC 881.
126. *Dudhiben Dharamshi v. New Jehangir Vakil Mills Ltd*, 1977 Lab. IC 10.

by a cyclist which resulted in his death. It was held that the place clearly came within the theory of notional extension because of the sufficient proximity both in time and place when he was obtaining access through the specified gate. The employer had specified the entry gate and it was only an ordinary incident of his employment that he had come to that place at the fatal hour.

Similarly, in another case,[127] a workman was murdered in a communal clash, while coming to the rice mill to attend the work. Death had occurred outside the work place before his work commenced; the cause of death bore apparently no relationship to the employment. He was wearing the mill's uniform, while coming to the mill. The Madras High Court found sufficient causal connection between the employment and the accident. It was held that if the workman has to be in a particular place because of his employment and he has to face a particular peril, and the accident is caused by reason of that peril then the causal connection will be said to be established. The latter case appears to be on the border line, but shows that by and large Courts have tried to stretch the cover of protection, often crossing the accepted boundaries of protection.

§4. Employer's Defences Against Liability

369. The employer can disown his liability to pay compensation in the following cases which have been envisaged by section 3 of the ECA:

(1) When the injury does not result in disablement to the employee (earlier workman) for a period exceeding three days.
(2) If the injury (not resulting in death) is due to any of the following reasons:
   (i) the employee is under the influence of drug or drink at the time of the accident, or
   (ii) the employee wilfully disobeyed an order expressly given or a rule expressly framed for the purpose of ensuring the safety of workers, or
   (iii) the employee wilfully disregards or removes any safety guards or safety devices which he knew to have been provided for the safety of the employee.

It is noticeable that, if the employee dies due to the accident, then the employer shall be liable even though the workman may himself have contributed to the accident by committing any of the three misconducts provided for. The intention of the ECA is to widen the concept of accident and thus, the scope of the social protection envisaged. Also, it is presumed that a disablement of not more than three days resulting from an accident should be considered as a natural corollary of industrial working and the workman should remain prepared to face such contingencies.

370. The three misconducts envisaged above relate to the principle of added peril. The doctrine of added peril contemplates that, if an employee while doing his

127. *TNCS Corporation Ltd v. S. Poomalai*, 1995 I LLJ 378 (Mad.).

employer's work undertakes to do something that involves extra risk, it is inequitable to hold the employer liable for its consequences.

371. Section 3(5) of the ECA disentitles an employee to claim compensation under this Act, if he has instituted a suit for damages against the employer or any other person in a civil court. Likewise, a workman is prohibited from instituting a suit for damages in any court of law (a) if he has made a claim for compensation before the Commissioner; or (b) if the workman and the employer have entered into an agreement for the payment of compensation as per provisions of the ECA. The employee does have the choice of accepting compensation under the Act or to avail himself of any other remedy against the employer in a tort of negligence or any other person. The idea, however, is that the workman cannot have the best of both the worlds. If the workman fails under one action, then he cannot choose the other. Therefore, there is a responsibility of being careful in choosing his remedy. The employer can disown liability if the alternative option has already been exercised by the employee. Of course, the word instituted in section 3(5) is something more than filing a claim. If a workman has done nothing except filing a claim and withdraws it before the proceedings actually begin, then the alternative claim would be available to him.[128]

§5. Employer's Liability for Contractor's Employees

372. Sometimes an employer may not do a work in respect of his trade or business by directly employing an employee himself, but assign it to a contractor. Ordinarily, the employer is not liable for injury sustained by employee employed by the contractor, as these employees are employed by the contractor, not by him. But section 12(1) of the ECA makes the employer liable in such cases if three conditions are fulfilled (1) the contractor has been engaged to do some work which is part of the trade or business of the employer; (2) the workmen were engaged for the purpose of employer's trade or business; and (3) the accident occurred in or about the premises on which the principal employer has undertaken to or undertakes to execute the work concerned. The idea underlying this provision is to make it easier for the workman to secure compensation. Such a provision assumes significance where the contractor does not have sufficient resources to pay the compensation under the Act.

373. In such cases where the employer has to pay compensation for the contractor's workmen, he shall be entitled to be indemnified by the contractor or any other person from whom the workman could have recovered compensation. This provision, however, does not prevent a workman from recovering compensation from the contractor directly, if he chooses to do so.

128. *S. Sappiah Chettiar v. Chinnathurai & Another*, AIR 1957 Mad. 216.

374. In case there exists an agreement of indemnity[129] between the employer and the contractor, it will not disentitle an employee to claim compensation from the employer. In a decided case,[130] a workman (now employee) was engaged by a contractor of the Public Works Department. He met with a fatal accident, while digging a plot. A claim was filed by the dependants against the Public Works Department. The Commissioner ordered that one-third of the compensation was payable by the contractor and two-thirds by the principal employer. His award was challenged by the employer. The High Court held that the Commissioner could pass such an award granting full or partial compensation to be paid by the principal employer. But, this can be done subject to the condition that the principal employer will be indemnified by the contractor.

§6. Employer's Remedy Against the Stranger

375. Section 13 of the ECA entitles an employer who has paid compensation to an employee to be indemnified by the person who was responsible for the accident that caused the injury or death resulting in the employer's liability.

§7. Occupational Diseases

376. The ECA treats personal injury resulting from an accident at par with a specified 'occupational disease', for the purpose of determining employer's liability to pay compensation under section 3. The Act enumerates occupational diseases in Parts A, B and C of Schedule III. Diseases which are not covered in this schedule are outside the purview of the Act. In order to succeed in getting compensation, the disease contracted must be an occupational disease peculiar to the employment specified in Schedule III.

377. For claiming compensation in respect of occupational diseases enumerated in Part A, no qualification period of employment is necessary. It would be enough, if the contracting of any disease is specified in this Part. But if a disease mentioned in Part A is contracted after an employee has left the employment, no compensation shall be payable to him.

378. For diseases mentioned in Part B the employee must be in continuous employment with the same employer for a period of at least six months in the employment specified in that Part. This period, therefore, shall not include a period of service under any other employer in the same kind of employment. In case a disease mentioned in Part B is contracted by an employee after he has left his employment, the employer shall be liable in the following conditions:

---

129. *Sarjerao Unkar Jadhav v. Gurinder Singh & Another* (1992) I LLJ 156 (Bom.).
130. *Executive Engineer PWD v. Subbiah Naicker* (1983) II LLJ 320 (Mad.).

(i) the employee has served under any employer for a continuous period of six months;
(ii) the employee has after his cessation of service contracted any disease specified in Part B as an occupational disease peculiar to that employment; and
(iii) it is proved that such disease arose out of the employment.

379. In case of an employee contracting any disease specified in Part C the qualifying period of employment would be such as is specified by the Central Government for each such employment either under one or more employers. The contracting of any disease provided in Schedule III shall be presumed to be an injury by accident arising out of and in the course of employment. And if such contracting was under more than one employment, all the employers concerned shall be liable for the payment of compensation in the proportion that the Commissioner may, in the circumstances, deem just.

The ECA empowers the State Government to add to the list of occupational diseases in Part A and B of Schedule III. Also, it empowers the Central Government to add to the list of occupational diseases that have been mentioned in Part C. Except as mentioned above, no compensation is payable to a workman in relation to any disease, unless the disease is directly attributed to a specific injury that results from accident arising out of and in the course of employment.

Chapter 2. The Computation and Disbursement of Compensation

380. The ECA provides for payment of compensation to the employee covered when he suffers permanent total disablement (PTD), permanent partial disablement (PPD) or temporary disablement in his earning capacity as a result of an employment injury. It also provides for compensation to dependants in case the employee dies. In all cases, the protection is provided, when the accident from which disablement or death is caused arises out of and in the course of employment. The Act has laid down the method for calculating wages on the basis of which compensation is payable, as also the method of calculating the compensation payable. In case there is no evidence by the employer or the claimant about the amount of wages, the compensation will be calculated on the basis of the minimum wages as laid down in the Minimum Wages Act 1948.[131] After the employer deposits the compensation payable with the Commissioner, a procedure is prescribed for disbursement of the compensation. This chapter deals with these issues.

§1. Incapacity to Work

381. Incapacity to work as a result of the industrial accident or contracting an occupational disease can be temporary or permanent. The incapacity can be further divided into total or partial. The ECA uses the word disablement, though it does not define it. Of course, it does define partial and total disablement.

I. Permanent Total Disablement (PTD)

382. In some cases the accident may lead to permanent injuries which may result in total loss of earning capacity. The ECA treats such cases as more serious than even the death of the employee. Section 2(1)(l) defines total disablement. It says that when a person is incapacitated of doing any work which he was capable of performing at the time of the accident resulting in such disablement, it is total disablement. The definition of total disablement speaks of incapacity of all work and not just the incapacity to do the work which the workman was doing before the accident.

383. Whether the accident has resulted in permanent total incapacity is determined after the condition of the employee gets stabilized. This can be agreed upon between the employer and the employee through an agreement. If no agreement is reached on this issue, it is determined by the Commissioner of Compensation, who is the quasi-judicial body under the ECA. For this purpose, the employee has to prefer a claim before him.

131. *Ganga Devi & Another v. M/S US Motors Ltd & Another* 2007 LLR 874.

384. The loss of degree of permanent capacity is expressed by a percentage figure which ranges between 0 and 100. In determining the percentage of incapacity, stress is laid on the loss in the notional competitive position of the employee in the labour market and not the actual loss of earnings. Therefore, there may be cases where an employee may be considered as having suffered loss in his earning capacity though in actual practice he may not have suffered any incapacity. On the contrary, an employee may lose his job or his job-seeking capacity in the market altogether even though as per the ECA his loss in earning capacity may be considered quite low. But the real drop in the earning capacity is not fully relevant in all cases.

However, courts see the impact of the accident in its totality. In one case,[132] a carpenter suffered an employment injury which led to the amputation of his left hand above the elbow. Since a carpenter cannot work with one hand, his disablement was held to be total and not partial. In another case,[133] when a truck driver lost his right hand fingers and right thigh it was held his disablement was permanent total as he had become unfit for a driver's job.

385. It is specified by section 2(1)(l) that permanent total disablement is deemed to result from every injury specified in Part I of Schedule I. This Part lists six types of injuries, which if suffered by the workman are deemed to result in permanent total disablement.

II. Permanent Partial Disablement (PPD)

386. Part II of Schedule I provides forty-eight types of injuries and specifies the loss of earning capacity in case of each of these. It is provided, that every injury specified in Part II of Schedule I shall be deemed to result in permanent partial disablement. An employee may suffer several injuries of permanent nature. In such cases, the loss of his earning capacity in respect of each of the injury is noted and added up. If the total comes to 100 or more, then he will be deemed to have totally lost his earning capacity.

387. The question of loss of earning capacity or the extent of earning capacity is a question of fact. In deciding this, it is important to take into account the reduction or destruction of physical capacity as discernible from the medical evidence. This will help to show the extent to which such diminution or destruction has disabled the affected workman from performing the duties which a workman of his class ordinarily performs.

388. In a decided case,[134] the court laid down four broad propositions for deciding the nature of disablement first, earning is not the same thing as earning capacity; second, the rise in earning capacity may be because of various factors and rise

132. *Pratap Narain Singh Deo v. Srinivasa*, AIR 1976 SC 222.
133. *P.K. Parmar v. Keval Constructions* (1985) I LLJ 98 (Guj.).
134. *Bengal Chambers of Commerce v. Md. Hussain*, 1969 Lab. IC 971.

in wages is not decisive of no loss of earning capacity; third, loss of physical capacity is not co-extensive with loss of earning capacity and fourth, loss of physical capacity or physical incapacity may be relevant in assessing to what extent there is a loss of earning capacity for every employment which the workman was capable of undertaking at that time or the employment in which he was engaged at the time of the accident.

389. The concept of permanent partial disablement (PPD) is related with the reduction in earning capacity. In one case,[135] a railway servant was working in A-1 post. He lost one eye and two teeth in an employment accident and was declared unfit to hold A-1 and B posts, but fit for doing jobs involved in C-2 posts because of the defective vision. The railway administration offered him a C-2 post which he refused. He claimed compensation on the basis of total disablement. It was held that he was entitled to compensation only on the basis of partial disablement. The court held that this was a case only of reduction in earning capacity not of loss of earning capacity, because he was offered an alternative employment by the employer. Sometimes, an accident may lead to a situation where the employee may not lose his earning capacity, but may stamp him with a visible mark of physical deficiency which may dissuade the likely employers to employ him. The court held that in such a case he would be deemed to be incapacitated as if his earning capacity is altogether destroyed. In another case,[136] it was held that 'if an employee suffers as a result of an injury from a physical defect which does not in fact reduce his capacity to work, but at the same time makes his labour unsaleable in any market reasonably accessible to him, there will be either total incapacity for work, when no work is available to him at all or there will be partial incapacity where such defect makes his labour saleable for less remuneration than it would otherwise fetch. The capacity of an employee may remain quite unimpaired, but at the same time his eligibility as an employee may be diminished or lost'. But sometime an employee may be retained in the same job with same pay, then the situation becomes difficult. In one such situation in a case,[137] the driver of a truck met with an accident and was awarded 35% loss in earning capacity. But, he was retained in the same job that he could do without any problem. On an appeal by the insurance company, it was held that, if the injured person was shifted to another job with same wages/salary, since the injury had made him misfit for continuing in the work that he was performing before accident, he could claim loss of capacity even though there was no actual loss of earning wage. However, when the injured person continues to do the same work without any difficulty and earned the same wage, he cannot be said to have suffered any loss of earning capacity. The appeal of the insurance company was dismissed.

---

135. *General Manager G.R.P. Railway, Bombay v. Shanker*, AIR 1950 Nag. 201.
136. *Sukhai v. Hukum Chand Jute Mills Ltd*, AIR 1957 Cal. 601.
137. *Prashanta Kumar Majhi v. Managing Director, Orissa Mining Corpn., Bhubaneshwar*, 2001 LLR 695 (Ori.).

§2. Compensation Payable in Disablement and Death

I. Determination and Distribution of Compensation

390. The temporary disablement can be total or partial. If the earning capacity of a workman is reduced in relation to the employment in which he had been employed at the time of the accident resulting in such disablement, it is called temporary partial disablement. This means the employee's earning capacity in relation to other employments is not affected. Whether a disablement is temporary or permanent and whether it results in reduction in earning capacity, the answer depends upon the fact of each case except when the injury is clearly included in Part II of Schedule I.

In case of temporary disablement, whether total or partial, an employee is entitled to half-monthly payment of a sum equivalent to 25% of the monthly wages of the workman.

391. Half-monthly payments are made on the sixteenth day from the date of disablement where such disablement lasts for a period of twenty-eight days or more. In case it lasts for a period of less than twenty-eight days, then the half-monthly payment is made after the expiry of a waiting period of three days from the date of disablement. Thereafter, it is payable half-monthly during the disablement or during a period of five years whichever is shorter. In case the disablement ceases before the date on which any half-monthly payment falls due, then a sum proportionate to the duration shall be paid in that half month.

392. In case of temporary disablement, the condition of the employee may either improve or deteriorate. Therefore, the compensation payable is always open to review and adjustment. Any agreement for half-monthly payment may either be arrived at by an agreement between the parties or it may be determined by the Commissioner for Employees' Compensation. Any party therefore may make an application for review to the Commissioner. The application should be supported with a certificate from a qualified medical practitioner suggesting that the condition of the patient has changed. On an application for review having been made, the Commissioner may continue or increase or decrease or end the half-monthly payments. If the Commissioner finds that the accident has resulted in permanent disablement, the Commissioner can convert the half-monthly payments into a lump sum compensation. When the Commissioner allows such conversion, the amount of half-monthly payments already received by the employee will be deducted from the lump sum compensation ordered to be paid. Rule 4 of the Employees' Compensation Rules (ECR) provides that when an application is filed by an employer for reduction or discontinuance of half-monthly payments and the Commissioner feels it justified, he may order withdrawing the half-monthly payments in whole or in part pending the application for review. Where a half-monthly payment is due to be payable to any person under a legal disability, the Commissioner may order that the payment in such a case may be made during his disability to any dependant of the employee or to any other person whom the Commissioner thinks best fitted in this regard so as to provide for the welfare of the employee.

393. After half-monthly payments have been made for six months, either the employer or the employee can get the recurring payments commuted into a single payment. Commutation can be done through an agreement between the parties or on order of the Commissioner. When the Commissioner receives an application for commutation, he estimates the probable duration of the temporary disablement and then determines the lump sum amount payable on the basis of half-monthly payments, which will have to be paid during the estimated period. He will deduct from this amount one half per cent of the total for each month comprised in the estimated period.

A. Permanent Disablement

394. It is provided by section 4 of the ECA that when permanent total disablement results from an injury, the amount of compensation shall be an amount equal to 60% of the monthly wages of the injured employee multiplied by the relevant factor or an amount of INR 140,000, whichever is more. The relevant factors are provided in Schedule IV. These factors are used to work out the lump sum equivalent of compensation, in case of permanent disablement and death. If the completed year of age on the last birthday of the employee immediately preceding the date on which the compensation fell due is not more than 16, the factor applicable is 228.54 (the highest figure in the Schedule) and, if the age is 65 or more the applicable factor is 99.37 (the lowest figure in the Schedule). Thus, the provision of relevant factor, which was for the first time included by the 1984 amendment, is intended to provide a higher sum of compensation for younger people than that payable to their older counterparts.

395. Where the monthly wage of a workman exceeds INR 15,000, his monthly wages for the purposes of calculation of compensation are deemed to be INR 15,000 only. Thus, the maximum compensation that can be payable for total disablement is INR 10.96 lakhs (presuming the application of the highest relevant factor in a case) in case of PDB. The minimum compensation in case of PTD has now gone up to INR 140,000, which before the amendment was INR 90,000.

396. In case an employee suffers permanent partial disablement resulting from an injury, specified in Part II of Schedule I, he will be paid such percentage of the compensation which would have been payable in the case of permanent total disablement as is specified therein as being the percentage of the loss of earning capacity caused by the injury. If the disablement is suffered from injuries not specified in Schedule I, the employee will be paid such percentage of the compensation payable in the case of permanent total disablement as is proportionate to the loss of earning capacity (as assessed by the qualified medical practitioner) permanently caused by the injury. Where more than one injury is caused by the accident, the amount of compensation payable under this head is aggregated. However, it shall not exceed the amount which would have been payable if permanent total disablement had resulted from injuries. Even medical practitioners have been directed by the ECA to have due regard for the percentages of loss of earning capacity in relation to different injuries specified in Schedule I, when they assess the loss of earning capacity in case of injuries not specified in this Schedule.

397. It has been held in a decided case,[138] that the Commissioner can order payment of compensation prescribed by the statute even though less compensation than was admissible is claimed.

B. Death

398. In case of death, the compensation payable is less than that would be payable in case of permanent total disablement. In case of death, it is 50% of monthly wages of the deceased employee, whereas in case of permanent total disablement it is 60%. The provision of multiplying the sum by the relevant factor as provided in Schedule IV is the same. The minimum sum that is payable in case of death is INR 120,000 and the maximum at the highest relevant factor (i.e., 228.54) comes to INR 9.12 lakhs.

399. The compensation in case of death is payable to the dependants. Section 2(1)(d) of the ECA defines dependant. It divides the dependants in three classes. But, they are not divided into different categories in the sense that those specified in category I will exclude others.[139] Unlike in the ESI Act, dependants under the ECA belonging to any category may claim the compensation simultaneously. In the first class, dependants include a widow, a minor legitimate son, an unmarried legitimate daughter and a widowed mother. This category of dependants is deemed to be known as dependants on the earnings of the deceased whether that is so, in fact or not. All three categories of dependants have been listed on the same pattern as has been done under the ESI Act.[140]

400. The compensation payable to a dependant of the deceased becomes the property of the dependant, after the compensation amount had been deposited with the Commissioner. In case the sole dependant to whom that sum was payable dies before the payment was actually made to him or her by the Commissioner, the sum is payable to the heirs of the dependant and not to the heirs of the deceased workman.[141]

401. On the death of an employee, only those dependants who are alive are eligible to get compensation. When a compensation amount has been allotted to a dependant or has been distributed among several dependants, the compensation so allotted or distributed becomes the property of the dependant. In such a case, if the

138. *Mohammad Koya v. Balan* (1987) II LJJ 86 (Kerala).
139. *New India Insurance Co. Ltd v. Man Singh and Others* (1984) I LLJ 186 (M.P.).
140. The details of these three categories of dependants can be seen in the next chapter of this part, under the heading 'ESI Act and Occupational Hazards'.
141. *Commissioner for Workmen's Compensation v. P.V. Mohan and Others* (1988) II LLJ 177 (Ker.).

dependant dies, the said sum being the property of that dependant, will devolve on his or her heirs and will not revert back to the employer.

402. Section 8 of the ECA provides for distribution of the compensation among the dependants of the deceased workman. It is provided that, all payments in case of death have to be made not directly to the dependants but through the Commissioner.

In case of a deceased workman, an employer may make to any dependant advances on account of compensation of an amount equal to three months' wage of such workman. But, the sum so paid must not exceed the compensation payable to that dependant. While making the payment to a dependant, the Commissioner shall deduct from the compensation payable to him or her any advances made by the employer on account of compensation. After making such permissible deductions from the compensation deposited, the Commissioner shall apportion it among the dependants of the deceased workman. The Commissioner can do so in such proportion as he thinks fit. He is authorized in his discretion to allot the entire amount of compensation to any dependant.

403. In case compensation is payable to a woman or a person under a legal disability, the Commissioner may pay the money in his discretion or may have the sum invested or otherwise dealt with for the benefit of the woman or such person during his disability in such manner as the Commissioner thinks fit. He is authorized to vary his order regarding the investment or apportionment of the amount deposited with him, if he is satisfied that on account of neglect or lack of prudence on the part of his parent or due to change in the circumstances of any dependant or for any other sufficient reason his earlier order needs such variation. Such an order can be passed only by serving notice to the parties which are prejudicially affected by such order.

404. The Commissioner may call upon the dependants to appear before him on a specified date for determining the distribution of the compensation. If after making an inquiry the Commissioner is satisfied that no dependants exist, he shall repay the sum of compensation amount to the employer by whom it was deposited, after deducting any amount permissible under the Act. The employer can demand from the Commissioner a statement showing details of all disbursements made by him. The provision of refund to the employer in the above situation shows that the Act intended to benefit only the workman and his or her dependants, and not others.

II. Payment of Compensation

405. The payment to the employee or his dependants as the case may be is to be made as soon as it becomes due.

406. If there is a dispute regarding the amount of compensation claimed by an employee and the employer accepts his liability but not to the extent claimed, the employer has to pay to the workman the amount accepted by him or deposit it with the Commissioner. He has to do so within one month from the date it fell due.

407. If the compensation is not paid within one month from the due date, the Commissioner may, in his discretion direct payment of simple interest at the rate of 12% per annum in addition to the amount of arrears. The Commissioner has the discretion to direct the employer in such cases to pay interest at such higher rate not exceeding the maximum of the lending rates of any scheduled bank. It has been held,[142] that the date of payment of compensation falls due on the date of the accident and not on the date of determination of the amount. In addition to the interest, the Commissioner is authorized to impose a penalty on the employer not exceeding 50% of the amount of compensation due. The interest due under this provision is payable to the workman or his dependant, as the case may be. The amendment 46 of 2000 provides that even the penalty shall be payable to the employee or his dependant as the case may be.

III. Compensation Not to Be Assigned

408. Section 9 of the ECA envisages that the compensation amount is not to be assigned, attached or charged, nor can any claim be set off against it. The idea underlying this provision is to give protection to the employee from being deprived of the benefit of compensation. It has been held[143] that this protection applies both to the employee concerned or his dependants in case of death, but not to the heirs of the deceased who are not his dependants.

142. *Superintending Engineer KEB Hubli v. Kadappa Mallappa* (1984) I LLJ 179 (Ker.); *Pratap Narain Singh Deo v. Srinivas Sabata* (1976) 1 SCC 289.
143. *B.M. Habeebullah v. Periaswami*, AIR 1977 Mad. 330.

Chapter 3. The ESI Act and Occupational Hazards

409. The ECA is known to be the oldest social security legislation in India. But, it certainly does not provide for a social insurance mechanism; it merely puts unilateral liability on the employer to compensate an employee who suffers occupational accidents. This is also the biggest drawback of the ECA; the implementation of this law remains poor mainly due to this limitation. In order to make the administration of employee's compensation more realistic the ESIS as envisaged in the ESIA was created. As noted earlier, this law provides protection against several contingencies including occupational accidents; and not just some of the contingencies as is the case with the ECA. In this chapter, we shall analyse the protection against occupational hazards as envisaged by the ESIA and how far this law is an improvement over the ECA. The Supreme Court has held this legislation to be a beneficial piece of legislation intended to provide benefits to employees in case of sickness, maternity, employment injury and for certain other matters in relation there to.[144] Even a sick industrial unit cannot be exonerated from payment of ESI contribution, under the ESI Act.[145]

410. The ESIS is a social insurance scheme. Both employers and employees contribute to the Employees' State Insurance (ESI) Fund. Those employees who are covered by the ESI Act are given compensation in case of employment-related disablement and death out of the ESI Fund, which is administered by the ESI Corporation or ESIC. When a person is covered by the ESI Act, he shall not be entitled[146] to receive or recover whether from the employer of the IP or from any other person any compensation or damages, under the ECA or any other law in respect of the employment injury sustained. It has, however, been held that this does not bar a suit for damages or compensation for injuries sustained, due to the employer's negligence.[147]

411. The coverage of establishments under the ESIA is limited. It applies to all factories including factories belonging to Government. But it does not apply to seasonal factories. Until recently, the term factory carried a restricted connotation as it covered any premises where twenty or more persons are or were employed for wages and where any manufacturing process is being carried on with the aid of power. This restricted definition was widened by the 1984 amendment to the ESI Act.[148] The definition has been further widened by the 2009 amendment to the ESI

---

144. *Mohammad Koya v. Balan* (1987) II LJJ 86 (Kerala).
145. *Employees' State Corporation, Sub Regional Office, Hubli v. APS Star industries Ltd*, Dharwad 2003 III LLJ 411.
146. Section 53, The Employees' State Insurance Act, 1948.
147. *P. Ashokan v. Western Indian Plywoods Ltd*, 1987 Lab. IC 310 (Ker.).
148. As per the definition of factory after the 1984 amendment to the ESI Act, it included factories run with power and employing ten or more persons and those carrying on manufacturing process without using power and employing twenty or more persons.

Act.[149] The amended definition covers all factories which employ ten or more persons, whether these are run with the use of power or without power. Seasonal factories continue to remain excluded from the definition of factory. The definition also excludes mines governed by the Mines Act. It also does not include plantations. It has been held that for the purpose of knowing the minimum number of persons employed for the application of the ESI Act, the employees at the head office and the work site can be combined.[150]

412. Section 1(5) of the ESI Act gives power to the appropriate Government to extend the application of the Act in consultation with the ESI Act and after giving six months' notice. But, since the ESI Corporation has the Central Labour Minister as its Chairman, the consultation envisaged for the purpose of extension, etc. is a mere formality. But, State Governments are also the appropriate Governments for the ESIA, in certain cases. They too have the power of extending the application of the Act. It is provided that, if a State Government wants to extend the application of the ESIA, it has to seek approval of the Central Government. Consultation with the ESIC is necessary in this case as well. Most of the State Governments have extended the ESI Act to hotels, restaurants, shops, cinema houses including preview theatres, road motor transport and newspaper establishments employing twenty or more persons.

413. Despite the large coverage of the ESI Act, due to passage of the 2009 amendment bill to the ESI Act, 1948, the ESI scheme still does not cover even the whole of the organized sector fully. Even several types of large establishments for which the Central Government is the appropriate Government have not been covered. They include railways, major ports, mines and oil fields. In this regard, it may be mentioned that certain employee groups in the unorganized sector have been demanding coverage under the ESI Act but their demand has not been accepted. For example, workmen in building and construction industry are making such a demand.

414. Unlike the ECA, the ESI Act puts a wage ceiling on its coverage, -which presently is INR 21,000 per month. Fixation of wage ceiling drives away from its applicability all those employees whose wages are above the ceiling fixed. Likewise, those who are covered go out of the coverage when their wages go above the ceiling. If the ceiling for coverage is raised, they may be brought back again. Suggestions have been made for removal of the wage ceiling for coverage but they have not been implemented. It is also suggested that, once an employee is covered by the ESI Act, he should continue to remain covered. But this too has not been accepted by the ESIC. It appears that the Central Government wishes to protect the interest

149. Parliament passed on 6 May 2010 the Employees' State Insurance (Amendment) Bill, 2009, which now will have the effect of including a large number of smaller factories in the coverage of the ESI Act, 1948 even though they may not be covered by the Factories Act, 1948. This is certainly a salutary development.

150. *Gauri Mohan Pohoomul v. Regional Director, Employees' State Insurance Corporation* 2005 LLR 52 (Bom).

of employees who are in the lower rung of salary brackets. But, in case an establishment is covered once, it remains so even if the number of persons employed goes below the minimum.[151]

415. Section 87 of the ESI Act provides that the appropriate Government may exempt any factory or establishment or class of establishments, from the operation of the Act for a period of one year at a time. The exemption can be reviewed from time to time, subject to specified conditions. The ESI Act also provides for granting exemption in favour of any person or persons employed in any factory or other establishment to which the Act applies. Exemption can be granted to any factory or establishment belonging to the Government or local authority, if the employees of such factory or establishments are in receipt of benefits substantially similar or superior to those provided under the ESI Act. The ESIC is quite opposed to granting exemptions for coverage as it considers that exemptions are antithetical to the concept of social security. But especially the State Governments have made liberal use of the exemption power. The ESI Review Committee 1982 was quite critical of granting exemptions by Government, but they continue to be made.

416. It may be noted that, when an employee or a class of employees is exempted from the application of the ESI Act, such employees may get covered under the ECA, if they fall within the definition of employee under that Act. For this purpose, one has to comprehend the definition of employee under section 2(1)(n) read with the Schedule II of the ECA. Even employees who get eliminated from the application of the ESI Act due to their reaching the wage ceiling may get covered under the ECA, if they fall in the definition of employee under that Act. However, the definition of employee in the ECA is quite restricted as it generally does not cover employee working in clerical or administrative capacity, which is not the case under the ESIA.

417. The term employee under the ESI Act has a wide coverage. By and large, it includes any person employed for wages in or in connection with the work of a factory or establishment to which the ESI Act applies. The employee may be employed directly by the employer or may be employed through a contractor. It also includes a person whose services are temporarily lent or let on hire to the principal employer by another person with whom he is employed. After an amendment to the ESI Act in 1966, even those who work elsewhere from the factory are covered as employees. This of course is so, provided that they are engaged in various types of work referred in section 2(9). But it does not include those whose wages (excluding remuneration for overtime) exceed INR 21,000 per month. Even casual employees have been held to be employees under the ESI Act.[152] Of course, now after the 2009 amendment, even the ECA has also been extended to casual employees. Managers, clerks and supervisors getting a monthly salary not exceeding INR 21,000 p.m. are

151. *State through the Manager, Employees' State Insurance Corporation, Gulbarga v. Kranthi Kumar* LLR 2005 LLR 376 (Kar.).

152. *ESI Corporation v. Chanambikai. Mills* (1974) Lab. IC 798 (Mad.); *ESI Corporation v. Oswal Woollen Mills Ltd* 1980 Lab. IC 1064 (Punj.).

covered under the ESI Act. Also, employees working in an administrative office, or those involved in purchase of raw material or sale of finished goods outside the factory too are covered by this Act. Even employees employed in the canteen and cycle stand by the contractor working for a factory come under the definition of an employee. Those working part-time in the garden are also included.[153]

§1. Employment Injury

418. The term employment injury under the ESI Act refers to a personal injury to an employee, caused by accident or an occupational disease arising out of and in the course of employment, being an insurable employment. This definition has been inserted by an amendment in 1966. Previously, the term was defined with reference to the ECA which though did not define employment injury, section 3 of that legislation served the purpose. The amended definition does not widen the scope of the term, but Parliament intended the ESI Act to have its own definition of the term so that the Act projects a spirit of social insurance.

419. Interestingly, the term employment injury under the ESI Act by and large carries the same connotation as it has been interpreted through the judicial decisions under the ECA. The terms accident, personal injury and occupational disease as discussed under the ECA carry the same connotations under to ESI Act as well. The phrase 'arising out of and in the course of employment' has also been construed similarly. Of course, as we noted in Chapter 1 of this part, there is not much clarity as to what injuries can be deemed to have arisen out of and in the course of employment. But the 1966 amendment to the ESI Act inserted sections 51-A, 51-B, 51-C and 51-D. These sections have somewhat altered the treatment of accidents under the ESI Act in favour of employees.

420. Section 51-A of the ESI Act gives an extended meaning to the term 'arising out of and in the course of employment'. This is on the basis of a presumption envisaged in it. The section provides that, if it is shown that an accident arose in the course of employment of an IP, it would be presumed also to have arisen out of employment. But the presumption is rebuttable. There is no such presumption under the ECA, where the burden of proof in all such cases is on the employee.

421. An explanation is provided by section 51-B of the ESI Act to the phrase 'arising out of and in the course of employment'. It says that an accident shall be deemed to arise out of and in the course of employment even if the employee at the time of the accident is contravening a law applicable to him or an order of the employer or is acting without employer's instructions. But this is so in those cases where the accident would have been deemed to have so arisen, if the act had not been done in contravention aforesaid or the employer's instructions referred, as the case may be.

153. *Modern Equipment Co. v. ESI Corporation, Punj. & Har. High Court* (1985), Award Digest, May 1985.

422. Section 51-C of the ESI Act enlarges the scope of the expression 'course of employment'. It incorporates the principle of notional extension of employer's premises. The section provides for the ESIC's liability in case of accidents taking place when an employee is traveling in a transport provided by the employer for going to or coming back from work. This applies subject to the conditions that the employee is traveling in the employer's transport with his express or implied permission; he must be going to or coming from his place of work; the vehicle must be operated by or on behalf of his employer; and the vehicle is not operated in the ordinary course of public transport service.

The effect of this section is that it obviates the need for examining whether it was the duty of the employee to go to his workplace and return from it by any particular means of transport. It has been held that section 51-C should not be construed to project that if an employee takes a public transport vehicle for his to and fro journey to the factory, the accident occurring therefrom should not be treated as an employment injury.[154] Another difference is in the interpretation of the term course of employment. The ESI (Amendment) Bill 2009 has added the benefit for workers for the accidents happening while commuting to and from the place of work and home. This is not so under the ECA.

423. Section 51-D provides that accidents happening to an IP on the premises of his employment shall be presumed to arise out of and in the course of employment. This is so, if three conditions are fulfilled i.e. the employee is on the premises employed for the employer's trade or business; the accident takes place when he is taking steps to meet an emergency and the accident happens when he is taking steps to rescue, secure or protect persons who might be injured, or when he is attempting to avert serious damage to property. This provision is sought to override the added peril performance of duty. Thus, when an employee takes extra danger while doing his duty and suffers injuries or dies, he is protected under the ESI Act.

424. It appears that these amendments are based on several decided cases under the ESI Act and the ECA where courts had taken views favouring employees in doubtful situations. So as to remove any doubt in similar cases happening in future, these inductions will help the employees in saving themselves from onerous legal prescriptions.

§2. Occupational Disease

425. Like the ECA, the ESIA also envisages lists of occupational diseases, the lists of which are revised from time to time. The two sets of lists are on the same pattern as in the ECA. We have already noted in Chapter 1 of this part, the three parts of Schedule III of the ECA. The Acts provide that the liability to pay compensation arises even in cases where a person contacts a disease after cessation of service, if the employee has rendered service with the employer for the specified period.

---

154. *Regional Director, ESIC v. L. Ranga Rao*, 1981 Lab 1C 1563.

§3. DISABLEMENT BENEFIT

426. As is so under the ECA, the ESI Act also divides disablement into two broad categories, i.e., temporary and permanent. The latter is further divided into permanent partial and permanent total disablement.

427. Section 54 of the ESIA provides that determination of disablement question shall be made by the Medical Board. Disablement questions include the following:

(i) whether the accident has resulted in permanent disablement;
(ii) whether the extent of loss of earning capacity can be assessed provisionally or finally;
(iii) whether the assessment of the proportion of the loss of earning capacity is provisional or final; and
(iv) in case of provisional assessment, the period for which such assessment shall hold good.

It is provided that when a Medical Board makes a provisional assessment about a disablement question it shall again be referred to the Medical Board before the period of provisional assessment expires.

If the IP or the ESIC is not satisfied with the decision of the Medical Board, there is a provision for appeal to the Medical Appeal Tribunal with a further right of appeal to the ESI Court. The appeal can also be made directly to the ESI Court.

428. While the ECA envisages the payment of compensation for permanent total or permanent partial disablement as a lump sum, in the case of the ESIA the payment is made in monthly instalments. There are no contribution conditions for the payment of disablement benefit. TDB is paid, if the disability continues beyond three days even as the payment is required to be made from the first day of the disability. TDB is payable, until the worker recovers fully. In case of permanent total or permanent partial disablement the employee gets the benefit for life at full rate. This may, however, change if the nature of permanent disability calls for a review. In the case of permanent partial disablement also the benefit is payable for life.

429. In case the disability certified by the Medical Board is total, the IP is paid at full rate. If it is partial, then only that percentage of the full rate is payable as is the percentage reduction in the earning capacity. Permanent Disablement Benefit (PDB) is payable from the date of resumption of duty, after the accident occurs. Until the date of recovery the employee will get TDB. Unlike the ECA, the PDB under the ESI Act is not related to the age of the IP, but merely on the wage slab and the commensurate SBR. The ILO Convention requires that the rate of cash benefits should be renewed, if there are substantial changes in the cost of living. There is no such provision either in the ECA or in the ESIA. However, under the ESIA the quantum of disability or dependant's benefits payable are renewed occasionally. These ad hoc increases are allowed to neutralize the impact of inflation. A more systematic approach would be to systematically link the increases to the consumer price index (CPI) rather than providing for ad hoc increases. Presently, the PDB rate is 40% over and above the SBR. Since the SBR is about 50% of the wage, in actuality PDB comes to 70% of the daily average wage of the IP. Interestingly, PDB rate under the ESI Act is higher compared to what the ILO has prescribed. It has advocated 60% of wages of the IP to be given as the PDB rate.

430. The claim procedure under the ESIA is like this: on occurrence of the accident, the IP will first submit the first medical certificate, and then the inter certificate if the period of abstention is extended by the Insurance Officer or Practitioner. Until he recovers, the local ESI office will start giving the TDB. If the TDB period is long, the officer sends the case for medical referee's opinion for knowing the percentage loss in the earning capacity. Then the IP fills up a form and submits it to the local officer. Then the payment of instalments starts.

§4. Dependants' Benefit

431. Dependants' benefit is payable to the dependants of an IP, if he dies as a result of an employment injury sustained as an employee under the ESIA. It is provided that this benefit is payable at the rates and for the period prescribed by the Central Government, and it is payable subject to conditions prescribed by the Central Government. The rate of benefit and its distribution among the dependants are laid down in the Employees' State Insurance (Central) Rules 1950. Presently, the dependants' benefit comes to about 70% of the average daily wage. It is the same as the PDB. The First Schedule, which earlier specified the rates of permanent and TDB, has been omitted by the 1989 amendment to the Act.

432. The definition of dependant under ESIA is the same as that in the ECA. The ESIA envisages three categories of dependants. The first category includes a widow, a minor legitimate or adopted son; an unmarried legitimate or adopted daughter and a widowed mother. For this category of dependants, it is not necessary that they should be actually dependent on the earnings of the deceased IP. The second category dependants include a legitimate or adopted son, who has attained the age of 18 years and is infirm and a legitimate or adopted daughter who has attained the age of 18 years and is infirm. For this category of dependants, it is essential that they should be dependent upon the earnings of the deceased IP at the time of his death. Dependants in the third category consist of a long list of relatives. They may claim benefit under the ESIA provided they are wholly or partly dependent on the earnings of the deceased IP at the time of the death. The relatives in this category are a parent other than a widowed mother; a minor illegitimate son; an unmarried illegitimate daughter; a legitimate daughter if married and is minor; an adopted daughter if married and is minor; an illegitimate daughter if married and minor; a legitimate daughter if widowed and minor; an adopted daughter if widowed and minor; an illegitimate daughter if widowed and minor; a minor brother; an unmarried sister; a widowed sister if a minor; a widowed daughter-in-law; a minor child of a predeceased son, a minor child of a predeceased daughter where no parent of the child is alive or a paternal grand-parent if no parent of the IP is alive.

433. The dependants' benefit is first paid to the first and second category of dependants stated above. In case an IP dies without leaving behind any dependant in the first or the second category, the dependant's benefit shall be paid to the other dependants of the deceased. It has been held[155] that on an IP's death as a result of employment injury, his dependants' claim to compensation under the Motor Vehicles Act 1939 will be barred.[156]

434. The dependants' benefit is payable to the widow and children of the deceased as follows: to the widow during life until remarriage an amount equal to three-fifths of the full rate (if there is more than one widow the amount is divided among them equally); to each legitimate or adopted son, an amount equal to two-fifths of the full rate until he attains the age of 25 years;[157] to each legitimate or adopted unmarried daughter an amount equal to two-fifths of the full rate until she attains the age of 18 years or until remarriage whichever is earlier. In the case of legitimate or adopted children who are infirm and are wholly dependent on the earnings of the IP at the time of his death, this benefit shall continue to be paid while the infirmity lasts.

In case of daughters, it lasts until they remain unmarried. If the total benefit distributed in this manner exceeds the full rate of the benefit, the share of each dependent will be reduced proportionately so that the total amount payable to them does not exceed the full rate. If the deceased IP does not leave behind a widow or a dependant child, the dependant benefit will be payable to the dependants of the lower order as per prescription in the rules framed under the ESI Act.

435. The procedure[158] to be followed is that first of all, the employer will send to the ESI local office the accident report. The manager of the local office makes an actual enquiry at the site whether it is an accident coverable by the protection cover of the ESIC. Then the manager sends the enquiry report to the regional director of the ESIC, who then informs the dependants to contact the local office and collect the payment. When the first payment is made, it is necessary that all dependants are present for identification marks. The local ESI office keeps on sending the benefit by money orders, or the beneficiary can collect it in person.

436. Unless the victims of occupational accidents are rehabilitated, the objective of accidents compensation cannot be realized fully. It is therefore necessary that the patient returns to his normal activity or finds a new employment, keeping in view his capacity of work. This requires a team of people to attend to various consequences arising out of the accidents. A bundle of social, educational, medical and vocational measures needs to be adopted to ensure rehabilitation of the IP. The ESIC has also started a Vocational Rehabilitation Scheme for disabled workers with effect from November 1994. The scheme aims at enabling the disabled IP to earn a living

155. *Annapurna v. G.M., K.R.S.T. Corporation*, 1984 Lab. IC 1355 (Kar.).
156. *See* s. 53, The ESI Act, 1948.
157. Earlier, in case of children, it was till the age of 18 years. The ESI (Amendment) Bill 2009 has hiked it to 25 years.
158. Debi S. Saini, *Redressal of Labour Grievances, Claims and Disputes* (New Delhi: Oxford & IBH, 1994), 76–77.

through gainful employment or self-employment, and to overcome the mental trauma. The willing disabled are referred to the Vocational Rehabilitation Centres (VRC) that are being run by the Ministry of Labour. Those persons who reside in the same place where the VRC is located, they are paid conveyance charges for the period of training at a rate which is admissible for attending an artificial limb centre. The IP who resides at a place other than where the VRC is located is paid second class railway or ordinary bus fare for journeys undertaken for training. The fair for an attendant is also fully reimbursed.

437. The ESIC also pays a rehabilitation allowance to an IP, for each day on which he remains admitted to an Artificial Limb Centre for fixation or repair or replacement of artificial limbs. This allowance is paid at the sickness benefit rate, which is the SBR fixed under the Act. There are no contribution conditions for eligibility to payment of the rehabilitation allowance.

Part VII. Unemployment Compensation

438. Post-Independence India has been grappling with the serious problem of poverty, unemployment and under-employment. But it has miles to go to eradicate or substantially minimize the problem.

439. The Indian Constitution envisages a proactive welfare state model of development that is discernible from its central philosophy as envisaged in the Preamble of the Constitution as well as the directive principles of state policy. As noted earlier, these constitutional directives to the state are considered fundamental in governance, and the government is politically accountable to the people for carrying out these directives. However, unlike the Fundamental Rights of citizens and groups as contained in Part III, the Directive Principles are not enforceable in any court of law. The right to work is contained only in Part IV[159] and not in Part III of the Constitution, and therefore is not enforceable in any court of law.

440. Considerable thinking has gone into the question of generation of employment opportunities in India. This is reflected in the creation of various schemes such as 'Food for Work Plan', 'Jawahar Rojgar Yojana (JRY)', and the Mahatma Gandhi National Rural Employment Guarantee Scheme (MNREGA), among others. Fiscal policies and licensing policies have also been used towards enhancing employment in specific regions. But the question of provision of right to work as a fundamental right has not received requisite attention. This is so, because of the large size of the population and a mammoth agenda of development before the country. The provision of unemployment benefit to the unemployed is also linked with the right to employment. Unemployment benefit, in a sense, complements the broader aspect of the national employment programmes.

441. Unemployment benefit is a broad concept. It involves provision of employment to the unemployed people as well as monetary benefit to them in period of unemployment. It is difficult to conceive a single form in which it is payable in various countries across the world. Some countries provide for work relief such as creation of special type of jobs. Others emphasize on cash relief-related schemes like 'cash transfers' in situations of unemployment. Also, the terms subject to which

159. Art. 41 of the Constitution reads as follows: Right to work, to education and to public assistance in certain cases: The state shall, within the limits of its economic capacity and development, make effective provisions for securing the right to work, to education, and to public assistance in case of unemployment, old age, sickness and disablement, and in other cases of undeserved want.

such benefit is available differ. These conditions may relate to the qualifying conditions, duration of the benefit, rate of benefits, methods of financing, etc. The socio-politico-economic conditions prevailing in a country also influence these matters.

442. Especially, developing countries find it difficult to provide unemployment benefit of any substantial magnitude. India is one such country where virtually no unemployment benefit worth the name is provided by the state directly or through the social security institutions. Significantly, however, Indian law through the IDA requires employers (not managers and administrators or even most supervisors) to pay to workers compensation in certain situations of lay-off, retrenchment, closure and transfer of their undertakings.

443. The provision for compensation in the above situations of unemployment did not exist in the IDA as originally enacted in 1947. It was for the first time made through an amendment to the IDA in 1953. Before this period, certain progressive employers used to pay voluntarily compensation in these situations. This they considered fair and reasonable, so as to reduce the hardships of workers in situations resulting from lay-offs, retrenchments and closures. The industrial tribunals envisaged under the IDA and courts also assumed the responsibility of decreeing grant of compensation in these situations. These bodies awarded 'severance pay' in cases of retrenchment and discharge on considerations of fairness and equity. But there was no uniformity in the payments awarded and the approach of various labour tribunals and courts. In 1953, the matter took a serious turn when the cotton textile industry faced the problem of accumulated stocks. Consequently, textile mills decided to retrench and lay-off a large number of workers, which caused industrial unrest. To cope with the situation, the Government of India promulgated an ordinance in October 1953 which made it obligatory on the employers in industries covered by the IDA to pay lay-off and retrenchment compensation to the effected workers. This followed an amendment in the IDA to this effect in December 1953. These compensations work as a protection to the workmen, to meet their immediate hardship resulting from loss of job. In this part, we shall study the provisions of the IDA relating to compensation payable by employers to workers in cases of lay-off, retrenchment, closure and transfer.

Chapter 1. Lay-Off Compensation

444. We shall examine the meaning of the term lay-off, applicability of the protection to industrial establishments, workers covered, quantum of compensation and permission of the appropriate Government for declaring lay-off in certain cases.

§1. Meaning of Lay-Off

445. Lay-off has been defined in section 2(kkk) of the IDA. As per this section, lay-off means the failure, refusal or inability of an employer to give employment to a workman, whose name is borne on the muster-rolls, of his industrial establishment, on account of

(i) shortage of coal, power or raw material; or
(ii) accumulation of stocks or the breakdown of machinery; or
(iii) natural calamity; or
(iv) any other connected reason.

It is also provided that a workman whose name is borne on the muster-rolls of the industrial establishment shall be deemed to be laid-off, if he is not given employment by the employer within two hours of his presenting himself for work at the establishment.

§2. Employer's Right to Lay-Off

446. The employer's right to declare a lay-off is severely controlled by the IDA. The employer is not free to resort to it as he pleases. Lay-off can be declared by an employer only when it is provided for in the standing orders approved under the Industries Employment (Standing Orders) Act 1946. The law has severely curtailed the common law right of employers in this regard. The right to lay-off can be exercised only if it is legal to do so.

§3. Entitlement to Lay-Off Compensation

447. Lay-off provisions are contained in Chapters V-A and V-B of the IDA. Chapter V-B applies only to factories, mines and plantations employing 100 or more workers. Chapter V-A applies to all industrial establishments which are not covered by Chapter V-B, i.e., factories, mines and plantations employing less than 100 workers and other establishments which are not factories, mines and plantations. However, lay-off provisions in Chapter V-A are applicable only to those factories, mines and plantations which employ less than 100 but at least fifty workers. Thus, those working in establishments employing less than fifty workers are not provided any lay-off compensation. Also, lay-off compensation is not available to workers employed in industrial establishments of seasonal nature, whatever may be the number of workers employed in them.

448. The lay-off compensation rights are available to those workers who are in continuous service of at least one year. But a worker will be deemed to be in continuous service, if during a period of the previous twelve months he has actually worked under the employer concerned for at least 240 days. This period of 240 days includes days on which the worker actually worked and also any period of sickness, authorized leave, accident, a strike which is not illegal, a lockout or maternity leave (in case of females).

449. A worker laid-off is not entitled to lay-off compensation in the following cases:

(i) if he does not accept an alternative employment offered by the employer in another establishment run by him which is situated within a radius of five miles from the establishment in which the worker is actually employed;
(ii) if he does not present himself for work during working hours at least once a day; and
(iii) if he is laid-off due to a workers' strike in another part of the establishment.

450. If a worker takes up a job in another part of the establishment during the period of lay-off, he is not entitled to any lay-off compensation.

451. A *badli*[160] worker or a casual worker is not entitled to lay-off compensation. A *badli* worker is one who is employed in an industrial establishment in place of another worker who is absent on a particular day or on some days.

452. A lay-off can occur in those cases where the business of the employer continues and the workers concerned remain on the muster-rolls. When the circumstances which necessitated the lay-off no more exist, the employer is expected to resume normal working of the establishment on full wages. The law does not lay down any specific period until the lay-off can continue. However, in case the lay-off has continued for forty-five days or more the employer may not pay lay-off compensation any more in case there is an agreement to this effect between the employer and the worker. Also, in such situations, the employer can retrench the worker(s) concerned and the lay-off compensation already paid can be set off against the compensation payable for retrenchment.

It is important to remember that lay-off can be declared only for purely trade related reasons. It cannot be used as a weapon of disciplining workers or as a weapon of collective bargaining to exert pressure on them.[161]

160. The word *badli* in Hindi means replacement; so, a *badli* worker is a replacement for a permanent one on a given day or days.

161. *Churakalam Tea Estate v. Its workmen*, 1969 II LLJ 407 (SC).

453. For resorting to lay-off, the employer is required to serve a notice of commencement of lay-off to the authorities. This notice should be given within seven days of the commencement of the lay-off. Notice is required to be given in those situations where the employer considers that the workers concerned would not be entitled to any lay-off compensation. He is also required to give a seven days' notice for terminating the lay-off.

§4. Amount of Compensation

454. A worker laid off shall be paid lay-off compensation by the employer for all those days during which he is so laid off, except for the weekly holidays that may intervene. The compensation shall be equal to 50% of the total of the basic wages and dearness allowance that would have been payable to him had he not been so laid-off. For the weekly holiday he will be paid full wages.

§5. Permission for Declaring Lay-Off

455. Until 1976, there were no provisions in the IDA to restrict or prevent lay-off and retrenchment. Employers resorted to large-scale lay-offs, retrenchments and closures especially in big establishments. The 1976 amendment to the IDA inducted in it Chapter V-B, to restrict these tendencies of the employers. This chapter puts strict curbs on the employers in factories, mines and plantations while affecting lay-offs, retrenchments and closures. It obliges them to obtain permission of the appropriate government to do so. The chapter was made applicable to establishments employing 300 or more workers. By an amendment in 1984, its applicability was extended to establishments employing 100 or more workers.

456. Even though, Chapter V-B of the IDA provides added security to workers, it has been bitterly criticized by employers and their federations, as creating substantial curbs on managerial prerogatives and rights. The criticism is more severe as this chapter hinders the globalization programme of the Government. Employers are finding it very difficult to cope with Chapter V-B, in the situation of tremendous competition that has resulted from the general opening up of the economy.

457. In cases covered by Chapter V-B, section 25-M provides that an employer is required to obtain the permission of the appropriate government or the prescribed authority in this behalf before resorting to any lay-off. Prior permission is not required, if the lay-off is due to shortage of power or any natural calamity.

458. In cases where the employer is required to obtain permission for lay-off, the application shall be made by the employer stating the reasons of the intended lay-off. A copy of the application is also to be given to the workers concerned. The Government's decision to refuse or grant the permission remains in force for one year.

The Government, however, can review its order or may refer it to an industrial tribunal for adjudication, which is obliged to decide the matter within a period of thirty days.

459. In exceptional circumstances such as an accident in the establishment or death of an employer or the like, the appropriate Government may direct that the provisions relating to prior permission in Chapter V-B shall not apply to such an employer.

Chapter 2. Retrenchment Compensation

460. We shall examine the meaning of retrenchment, conditions for retrenchment, retrenchment compensation, and permission of appropriate Government for retrenching workers in certain cases.

§1. What Is Retrenchment?

461. The term retrenchment has been defined very widely in section 2(oo) of IDA, and is in two parts. The first part, which is quite exhaustive, lays down that retrenchment means termination of the services of a workman for 'any reason what so-ever, otherwise than as punishment inflicted by way of disciplinary action'. The second part says that retrenchment does not include the following:

(i) voluntary retirement of the workman; or
(ii) retirement of the workman on reaching the age of superannuation; or
(iii) termination of the workman as a result of non-renewal of the contract of employment; or
(iv) termination of service on the ground of continued ill health of the workman.

Traditionally, retrenchment is understood to be a situation where one or more workers is/are surplus. But controversy is created by the term 'any reason whatsoever' appearing in the first part of the definition. The SC interpreted this term as including 'a variety of reasons, e.g., for economy, rationalization in industry, installation of a new labour-saving machinery, etc.'[162] The Court accepted the term retrenchment as no wider than its ordinary and accepted connotation, i.e., discharge of surplus labour or staff by an employer for any reason otherwise than as punishment inflicted by way of disciplinary action. Thus, it was said that 'it has no application where the services of all workman have been terminated by the employer on a real bona fide closure of business ... in no case there is any retrenchment unless there is discharge of surplus labour or staff'. Later judgment of the SC, however, gave a much wider interpretation to the term retrenchment.[163]

Termination of even temporary workers was held to be retrenchment, as also cases where an appointment ended with efflux of time. The court held that all terminations except those specifically excluded by sections 2(oo) are retrenchment. Thus, when the service of a probationer clerk was terminated because she failed to pass the confirmation test it was held that the termination was a retrenchment, because it did not fall in any of the exclusionary clauses in section 2(oo). These judgments sent shock waves in the employer's circles, which led to amendment of the definition of retrenchment. A new clause (bb) was added in section 2(oo) which excluded from the definition 'termination of the service of a workman as a result of

162. *Barsi Light Railway Co. Ltd v. Jogleka* (1957) I LLJ 243 (SC).
163. *State Bank of India v. N. Sundramoney* (1976) I LLJ, 478 (SC); *Santosh Gupta v. State Bank of Patiala* (1980) II LLJ 72 (SC).

the non-renewal of the contract of employment between the employer and workman concerned on its expiry or of such contract being terminated under a stipulation in that behalf contained therein'.

In the post-amendment (1984) situation, a contract of employment which comes to an end by efflux of time will not be considered as retrenchment.[164] However, the Supreme Court cautioned that clause (bb) in section 2(oo) should be so construed as to result in fair and just deal to the workers. Thus, in *Shailendra Nath Shukla* v. *Vice Chancellor, Allahabad University*,[165] it was held that, if the contractual employment is resorted to as a mechanism to frustrate the claim of the employee to become regular or permanent against a job which continues or the nature of duties is such that the colour of contractual agreement is given to take it out from section 2(oo), then such agreement cannot be regarded as fair or bona fide. In this case, the workmen had been working in their job continuously for five years and their duties were like those of regular employee, the termination of their service was held not to be covered by clause (bb) of section 2(oo), and it was held to be a case of retrenchment.

§2. Conditions for Retrenchment

462. For effecting the retrenchment, the employer must make a seniority list of workmen in the categories involved. This list should be displayed at least seven days before the actual retrenchment. It is now important to know as to which workers should be subjected to retrenchment in case the employer has the right to lawfully retrench in a certain situation. (Rule 77 of the Industrial Disputes (Central) Rules 1947). Also, retrenchment should take place on the basis of the rule 'Last come, first go' for various categories of workmen. The principle of 'Last come, first go' is considered to be a healthy safeguard against discrimination.[166] However, there can be exceptions to this, but the management must have cogent reasons for deviating from this principle and also must act in good faith. Thus, where the employer in a bona fide manner retains the staff possessing special aptitude in the interest of business, he cannot be assumed to have acted unfairly merely because the rule of 'last come, first go' is not observed.[167]

463. Where any retrenchment is made and subsequently the employer proposes to take into employment any persons, he shall first give the opportunity to the retrenched workmen to offer themselves for re-employment. In that case, persons who offer themselves for re-employment will have preference over other persons.

464. An employer wanting to retrench any workman must give a notice to the appropriate government to this effect.

---

164. *Life Insurance Corporation of India and Another v. Rajeev Kumar Srivastava* (1994) II LLJ 97 (All.).
165. (1987) II LLJ 351 (SC).
166. *Swadesamitram Ltd v. Workmen*, 1960 I LLJ 504(SC).
167. *Om Oil & Oil Seed Exchange Ltd v. Workmen* (1966) IILLJ 324(SC).

§3. RETRENCHMENT COMPENSATION

465. Section 25-F of the IDA envisages that every workman who is employed in industry and is in continuous service for not less than one year shall not be retrenched by the employer unless he has been given one month's notice in writing to this effect. This notice must contain the reasons for retrenchment. If such a notice has not been given, the workman must be given one month's wages *in lieu* of such notice. Along with this, the workman must be paid retrenchment compensation, which shall be equivalent to fifteen days' average pay for every completed year of service or any part thereof in excess of six months. Even temporary or daily workers who have put in 240 days of service with the employer in the past year will be entitled to retrenchment compensation, and they will be deemed to be in continuous service.

466. Any retrenchment without paying retrenchment compensation under section 25-F will be void *ab initio*. Such action would entitle the workman to a declaration by the tribunal that he is in continuous service and he will also be entitled to full back wages.[168]

467. As in case of lay-off, those working in establishments employing 100 or more workmen are governed by Chapter V-B. Under this chapter, no workman who has been in continuous service for not less than one year can be retrenched until

(i) the workman has been given three months' notice in writing or has been paid wages *in lieu* thereof;
(ii) the prior permission of the appropriate government has been obtained on an application made in this behalf; and
(iii) where permission for retrenchment has been granted, the workman being retrenched has been paid compensation at the rate of fifteen days' wages for every completed year of service.

468. Courts have established certain important principles regarding payment of retrenchment compensation. Retrenchment will become inoperative, if a workman has not been given retrenchment compensation. Retrenchment is complete only when the compensation has been paid.

469. Especially in the post-globalization India (1991 onwards), it is a common practice among managements to reduce their labour force. The management does so by entering into an agreement with the union by devising voluntary retirement schemes (VRS). Usually, such VRS contain better plans of retrenchment compensation. In many such cases, compensation is paid at the rate of one month's (and not fifteen days' wage as provided by law) pay for every completed year of service.

168. *Narotam Chopra v. Presiding Officer, Labour Court* (1989) SCC 97; *Mohan Lal v. Bharat Electronics Ltd* (1981) 3 SCC 225.

§4. Permission for Retrenchment

470. The amendment to the IDA in 1976 resulted in, among others, creation of Chapter V-B. Analogous to section 25-M in it, which deals with permission for lay-off, section 25-N has been provided for dealing with retrenchments in establishments employing 100 or more workers.[169]

471. Section 25-N provides that in case where Chapter V-B is applicable, the period of notice of retrenchment shall be three months or the employer shall pay wage *in lieu* of that. It also provides for obtaining the prior permission of the appropriate government before making a retrenchment. The application for permission under section 25-N must be made by the employer as stating clearly the reasons for the intended retrenchment. The government decides the granting of permission, having regard to the genuineness and adequacy of the reasons stated by the employer, the interest of the workmen and all other relevant factors. The Government's order granting or refusing such permission must give reasons. Such an order remains in force for one year. The Government can review its order or may refer it to a labour tribunal for adjudication. The tribunal must give its decision within a period of thirty days.

472. In certain cases, the appropriate Government may decide that in relation to a certain establishment permission provision will not apply for a specified period. This it can do, if it is satisfied about the existence of such exceptional circumstances as accident in the establishment or death of the employer.

169. The limit of 100 or more workmen for the purpose of obtaining permission of the appropriate Government was provided by the 1984 amendment to the IDA. The 1976 amendment had provided for such permission in all cases where an establishment employs 300 or more workmen.

Chapter 3. Closure Compensation

473. As in situations of lay-off and retrenchment, closure of the establishment too causes grave concern for workers as it results in discharge, unemployment and loss of income. The IDA treats unemployment resulting from closure on similar footing as that related with retrenchment. The payment of closure compensation creates a sense of security in a worker to a reasonable extent. In this chapter, we shall examine meaning of closure, legal requirements of closure, closure compensation payable to workers and the permission to be obtained from the appropriate Government for closure, under Chapter V-B of the IDA.

§1. What Is Closure?

474. The word closure was not originally defined in the IDA. This resulted in a lot of discussion and litigation on the subject. The 1982 amendment to the IDA defined this term.

475. Section 2(cc) of the IDA defines closure as 'the permanent closing down of a place of employment or part thereof'. It is not necessary that the whole establishment is closed down for the purpose of section 2(cc). Closure can even be partial. But partial closure must be of such a part of the undertaking as is distinct and independent.[170] Also, it should be a closure in fact, and should not be a ploy adopted for carrying on the same business in a different manner.[171]

§2. Closure Notice to Government

476. It is provided in section 25 FFA that an employer who intends to close down an undertaking shall serve at least sixty days' notice on the appropriate Government stating the reasons for the intended closure. Such a notice is not required in two situations

(i) where the undertaking employs less than fifty workmen,
(ii) where the undertaking is engaged in the construction of roads, dams, bridges, canals, etc.

Even in cases other than these, the appropriate Government may waive the requirement of giving of sixty days' notice by the employer, if it is satisfied that the employer could not do so due to exceptional circumstances such as accident in the undertaking or death of the employer or the like. It has been held that such a waiver cannot be given, if the closure is merely due to: (i) financial difficulties; (ii) accumulation of undisposed stocks; (iii) expiry of the lease or license; or (iv) closure of

170. *Raj Hans Press v. K.S. Sidhu* (1977) Lab. IC. 1633.
171. *Rajasthan Small Scale Industries Employees Union v. State of Rajasthan* (1990) Lab. IC. 1668.

mining operations because of the exhaustion of the minerals of the area. In one case, the circumstances were such that there was real danger of physical violence or lack of safety to the employers. It was held that, in such a situation a final closure can be on account of unavoidable circumstances beyond the control of the employer.[172]

§3. Closure Compensation

477. Section 25 FFF of the IDA provides for notice and payment of compensation, when an undertaking is closed for any reason whatsoever. Such compensation is payable to every workman who has been in continuous service for not less than one year. The rate of compensation is the same as in case of retrenchment. In one case, closure compensation will not be the same as it would be in case of retrenchment in a similar situation. This is so where the undertaking is closed on account of unavoidable circumstances beyond the control of the employer. In such situations the compensation shall not exceed the average pay of three months.

§4. Permission for Closure

478. As in case of lay-off and retrenchment, Chapter V-B of the IDA also applies to cases involving closure. This chapter envisages prior permission of the appropriate Government for lay-off, retrenchment, closure and transfer of an undertaking.

479. The procedure for closing down an undertaking to which Chapter V-B applies is laid down in section 25-O. This section provides that an employer who wants to close an undertaking shall apply for prior permission at least ninety days before the date on which the intended closure is to become effective. The application to the government should state the reasons for the intended closure. However, there is no need for permission in case of undertakings involved in construction of buildings, bridges, roads, canals, dams or other construction works.

480. The Government makes an enquiry into the matter, and in doing so it has to give an opportunity to hear the employer and the workers. As in case of lay-off and retrenchment, the Government grants or refuses to grant the permission considering the genuineness and adequacy of the reasons stated by the employer, the interest of the general public and other relevant factors. The order of the government remains in force for one year, but it can review the order or can refer it to a labour tribunal for adjudication. The tribunal shall pass an award on such a reference within thirty days. The permission provision does not apply, if the government feels that in a particular situation the circumstances were exceptional such as accident in the undertaking or death of the employer or the like.

---

172. *Kalinga Tubes Ltd v. Their Workmen* (1969) I LLJ 557 (SC).

Chapter 4. Transfers

481. Sometimes, the ownership of an undertaking is transferred from one employer to another. This too causes tremendous anxiety among the workers. Section 25 FF of the IDA deals with such a situation. Under this section, no retrenchment compensation is payable to the workmen concerned, if the new employer employs the workmen subject to the following three conditions:

(i) the service of the workman has not been interrupted by such transfer;
(ii) the conditions of service applicable to the workman after the transfer are not less favourable than before;
(iii) the new employer undertakes the liability to pay, in the event of future retrenchment, compensation on the basis that his original service is continuous and uninterrupted.

It may be noted that all the three conditions exist conjunctively. The employer's liability is not discharged by providing any one of these conditions. If the employee does not undertake these conditions, the old employer must give notice and compensation to every discharged workman who has put in service of one year or more. The compensation must be at the same rate as it is in case of retrenchment.

482. By virtue of section 25F, section 25FF has been made applicable to all cases falling in Chapter V-A or V-B, for this is the only section in the IDA which deals with payment of compensation to all workmen in case of transfer of undertakings.

Chapter 5. Unemployment Allowance Scheme under the ESI Act, 1948

483. A novel development in the history of protection to workers in India against unemployment took place on 1 April 2004, when an unemployment allowance scheme called '*Rajiv Gandhi Shramik Kalyan Yojana*'[173] was launched by the ESIC. It provides a very limited protection against unemployment, but nevertheless is a salutary development. The scheme covers those IP who get rendered jobless due to retrenchment or closure of factory/establishment, etc., or on suffering of at least 40% permanent disablement arising out of non-employment injury. The employments covered under this scheme are as follows: retrenchment as defined in the IDA; closure of the factory/establishment as defined in the IDA; and permanent invalidity[174] not less than 50% arising out of non-employment injury.

484. The eligibility conditions for availing this benefit include the following: The person concerned should have been an IP under the ESI Act 1948 on the date of loss of insurable employment on account of retrenchment, closure of the factory/establishment or permanent invalidity arising out of non-employment injury. Also, contribution in respect of the applicant should have been paid/payable for a minimum period of three years[175] prior to the loss of employment.[176] Further, the period of service of an IP need not be with one employer. She/he will be entitled to this allowance, even if part of his/her service was with an employer in the same or in any other region. There are no qualifying conditions afresh for claiming unemployment allowance for any subsequent spells provided to him/her, except that he/she should be an IP on the subsequent dates of unemployment. The unemployment allowance in the subsequent spells shall be at the same rate as has already been decided/paid. However, (as specified in section 65 of the ESI Act) an IP shall not be entitled to any other cash benefit and the unemployment allowance simultaneously for the same period concerned. But choice is given to her/him to opt for either of the two, i.e., cash benefit or unemployment allowance. The term 'cash benefit' excludes periodical payments of PDB under ESI Act and Regulations.

485. For entitlement to allowance under this scheme, there will be one month waiting period after the retrenchment. The rate of this allowance as provided by this scheme is 50% of the last pay drawn up to a period of one year. When the person concerned gets re-employment or attains the age of superannuation or 60 years of age, whichever is earlier, the person concerned ceases to get this allowance.

---

173. Shramik Kalyan Yojana (in Hindi) means labour welfare scheme.
174. It is provided that the invalidity of the person should be duly certified by a Medical Board constituted by the Central or State Government.
175. At the beginning of the scheme this was five years, but has been reduced to three years with effect from 11 Sep. 2009.
176. The duration of a year in this context, would mean a period of 156 days or more. An IP who has lost employment and in respect of whom the contribution was paid/payable for 156 days or more in any two consecutive contribution periods in this reckoning will be deemed as having worked for one full year. Similarly, those who have paid contribution for seventy-eight days more in a contribution period will be deemed as having served for a half year.

486. Under this scheme, provision has also been made for medical care for a period of one year from the date of unemployment for the IP and his/her dependant family members. It also focuses on re-employability, as a Vocational Rehabilitation Skill Development Scheme has been included in it.

487. Unemployment allowance shall not be admissible to the IP concerned in the following circumstances:

(1) During lock out.
(2) Lay off/temporary closure of factory/establishment.
(3) Strike resorted to by the employees.
(4) Voluntary abandonment of employment/voluntary retirement/premature retirement.
(5) Less than three year's contributory service.
(6) On attaining the age of superannuation or 60 (sixty) years whichever is earlier.
(7) Convicted (i.e., punished for false statement) under the provisions of section 84 of the ESI Act read with Rule 62 of the ESI (Central) Rules, 1950.
(8) On being re-employed elsewhere during the period he/she is in receipt of unemployment allowance.
(9) Dismissal/termination under disciplinary action.
(10) On death of IP.

488. The rate of unemployment allowance in respect of a person concerned who becomes unemployed is calculated on the basis of average daily wage during the last four completed contribution periods, immediately preceding the date of unemployment. The daily rate of unemployment allowance is payable at the SBR as specified in the Table of Standard Benefit under Rule 54 of ESI (Central) Rules 1950 corresponding to the average daily wage so arrived.

489. Till very recently, the maximum duration of period for getting this benefit by an IP during his/her entire life time, could not be more than six months. But w.e.f. 1 April 2009 it has been raised to twelve months. At the same time, the unemployment allowance cannot be admissible for a period less than one month at a time. In case the beneficiary gets gainful employment subsequently, she/he can avail the balance allowance in case the contingency so arises, but she/he should again be IP to be eligible for unemployment allowance for subsequent spells.

490. The scheme also provides for medical care of the IP eligible for unemployment allowance, under the Scheme for himself/herself and his/her family from the ESI dispensaries/ESI hospitals/IMPs clinics. This can be for a period corresponding to contribution period before unemployment, whichever is later. In the event of death of the IP on any date prior to the expiry of six months period of unemployment allowance, the family of the deceased IP shall continue to be entitled to medical care for eight months as the case would have been, had the IP remained alive. Medical care under this scheme shall, however, be restricted only for the first spell of unemployment.

491. The amount of unemployment allowance up to and including date of death of IP, is payable to his/her nominee or legal heir.

492. Due to the enhanced competition because of globalization, employers tend to reduce cost. In this regard, they tend to shift from employing labour on long-term basis to offering fixed-term employment. This has adversely affected job security in general. To cope with the effects of this development, the ESIC launched a scheme for IPs covered under the ESI Act on 18 September 2018; it has been named as Atal Bimit Vyakti Kalyan Yojna. The scheme aims at direct cash transfer to the affected IPs when they become unemployed and are searching new employment. The benefit envisaged under the scheme for the unemployed persons searching employment will be 25% of the average earning of the IP for 90 days. About 20 lakh workers are estimated to benefit from this scheme annually, which will cost the exchequer about INR 1,600 crores every year.

Chapter 6. Towards Comprehensive Unemployment Insurance

493. The provisions of the IDA in Chapters V-A and V-B and the unemployment allowance payable under the ESI Act, 1948 certainly provide some relief to workers in times of need when they find themselves laid-off, or retrenched or a situation of facing closure of their employer's undertaking. The IDA puts a check on the employers who may indulge in hasty retrenchment and lay-off. In actuality however, employers find various loopholes to subvert the legislative intention. Also, the protection provided under these chapters of the IDA is meagre. State agencies have made sporadic attempts to improve the situation, but these attempts lack any serious concern.

The issue of unemployment compensation became a point for consideration at the State Labour Ministers' Conference in 1981, when the textile mills in the country faced closure and a large number of workers faced serious problems. A Committee set up by it to draw up a scheme recommended establishment of a multipurpose fund to be named as Gratuity and Miscellaneous Payments Guarantee Fund. It aimed to ensure expeditious payment of all statutory payments including those under the IDA. It sought to create an Insurance Fund to be administered by the EPFO. The fund was to be built out of a levy on the employers, on the basis of an actual study. However, nothing fruitful actually came out of these efforts, and the present situation is one of status quo.

494. No system of social security can ignore the issue of unemployment insurance. Merely putting the burden on the employer as is envisaged in the IDA does not provide any realistic solution. Expressing itself on the framework of legal protection, the first National Commission on Labour (NCL) observed as follows:

> The present arrangement by which the lay-off and retrenchment compensation is required to be borne by the employer at a time when he is really in difficulties ...works somewhat harshly on him but more harshly on workers who are on many occasions deprived of the benefits provided under the Act ... . The long-term solution lies in adopting a scheme of unemployment insurance for all employed persons. The present scheme of benefit against retrenchment and lay-off must continue during the transition.[177]

495. The NCL-I wished to tackle the question by advocating development of a comprehensive social security scheme which would include the contingency of unemployment. It hoped that the country would be able to evolve soon an integrated social security scheme. The commission opined that a more comprehensive scheme providing, among others, for provision of unemployment insurance benefit would be possible with some marginal addition to the current rate of contribution. But the NCL-I addressed itself to applying the unemployment insurance scheme only to those who were employed and faced the risk of unemployment, and not to

177. *Report of the National Commission on Labour, Government of India* (New Delhi: Ministry of Labour and Employment and Rehabilitation, 1969), 176.

those persons who have not entered employment at all. But even after 50 years of NCL-I recommendations in this regard, there has been virtually no progress towards this goal.

496. Several private and autonomous bodies have also expressed themselves towards setting up an unemployment insurance scheme. Sometime back in 1991, the Federation of Indian Chamber of Commerce and Industry (FICCI) suggested to the Central Government an unemployment scheme. This envisaged a mutual fund to be raised from contributions from employers and employees at the rate of 1% of the gross wages. A similar proposal was also put forward before the Government by the National Labour Law Association, and the Social Security Association of India. However, nothing concrete has actually taken place.[178] Perhaps, the virtual withdrawal by the state from various spheres of its involvement consequent to the globalization euphoria has led to putting the issue in the cold storage.

497. The adoption by the Central Government of the New Economic Policy (NEP) in July 1991 expectedly led to a large number of industries becoming sick. The NEP envisaged a policy of globalization and liberalization. To cope with the situation, the Government created a National Renewal Fund (NRF). The fund was intended to be used to provide assistance to employees affected by technology upgradation and restructuring. It was to finance the schemes related with retraining, redeployment, and counselling and placement services. It also funds the compensation payment, in view of closure or sickness of the undertakings. The NRF was also to be used for designing employment generation schemes. The Fund is being administered by a steering committee whose members are from Government departments such as industry, labour, finance, education, planning, etc.

498. In actuality, the NRF became merely a National Retirement Fund. Its activities have been confined to funding VRS for public sector employees. Aiding of rehabilitation and renewal has slipped into oblivion. These schemes have usually envisaged more attractive voluntary retirement benefits than the retrenchment compensation available under the IDA.

499. It appears that provision for a general unemployment insurance scheme is a far cry in a country like India where the figure of unemployed persons runs into millions and the growth rate in employment is very low. The key problem is of the availability of funds before a state which is increasingly withdrawing itself from several spheres of peoples' lives, especially to pave the way for the globalization of the economy. Some State Governments have at their own level made efforts in this regard, especially Kerala and Maharashtra.

500. Experts have felt that unemployment benefits as a major component of formal social security model are not feasible in the Indian context mainly, due to the financial and administrative reasons. A huge workforce faces underemployment. As

---

178. R.K.A. Subrahmanya, *Social Security – A Critical Survey* (New Delhi: B.R. Publishing Corporation, 1998), 194.

per the data released by the Centre for Monitoring Indian Economy (CMIE), there were 31 million people looking for jobs in February 2018; with an employment rate of 6.1%.

Thus, as is true in relation to other developing countries, the issue of unemployment benefit in Indian context as well is intimately intertwined with the state of the Indian economy. Of and on, one hears of making the right to work a fundamental right for all sections of society. But it is difficult to operationalize that dream at least in the short run. The Indian State is showing greater concern to ensuring minimum wages to workers in the huge unorganized sector, rather than debating an issue such as unemployment insurance.

501. The Second National Commission on Labour (NCL-II), which gave its report in 2002 had suggested an umbrella legislation, to provide some protection to the unorganized sector workers.[179] This has resulted in the government espousing the enactment of the UWSSA. Interestingly, there is a provision for unemployment allowance in MNREGA scheme, if the State Government is not able to provide work to a willing worker who is prepared to offer herself or himself for manual work under that Act.[180]

179. Government of India, Report of the National Commission on Labour (2nd), Ministry Labour, New Delhi, 2002, vol. I and II., para 7.433.
180. *See* Ch. 2 of Part X in this part of IEL.

Part VIII. Provident Funds and Pensions

502. Provident Funds exist mainly in developing countries.[181] A provident fund scheme seeks to provide economic security to a person or his family members, in the event of retirement or death. It motivates people to save compulsorily. A provident fund involves a system whereby employee-members of the provident fund scheme and their employers make regular contribution of a specified percentage of the employee's wages to a fund. The contributions so made in respect of each member are separately credited in the account of each member. Interest amount is added to the balance in the member's account periodically, usually on an annual basis. In the event of a specified contingency, the sum standing to the credit of a subscriber is paid out. In case of retirement, due to old age or voluntary retirement for other reasons, the amount is paid to the subscriber-member.

If the member dies, the amount standing to his credit is paid out to the survivors. Withdrawals from the fund are also usually permitted subject to certain conditions.

503. Especially in the organized sector, provident funds are considered as the key mechanism of social security in India apart from pension plans, which too are connected with the provident funds. Gratuity is another important retirement benefit in the country, which is payable under the Payment of Gratuity Act 1972; it will be discussed in Part IX.

504. The Central and State Governments in India have been providing pension facilities to their employees since long. Earlier, the option for pension was discretionary. But later on it was made compulsory for all government employees. Recently, a pension scheme has been introduced by the Central Government for employees employed in private and semi-government establishments, through amendment in the EPFA in 1995. This part mainly deals with EPF Act and the three schemes framed under it are the provident fund scheme, the pension scheme, and the deposit-linked insurance scheme. Undoubtedly, the EPF Act is considered as a key social security legislation in India.

181. Some of the developing countries in which provident funds exist are Fiji, India, Indonesia, Kiribati, Malaysia, Nepal, Papua New Guinea, Singapore, Solomon Islands, Sri Lanka and Western Samoa. *See*, R.K.A. Subrahmanya, *Social Security – A Critical Survey* (New Delhi: B.R. Publishing Corporation, 1998), 87.

Chapter 1. Provident Funds

505. The EPF Act is the principal legislation, which envisages provident fund and related facilities in the non-government sector in the country. An older legislation, the Indian Provident Fund Act 1925 is still on the statute book though it has an extremely restricted application. This Act is said to be the mother enactment on provident fund in India. Recognition to provident fund in the country began with this law for the purpose of relief in income tax and protection against attachment, among others. The EPF Act has a very wide coverage and has considerably expanded since its inception. There is provision for subscribing to a public provident fund (PPF) for people who are not employed or if employed who want to avail of additional facilities for separate provident fund. Contributions to PPF are also adjusted for income tax relief, as is the case with contributions to EPF.

There also exist some separate provident fund schemes, for specific categories of employees. These are, for example, envisaged in the Coal Mine Provident Funds Act 1948, the Sea Men's Provident Fund Act 1966; and the Assam Tea Plantations Provident Fund Act 1955. The first two are Central Acts and the third is a State Act. The Government employees are governed by separate rules which have been framed under Article 309[182] of the Constitution. There are also other provident funds recognized by the Income Tax Act, which relate to persons not covered by statutory schemes.

506. It is noticeable that several provident fund enactments exist in the country. Their provisions are by and large similar with some variations. There is an urgent need for consolidating these into a single integrated scheme, covering all establishments.

182. This article is titled: 'Recruitment and Conditions of Service of Persons serving the Union or a State'. The article reads as follows: 'Subject to the provision of this Constitution, Acts of appropriate Legislature may regulate the recruitment, and conditions of service of persons appointed, to public services and posts in connection with the affairs of the Union or of any State: Provided that it shall be competent for the President or such person as he may direct in the case of services and posts in connection with the affairs of the Union, and for the Governor of the State or such person as he may direct in the case of services and posts in connection with the affairs of the State, to make rules regulating the recruitment, and the conditions of service of persons appointed, to such services and posts until provision in that behalf is made by or under an Act of the appropriate Legislature under this Article, and any rules so made shall have effect subject to the provisions of any such Act.' The vision statement of the EPFO envisages repositioning itself as a world class Social Security Organisation providing futuristic services meeting the growing requirements of all categories of its stakeholders. Its Vision 2030 reads as follows: a) Universal Social Security Coverage on mandatory basis by way of Provident Fund, Pension and Life Insurance for all workers of the country; b) Online Services for all EPFO benefits with State-of-the-Art Technology; and c) Implementation of policies for a benefit structure with adequate support level of social security.

Its mission statement reads as follows: "to extend the reach and quality of publicly managed old age income security programs through consistent and ever-improving standards of compliance and benefit delivery in a manner that wins the approval and confidence of members in our methods, fairness, honesty and integrity, thereby contributing to the economic and social well-being of the nation.

§1. Object

507. The EPFS is one of the three schemes that have been framed under the EPF Act. This scheme is known to be the principal component of this legislation. This Act provides for the institution of a provident fund for employees in factories and other establishments. The provident fund benefits the industrial worker (after the worker retires) or his or her dependants (in case of member's death while in service). It envisages a compulsory contributory provident fund to which both the worker and the employer make contributions. This law inculcates among the workers a spirit of savings regularly. It also encourages the stabilization of a steady working force in the establishments to which the Act applies. In case a provident fund exists in an establishment which offers equal or more advantageous terms and is operating efficiently, provision has been made in the EPF Act to allow such arrangements to continue. However, this can be allowed subject to certain conditions to safeguard the interest of the employees.

§2. Applicability of the Act

508. The EPF Act extends to the whole of India except the State of Jammu and Kashmir. The Act is at present applicable to (a) Every establishment, which is engaged in any one or more of the industries specified in Schedule I of the Act or any activity notified by the Central Government in the official Gazette and (b) Employing twenty or more persons.

Courts in India have been taking a proactive stand in deciding the applicability of the Act, in favour of the employees who are meant to be benefited by the EPF Act. In a case, the management, control and supervision were with one person. The employer divided employees between two firms; it was held to be merely a way to escape the liabilities under different labour laws including Provident Fund law. So the two establishments were treated as one.[183]

The Act empowers the Central Government to extend the provisions of this Act to any establishment that employs twenty or more persons. However, the Government must give at least two months' notice of its intention of so extending the applicability of the Act.

509. The EPF Act permits voluntary coverage to establishments in cases where the Act is not applicable otherwise. For voluntary coverage, the mere making of an application by an employer and the majority of his employees is not enough, though such an application is the starting point in this exercise. The decision to allow voluntary coverage of the Act has to be made by the Central Government, through a notification in the official gazette. The notification normally takes effect from the date of its publication, unless the authority concerned decides to apply it retrospectively. But an amendment in 1988 to the EPF Act provides that the voluntary application of the EPF Act can be made from the date of the agreement (and not before

183. *Regional Provident Fund Commissioner v. Nath Traders* 2007 LLR 378 (Del.).

it) or from any subsequent date specified in such agreement. The voluntary coverage through this procedure can also be made in case of infant establishments. Such establishments are those which are allowed an initial vacancy period to prevent the application of the EPF Act during this period.

510. Three categories of establishments have been excluded from the application of the Act

(i) Cooperative societies employing less than fifty persons and working without the aid of power.
(ii) Establishments belonging to or under the control of the Central Government or a State Government and whose employees are entitled to the benefit of contributory provident fund or old age pension in accordance with any scheme or rule framed by the Central Government or the State Government governing such benefit.
(iii) Other establishments set up under any Central, provincial or State Act and whose employees are entitled to the benefit of contributory provident fund or old age pension in accordance with any scheme[184] or rule framed under that Act.

511. As on 31 October 2020, there were 4.46 crore members from 8,29,362 establishments covered under the Act[185] falling under 197 scheduled industries[186] or classes of establishments. Initially, the Act was made applicable only to six scheduled industries. In 1952 it covered only 1.2 lakh employees employed in 1,400 establishments.[187] The EPF organization is one of the largest provident fund institutions in the world in terms of members and volume of financial transactions. So far as the employees are concerned, at the inception of the EPFS an employee who was in receipt of pay up to INR 300 per month and who had worked for one year was eligible for membership of the fund. As a result of the amendments made from time to time, the conditions of eligibility for membership have been changed in favour of the employee by amending the Act and the schemes. Presently, employees who are in receipt of wages up to INR 15000 per month are covered under the EPF Act. Voluntary coverage is possible even for employees who receive wages exceeding INR 15,000 per month.

512. A review of the extension of the EPF Act to new industries in the past shows that the Government does not have a systematic policy on its extension. Its decisions in this regard appear largely piecemeal and ad hoc. There does not appear any rational basis for extending the Act or any well-formulated guidelines to direct the decisions of extending the Act to new industries or class of establishments.

184. In the absence of any such scheme, the establishment concerned cannot be exempted. This was held in *Himachal Pradesh Nagar Vikas Pradhikaran v. Regional PF Commissioner*, 1998 II LLJ 267.
185. *Annual Report 2020-21,* Ministry of Labour (New Delhi: Government of India).
186. Scheduled industries refer to those which have been included in Sch. I of the EPF Act (*See* s. 1(2) of the EPF Act). As per s. 4 of this Act the Central Government is empowered to add to Sch. I.
187. Initially, the EPF Act was applicable to all establishments employing fifty or more persons. The employment limit for the purpose of coverage was reduced to twenty, in 1960.

Extension decisions are usually based on specific demands from workers or trade unions, and sometimes even on extraneous considerations. Of course, extensions are examined by the Ministry of Labour in consultation with the minister concerned in the Central Government and the State Governments.

The EPF Review Committee, 1981 had recommended that a better method will be to make the EPF Act applicable to all industries and classes of industries and putting in Schedule I only those establishments which are excluded from the Act's coverage. This will remove all doubts and ambiguities about the application of the Act. However, there does not appear to be any initiative on the part of the Government to take action in this regard.

513. Despite the laudable objectives and claims of coverage on the part of the Central Government and the EPF organization, a large number of establishments (especially smaller ones) still remain outside the ambit of the Act even though they fall in the category of scheduled industries and employ twenty or more persons. There is an urgent need to strengthen the working of the inspectorate and the administration of the Act so that such establishments are brought under the ambit of the Act. Also, keeping in view the applicability of other labour laws, there is a case for extending the applicability of the Act to establishments employing ten or more persons.[188]

514. The EPF Act does not apply to cooperative societies which employ less than fifty persons and work without the aid of power. It is difficult to comprehend the logic of such an exclusion. There is a need to withdraw this exemption in the interest of benefiting the employees working in these cooperative societies.

515. The application of the Act is also limited by defining the 'excluded employee' in the EPF scheme to be a person whose pay exceeds INR 15,000 per month. This pay limit is revised from time to time. Interestingly, the EPF Act by itself does not make any provision to limit the coverage of the Act, on the basis of wages of the employees. This becomes a serious limitation of the Act. This is more so because the revision of pay ceilings do not keep pace with inflation. For example, during the period 1961 to 1984 the ceiling was raised only by 150% whereas the CPI rose by 600%.[189]

516. The EPF Act is applicable to every employee who is employed in or in connection with the work of a factory or other establishment covered under the Act from the date of joining the factory or establishment. Thus, even persons employed on ad hoc, temporary or casual basis are covered from day one. At the inception of the EPF Scheme in 1952, an employee was eligible to be covered, if he or she was in receipt of pay up to INR 300 per month and who had worked for one year. This

---

188. Both the National Commission on Labour (1969) and the Ramanujam Committee (1982), which was appointed to review the working of the EPF Act, had recommended that the applicability limit of the Act should be lowered from 20 to 10 persons. But no action has been taken in this regard.
189. *See* R.K.A. Subrahmanya, *Social Security – A Critical Survey* (New Delhi: B.R. Publishing Corporation, 1998), 92.

wage limit was raised from time to time as also the condition related to period of employment required, before applying the scheme to an employee. With effect from 1 November 1990, the EPF Act has been made applicable to an employee from the date of joining itself. Experience, however, shows that this provision has caused more problems than it has solved. In several industries, workers are employed on casual or contract basis for a long time, with periods of discontinuity. Many of them are highly mobile in terms of place and employment. Provident fund accounts are maintained by the EPF organization on establishment basis. When members change employment from one industry to another, their files (which are not too professionally maintained) are to be transferred from one to the other establishment. In several cases of bureaucratic inertia and indifference, these files are not transferred, thus causing immense problems to the subscriber. A large number of such workers do not want to be covered under the EPF Act. Such problems are frequently noticed in the brick kiln industry and the building and construction industry, which employ most workers on temporary and casual basis.

This problem shows that the social security requirements of this category of employees have to be provided on the basis of schemes that are differently designed. In fact, the social security needs of employees in the unorganized sector in a country like India have to be based on different assumptions. But there does not appear to be any initiative being taken in this regard at the level of the Governments, the EPF organization or outside agencies.

§3. Exemptions

517. The EPF Act contains provision, through section 17, for granting exemption to any establishment to which the Act applies from the application of the Act or any scheme under the Act. Such exemption is intended to enable the employees concerned to continue to enjoy the better benefits available to them under the private provident fund scheme. Such exemption does not mean total exclusion from the provisions of the Act. The exempted establishments continue to be covered under the Act. The exemption can be granted, if such an establishment has a PF scheme of its own and the rates of contribution of such PF scheme of the employer are not less favourable than those specified in the Act. The Act also envisages granting of exemption to an establishment if its employees are enjoying provident fund, pension or gratuity benefits which taken as a whole, separately or jointly, are not less favourable than the benefits provided under the Act. Provisions also exist for granting exemption to individual employees or class of employees, if they are presently enjoying benefits not less favourable than those available under the Act. The exemption can be granted with retrospective effect.[190]

518. Section 17 of the EPF Act lays down certain conditions to be fulfilled before an exemption on the above lines can be granted. The exempted establishment should constitute a BOT for administering the funds. It is also provided that the balance in the PF account should be invested according to the pattern prescribed

190. *Indian Seamless Metal Tubes Ltd, Pune v. Union of India*, 1995 LLR 773 (Bom.).

by the government. While considering an application for exemption, the EPF organization takes into consideration[191] mainly the rate of contribution made by the employer and the employee, the eligibility clause, and the interest rates payable to the members on their accumulation. In case an establishment violates any of these conditions, the exemption granted to it is liable to be cancelled. In case of any such cancellation, the amount of accumulations standing to the credit of every employee to whom such exemption applied, together with the amount forfeited from the employer's share of contribution in respect of that employee concerned, shall be transferred to the concerned fund under the EPF Act.

519. Even though, the BOT in the establishment concerned is responsible for the management of the exempted funds, the EPF organization exercises control over these funds by conducting regular inspections. Despite this, however, several shortcomings in the system of exemptions are noticeable. In several cases, BOT are not constituted. Cases of misuse of funds and non-investment of PF balances are also not few and far between. The EPF Organization has formed a committee of exempted establishments. This Committee has constituted a sub-committee of the CBOT to oversee the working of the exempted establishments and to make suggestions for consideration of the Board so as to improve the working of the exempted establishments. This sub-committee also considers and suggests additional guidelines for grant of exemption/regulation.

520. As on 31 October 2020, there were 14,87,572 establishments and factories covered under the Act with a membership of 25.26 crores, both in the Exempted and in the Unexempted sectors.

§4. Employers' Duties

521. The EPF Act requires the employers to maintain a contribution card for every member, which contains information about the amount deducted from the employee's wages. It is the employer's duty to pay to the fund, his own contribution and the contribution of the employee within fifteen days of the close of the month. The employer is to allow any member to inspect this card. Also, the card and other records of a member may be inspected by the PF Commissioner or any authorized person on his behalf. It is provided that, if the employer defaults in payment of any contribution to the fund, such an employer shall be liable to pay damages for violation of these provisions, which may be decided by the Government.

§5. Nomination

522. After an employee joins the EPF Scheme, he or she should fill up a nomination form whereby he or she nominates his or her family person(s) who would

191. *56th Annual Report 2008-09, Employees Provident Fund Organization*, Ministry of Labour (New Delhi: Government of India).

receive payment in the event of the death of the member. While doing so, the employee should give a declaration providing details of his or her family members. As and when there is any change in the list of family members, it should be intimated to the Regional PF Commissioner.

§6. Employer not to Reduce Wages

523. Section 12 of the EPF Act prohibits an employer from reducing directly or indirectly the wage of any employee who is governed by the EPF Act simply by reason of his liability for the payment of any contribution to the Provident Fund or any charges under the EPF Act or any schemes framed under it. It has been held in a decided case,[192] that the employee can get his or her contribution reduced by a proper application. However, employer's contribution cannot be reduced. Even on execution of transfer from the statutory scheme to a voluntary scheme, which is more beneficial to the employee in terms of reduced contribution of the employee, the employer cannot reduce its contribution that it has been paying to the employee's PF account under the statutory scheme.

§7. Protection Against Attachment

524. The EPF Act provides protection to the provident fund accumulation against any assignment or charge. The protection against attachment of provident fund is available even against liability to government. Such accumulation shall also not be liable to attachment under any decree or order of any court, in respect of any debt or liability incurred by the member or the exempted employee. Any receiver appointed under the Provincial Insolvency Act or any official assignee appointed under the Presidency Towns Insolvency Act shall not be entitled to or have any claim on the amount standing to the PF Account of the member.

§8. Provident Fund Balance When Payable to the Member or Nominee

525. The EPF scheme specifies the circumstances when the full amount standing to the member's credit along with his interest is payable to the member or his/her survivors on the occurrence of any of the specified events. These events include (i) retirement or attaining the age of 55 years; (ii) disablement; (iii) migration; (iv) retrenchment and (v) death.

The EPF scheme provides that when the amount of the provident fund becomes payable, it is the duty of the CPFC to make prompt payment to the member or nominee as the case may be. The CPFC must give notice to the person to whom the amount is payable and tender the payment after closing the account.

---

192. *Consolidated Crop Protection (P) Ltd v. Hema Chandra Rao & Another*, 1977 Lab. IC 251 (Bom.).

§9. ADVANCES

526. The EPF Scheme also provides that a member can take advances from the provident fund account for certain specific purposes, which can be summarized as under

(i) *House building advance* – The EPF Scheme allows non-refundable advance for purchase of house site and/or construction of a house, purchase of a house/ flat from an individual or through a government/semi-government organization or a cooperative institution or a local body or housing finance corporation, or making addition/improvement to the existing house owned by the owner after fulfilling the eligibility conditions and producing supporting documents described under the scheme. The scheme has also specified the amount admissible, in respect of each advance.

(ii) *Loan Repayment Advance* – An employee who has completed fifteen years of membership is eligible to get a refundable advance for repayment of loans in special cases to an agency. The amount admissible is twenty-four months' basic wage plus DA or employee's and employer's share of contributions and interest thereon or the amount to be refunded to the agency whichever is the least. In this respect, the payment of advance is made to the agency and is not given to the member directly.

(iii) *Other Advances* – A member is entitled to receive refundable advance from the provident fund in the following events or requirements:

The EPF scheme prescribes conditions for eligibility, supportive documents to be furnished, and the amount admissible for such advances.

(a) closure/lockout of the establishment for more than fifteen days for reasons other than strike;
(b) the employee not in receipt of wages for a continuous period of two months or more for reasons other than strike;
(c) illness of the member or his family;
(d) member's own marriage or marriage of any specified relatives;
(e) post-matriculation education of son/daughter;
(f) abnormal conditions like flood, riots, earthquakes, etc. by which the property of the member is damaged;
(g) member affected by power cut in the factory/establishment;
(h) purchase of equipment in case of physically handicapped member; or
(i) for financing a life insurance policy.

Chapter 2. Employees' Deposit-Linked Insurance

527. One of the three schemes envisaged by the EPF Act is the EDLIS. Section 6C of the Act has authorized the Central Government to frame a scheme such as the EDLIS. This scheme was made in 1976 has been in force since 1 August 1976. It seeks to provide an insurance cover to the members of the EPF without payment of any premium by its members. The insurance cover provided by the EDLIS is linked to the amount standing to the credit of an employee in his or her provident fund.

528. The scheme has established a deposit-linked insurance fund into which are paid by the employer contribution from time to time, in respect of all his employees who are entitled to be covered. Interestingly, even the Central Government contributes to this fund.

§1. Application and Coverage

529. The EDLIS applies to all factories and establishments to which the EPF Act applies. All the employees who are members of the provident fund are required to become members of this scheme.

§2. Exemptions

530. The EDLIS provides that the CPFC may grant exemptions to an employer who makes a request in this regard. Such an exemption can be granted from the operation of all or any of the provisions of the insurance scheme, if the CPFC is satisfied that the employees of such establishment are in enjoyment of benefits in the nature of life insurance without making payment of any premium or contribution. Such life insurance benefit provided by the employer may or may not be linked to their deposits in the provident fund.

Also, such benefits should be more favourable to the employees concerned than the benefits admissible under the EDLIS. Further, the CPFC while granting the exemption may impose any conditions to be observed by the employee. A notification about the exemption has to be given in the official gazette. The Central Government can exercise the power of inspection and control about the proper investment of any such insurance fund and related matters. These inspection powers have been conferred by the scheme on the CPFC or any inspector appointed. The CPFC is also authorized to control the exemption, if the employer fails to comply with the conditions subject to which such exemption was granted. On cancellation of any such exemption any amount payable by the employer in respect of the employee concerned shall be transferred to the Deposit-linked Insurance Fund Account created under the EDLIS.

531. In this regard it may be noted that the Life Insurance Corporation of India has introduced a similar scheme offering somewhat better benefits to the persons covered. Consequently, a large number of establishments covered under the EDLIS have obtained exemption from this scheme.

§3. Benefits under the Scheme

532. The benefit envisaged in the EDLIS is payable in the event of death of an employee who is a member of the Provident Fund under the EPF Scheme. The payment is to be made to the nominee/family members of the deceased member. This amount is also called additional assurance benefit.

The benefits provided under the EDLIS are paid in case of death of an employee who was member of the scheme at the time of death. The family will get an amount linked to either the average balance in PF account during preceding 12 months or 20 times of the average wages of INR 15,000 of the last 12 months of the member subject to a maximum of INR 700,000 whichever is higher.

This scheme is intended to encourage the members of the EPF scheme to maintain a high sum of money in his or her PF account and not indulge in unnecessary withdrawals from it. Yet the latest amendment to the scheme puts primacy on protection that is analogous to a life insurance policy.

§4. Payment of Assurance Benefit

533. On the death of a member, the assurance benefit is payable to his or her nominee or nominees as have been mentioned in the nomination made by the member. The nomination made by an employee under the EPF scheme or under the exempted provident fund is also treated as nomination under the EDLIS. The assurance amount becomes payable to such nominees. If no nomination subsists or if the nomination relates to part of the amount standing to the credit of the account, in that case the amount becomes payable to the members of his family.

534. No part of the amount payable under the scheme is liable to be attached, whatever may be the extent of the debt or liability incurred by the deceased member. It has been held that the amount payable under the group insurance scheme of the Life Insurance Corporation of India is also payable under an insurance scheme and it cannot be attached.[193]

193. *Ratnakumar v. Katta Subbaravamma*, 1994 II LLJ 81.

Chapter 3. Pensions

535. A very bold and significant development in the social security system in India has been the introduction in 1995 of a pension scheme for employees covered by the EPF Act. Pension schemes already existed for employees of Central Government and State Governments. Some public sector undertakings had also provided for pension schemes, as a retirement benefit for their employees. But a very large number of private and public sector organizations were still not covered under any pension scheme. To fill these *lacunae*, the Employees' Provident Funds and Miscellaneous Provisions (Amendment) Ordinance 1995 was promulgated by the President of India which came into force w.e.f. 16 November 1995. This ordinance conferred powers upon the Central Government to frame a suitable pension scheme providing for the following: superannuation scheme, retiring pension or permanent disablement pension to employees to whom the Act applies, widow or widower's pension, children pension or orphan pension payable to the beneficiaries of such employees in the event of death.

536. The new pension scheme applies to all employees who were covered by the earlier Family Pension Scheme (FPS) and also to new members. The FPS broadly provided for three benefits for its members, which are

(a) family pension (pension payable to the widow or minor children on the death of the employee before attaining the age of 60 years);
(b) life assurance benefit; and
(c) retirement-cum-withdrawal benefits.

The pension scheme of 1995 created a pension fund without requiring any extra contribution from the employees or the employers. From and out of the contributions payable by the employer in each month under the EPF Act and rules framed under it, contributions representing 8.33% of the employee's pay are remitted by the employer to the pension fund. The Central Government also contributes to the pension fund at the rate of 1.6% of the employee's pay. All assets and liabilities of the existing family pension fund have been transferred to the proposed pension fund.

The salient features of the Employee Pension Scheme are as follows:

- It is a guaranteed pension plan whereby the stipulated amount will be remitted to the employee upon retirement.
- Every employees who is a member of the EPF scheme automatically gets enrolled into the EPS scheme.
- All employees whose monthly salary combined with DA is INR 15,000 or less must enrol themselves into this scheme.
- The monthly pension amount will not be less than INR 1,000.
- Pensions can be availed when the employee attains the age of 50, but in such situation there will be a reduction in the amount of eligible pension.
- In case the EPS member dies the widow/widower of the deceased employee will receive pension. Children will receive pension till they attain 25 years of age.

- If case the widow/widower remarries, the children of the employee will be the recipients of enhanced pension as such children are categorized as orphans.
- Any child who is physically challenged will receive pension for his/her entire lifetime.

§1. APPLICABILITY

537. The Pension Scheme applies to all employees employed in factories and other establishments to which the EPF Act 1952 applies. It also applies to employees in other factories and establishments which have been covered by the EPF Act by an extension done by the Central Government. Apart from the persons who were members of the FPS, the EPS is also compulsory for persons who become members of the Provident Fund from 16 November 1995, i.e., the date of introduction of the scheme. The PF subscribers who were not members of the FPS have an option to join this Pension Scheme. The types of benefits available to members under the EPS are given in Table 3.

Table 3 Employees' Pension Scheme: Benefits

S. N.	*Type*	*Eligibility Conditions*
1	**Withdrawal Benefit**	Less than 10 years of eligible service/ membership ***(more than 6 months and less than 9½ years of eligible service)***
2	**Scheme Certificate**	On leaving employment below 58 years of age
3	**Superannuation Pension**	In case of Superannuation with minimum eligible service of 10 years
4	**Reduced Pension**	On leaving service between the age of 50 and 58 years with minimum eligible service of 10 years.
5	**Disablement Pension**	Loss of job on account of total and permanent disablement during service
6	**Widow/Widower and children Pension**	On the death of the member before obtaining the age of 58 years or on the death of the pensioner
7	**Orphan Pension**	On the death of the member and his/her spouse or remarriage of the spouse before attaining the age of 58 years of member.
8	**Nominee Pension**	On the death of the member while in service who is not having any family. On the death of member who is not having any family but rendered more than 10 years of eligible service.

S. N.	*Type*	*Eligibility Conditions*
9	**Dependant Parent Pension**	In case of member not having any family or any nominee: (a) On the death of the member while in service before attaining 58 years of age. (b) On the death of the member before 58 years of age and leaving service with at least 10 years of eligible service.

§2. Employers' Duties

538. The pension scheme provides various duties of the employers which are described below.

Before taking any employee into employment, the employer has the duty to ask him or her to state, in writing, whether he or she is a member of the Pension Fund. If he or she is a member, the employer shall also require from the employee to furnish a copy of the scheme certificate issued by the EPF Commissioner relating to his or her past employment. If the employee was not in employment before joining the employer or had availed return of contribution in respect of his or her previous employment, he or she shall supply to the employer necessary particulars for the purpose of becoming a member of the Pension Scheme.

539. Every employer covered under the Scheme shall furnish to the Commissioner particulars of all branches and departments, owners, directors, partners, managers or any other person or persons having the ultimate control over the affairs of such factory or establishment.

540. Every contractor shall submit to the principal employer a statement showing the particulars of employees employed by or through him, in respect of whom contributions to the pension fund are payable. The contractor shall also furnish to the employer such information which the principal employer is required to furnish to the EPFC under the EPS.

541. The employer shall prepare an Employees' Pension Fund Contribution card in respect of each employee who has become a member of the EPS.

542. Every employee shall send to the Commissioner within fifteen days of the close of each month a return in respect of the employees leaving services of the employer during the preceding month. If there is no such employee, the employer shall send a nil return.

543. The Central Board may issue any direction to the employers generally as it may consider necessary for the purpose of implementing the scheme. It shall be the duty of the employer to carry out such directions.

§3. CONTRIBUTION

544. Every employer shall pay the contribution payable to the Employees' Pension Fund in respect of each member of the EPF employed by him directly or through a contractor. Out of the contributions payable by the employer in each month under the EPF Act and the Rules framed under it, a part of the employees' pay shall be remitted by the employer to the employees' pension fund within fifteen days of the close of every month. This shall be done by a separate bank draft or cheque on account of the employees' pension fund contribution. The employer shall bear the cost of remittance, if any. The Central Government shall also contribute at the rate of 1.6% of the pay of the members of the pension scheme. Where the pay of the member exceeds INR 15,000 per month, the contribution payable by the employer and the Central Government shall be limited to the amount payable on his or her pay of INR 15,000 only.

§4. PENSIONABLE SALARY

545. The term 'pay' includes basic wages, dearness allowance, retaining allowance and cash value of food concessions admissible, if any. Pensionable salary of an employee is the average monthly pay drawn by him or her during the contributory period of service in the span of twelve months preceding the date of exit from the membership of the EPF. If, during this period of twelve months there are non-contributory periods of service, the total wages during the twelve months span shall be divided by the actual number of days for which salary has been drawn and the amount so derived shall be multiplied by 30 to know the average monthly pay. The maximum pensionable salary of a person shall be limited to INR 15,000 per month. If at the option of the employer and employee, contribution paid on salary exceeding INR 15,000 per month and 8.33 share of the employer is remitted to the pension fund, the pensionable salary in such cases shall be based on such higher salary.

§5. AMOUNT OF PENSION

546. The amount of monthly pension of a member depends upon his or her pensionable salary and pensionable service. The scheme prescribes the following formula for calculating the monthly pension payable to a member, i.e., multiply the pensionable salary by pensionable service; and then divide this figure by 70 as is done in the formula below:

$$\text{Member's pension} = \frac{\text{Pensionable salary} \times \text{Pensionable service}}{70}$$

A member shall be entitled to retirement pension or short service pension. The pension is calculated on the basis of eligible service. A person should have put in a minimum of ten years of contributory service, to be eligible for pension. A member shall be entitled to retirement pension (i) if he or she has rendered eligible service of twenty years or more and retires on attaining the age of 58 years; or (ii) if he has rendered eligible service of twenty years or more and retires or otherwise ceases to be in the employment before attaining the age of 58 years. In case a member has put in eligible service of ten years or more but less than twenty years, he or she shall be entitled to short service pension. While the normal superannuation pension is payable on attaining the age of 58 years, pension at a discounted rate is payable on attaining the age of 50 years. Where the pensionable service is less than ten years, the member has an option to remain covered for pensionary benefits until the age of 58 years or claim return of contribution/withdrawal benefit. In cases of superannuation and in cases where service is more than twenty years, a member's pensionable service is increased by granting two bonus years. Therefore, a member who has put in twenty years of service will get benefit of twenty-two years; one who has put in thirty-two years will get benefit of thirty-four years.

The long awaited demand for implementation of the minimum pension was granted during 2014–2015. It provides a minimum pension of INR 1,000 per month for member/widow(er)/disabled/nominee/dependant parent pensioners, INR 750 per month for orphan pensioners and INR 250 per month for children pensioners.

547. For members of the ceased FPS, a separate formula for pension calculation has been prescribed.

548. A member who is permanently and totally disabled during the employment, shall be entitled to pension per month even if he/she has not rendered the pensionable service entitling him/her to pension. But for being entitled to this, he or she must have made at least one month's contribution to the pension fund. The monthly member's pension in such cases shall be payable from the date of permanent total disablement and shall be tenable for the lifetime of the member. A member who applies for this benefit shall be required to undergo medical examination, as prescribed by the Central Board. Such examination is conducted to determine whether or not he or she is permanently and totally unfit for the employment which he or she was doing at the time of such disablement.

549. The EPS also envisages benefits to the family on the death of a member. In the event of death of the member, while in service or away from employment before attaining the age of 58 years, the widow pension shall be payable as under:

(i) member's pension as would have been payable had he retired on the date of death; or
(ii) widow pension payable as per Table C appended to the EPS, whichever is higher.

The monthly widow pension shall be payable up to the date of death of the widow or remarriage, whichever is earlier. In cases where there are two or more widows, family pension shall be payable to the eldest surviving widow and on her death it shall be payable to the next surviving widow, if any. The term eldest refers to seniority in relation to the date of marriage and not age.

550. If there are any surviving children of the deceased member falling within the definition of family, they are entitled to receive a monthly children pension, in addition to the monthly widow/widower pension. Monthly children pension for each child shall be equal to 25% of the amount admissible to the widow/widower of the deceased member as monthly widow pension payable. Children's pension is payable, until the child attains the age of 25 years. Such pension shall be admissible to a maximum of two children at a time. It will be payable from the oldest to the youngest child in that order.

551. In case the deceased member is not survived by any widow but only children falling within the definition of family, or in case the widow pension is not payable, in such cases children shall be entitled to a monthly orphan pension. Such a pension shall be equal to 75% of the amount of the monthly widow pension.

Also, in case the widow/widower dies or remarries after sanctioning of widow/widower pension, the children shall be entitled *in lieu* of monthly children pension to a monthly orphan pension. This will be with effect from the date following the date of death or remarriage of the widow or the widower. The monthly orphan pension shall be admissible to a maximum of two orphans at a time. The orphan pension shall run from the oldest to the youngest orphan.

552. The EPS provides for payment of monthly pension to a nominee in case a member is not married or who does not have a living spouse and/or an eligible child. This pension shall be equal to the monthly widow pension as admissible. This is however, subject to the proviso that in case the member acquires a family subsequently the nomination so made shall become void.

553. EPFO launched in March 2018 a dedicated Pensioners' Portal. The pensioners may get the details about their pension payment order (PPO), passbook, and various other fields such as pension credit date or life certificate submission. The organization has made a good use of IT tools which has helped and simplified the interactions with stakeholders including members, employers, or pensioners. Many digital services have been launched recently. EPFO has also made the claim online settlement process more member-centric and hassle free. This has helped the members a great deal.

§6. Date of Payment of Pension

554. The monthly pension payable to a member shall be payable from a date immediately following the date of completion of 58 years of age, even in cases where the member has retired or ceased to be in employment before that date. However, a member, if he or she so desires, may be allowed to draw a monthly reduced pension from a date earlier than 58 years of age, but not earlier than 50 years of age. In such a case, the member's monthly pension shall be reduced at the rate of 3% for every year the age falls short of 58 years.

555. Where a member ceases to be in employment by way of retirement or otherwise at a date earlier than the date of superannuation from which pension can be drawn, then he or she has a choice. In such a case, the member may on his or her option be paid pension as admissible under this scheme on attaining the age exceeding 50 years. Alternatively, he or she may be issued a certificate of pensionable salary and the amount of pension due on the date of exit from the employment. If the person is subsequently employed in an establishment covered under the EPS, his or her earlier service as per the scheme certificate shall be reckoned for pension along with the fresh spell of pensionable service.

§7. Benefit on Leaving Service

556. If a member has not rendered the eligible service prescribed on the date of exit or on attaining 58 years age, whichever is earlier, he/she shall be entitled to a withdrawal benefit. The rates of withdrawal benefit are laid down in Table D of the EPS. If the person has not attained the age of 58 years he or she may opt to receive the scheme certificate. In such a case, if the member does not take up an employment coverable under the EPS, but dies before attaining the age of 58 years, the amount of contributions received in respect of his or her case shall be converted into a monthly widow pension and children pension. The widow pension in these cases shall be calculated as per the rates in Table C appended to the EPS. Children pension shall be payable at 25% of widow pension for each child, up to two children. If there is no widow, then the orphan pension shall be payable at the rate of 75% of the amount payable as widow pension.

§8. Option for Commutation

557. The EPS earlier provided for commutation of pension up to one-third of its quantum. The idea was to enable the pensioner to receive an amount which is one hundred times the monthly pension so commuted as the commuted value of the pension. He or she could regularly receive only the not transposed value of the pension per month, i.e., two-thirds pension. This facility has now been withdrawn w.e.f 26 September 2008, after notification of the amendment to the EPS.

§9. Private Pension Scheme

558. It is possible to exempt any establishment or class of establishments from the operation of the EPS. The exemption can be granted by the appropriate government. In doing so the appropriate Government may impose conditions on the pattern of investment of the pension fund or otherwise. The exemption can, however, be granted only if the employees of the establishment are members of any other pension scheme wherein the pensionary benefits are at par or more favourable than those envisaged under the EPS.

An exemption so granted can be cancelled by the authority which granted it by order in writing, if an employer fails to comply with any of the conditions imposed while granting the exemption.

§10. COMMENT

559. When the EPS was introduced in 1995, several sections of workers' organizations opposed it. They criticized it as a mere eye wash. On the contrary, some finance experts doubted its viability, given the contribution and benefit structure envisaged by the Scheme. It appears that with the passage of time its criticism has almost died down. At the same time, the EPS has stood the test of time. It is heartening to note that as on 31 March 2020 there were 66,82,717 pensioners under EPS in different categories. Undoubtedly, the launching of the EPS is a good beginning in the history of Indian social security system. For, any real social security for the old and the retired is regular receipt of income through a pension scheme. In order to be meaningful, however, it is essential that the amount of pension is linked to the price index. The Central Government has promised to review the EPS annually and to revise the pension rates so as to neutralize the price rise. Pension rates have been revised once on the basis of advice from the actuary. It is hoped that in the time to come the Pension Scheme shall make available protection to the elderly people against the contingency of old age in a realistic sense.

Part IX. Gratuity

560. The Indian social security system gives an important place to gratuity payment by employers to their employees on retirement, death and resignation. Gratuity payments are also made by the Central and State Governments to their employees. Further, such payments are also made by employers to employees employed with public sector undertakings as well as those employed in the private sector.

A gratuity is intended to provide cash benefits to the employees leaving the job or to their dependants in case of death, so as to compensate for at least part of the loss of income of the employee occurring due to old age, invalidity and death. Technically speaking, it is a lump sum payment made by an employer to an employee, in consideration of the latter's past services when his or her employment is terminated. Gratuity schemes serve as important instruments of social security in developing countries like India where the general level of income is quite low, and effective social security is also not quite substantial. To begin with, gratuity payments were made by the employer to its employees at its pleasure[194] in order to keep them content. Thus, every employee was not entitled to gratuity as of right.

561. The payment of gratuity in India got transformed from a gratuitous payment by the employer to an established practice. It is related with the introduction of the system of industrial adjudication during World War II, which culminated in the enactment of a central law in the form of the IDA. The IDA is the principal industrial relations law in the country. It envisages adjudication mechanisms for deciding both interest and rights disputes through quasi-judicial bodies called industrial tribunals and labour courts. Appropriate Governments (both Central and State Governments in their jurisdictions) faced situations of workers raising industrial disputes related to payment of gratuity, which were referred by the appropriate government to industrial tribunals for adjudication. Tribunal awards granting employees' claims of gratuity legitimized the system of gratuity payment in the country. As the practice of demand for gratuity payment was becoming widespread, the judiciary conferred legitimacy when the Supreme Court referred to it as a retiring benefit to the workmen who have rendered long and unblemished service to the employer and thereby contributed to the prosperity of the employer.[195] Several other

194. *Express Newspapers v. Union of India* (1961) I LLJ 334 (SC).
195. *Delhi Cloth and Gen. Mills Co. Ltd v. Their Workmen* (1968) 36 FJR 247.

developments[196] led to the emergence of gratuity payment becoming an accepted practice, eventually leading to the enactment of the Payment of Gratuity Act in 1972 (PGA). The Act is administered by the 'Controlling Authority (CA)' which exercises administrative as well as quasi-judicial powers in relation to determination and payment of gratuity. This part deals with the application of the Payment of Gratuity Act, the benefit envisaged in this Act and conditions for payment of gratuity.

196. Statutory provision for payment of gratuity started with the enactment of the Working Journalists (Conditions of Service and Miscellaneous Provisions) Act 1955. The provision of gratuity in it was declared ultra vires by the SC in a decided case in 1961. The concerned section in the Act was reworded in 1962 so as to give effect to the decision of the apex Court. In 1962 the Central Wage Board recommended the introduction of industry-wide gratuity scheme in coal industry to be financed out of a fund to be created by levying a cess on dispatches of coal. In 1965, a uniform scheme of gratuity was framed by the Ministry of Finance, Government of India, for undertakings in the public sector. In its report in 1969, the Committee on Labour Welfare suggested that while computing the quantum of gratuity, the element of dearness allowances should also be taken into consideration along with basic wages (Government of India, Report of the Committee on Labour Welfare, 1969, 269). In a significant judgment in 1969, the Supreme Court recommended that the legislature should evolve a reasonably uniform scheme of gratuity so that litigation in the matter of its payment could be minimized. Following this, Kerala, Uttar Pradesh and West Bengal States enacted Gratuity Acts. Other States also expressed the desire to enact a law on those lines. As per the call of the Supreme Court, Parliament enacted a central legislation on gratuity, which was named, the Payment of Gratuity Act 1972 (PGA). The PGA overrides the State laws on gratuity and is applicable throughout India. It came into force on 16 Sep. 1972. Apart from the usual amendments, this Act was substantially amended in 1984 and 1987.

Chapter 1. Nature of Gratuity

562. The Indian judiciary has treated gratuity as a kind of retirement benefit, like the provident fund or pensions. However, it has clarified that its purpose is different from these two benefits. In an important decision, the Supreme Court[197] observed that gratuity and pensions 'are both efficiency devices, and are considered necessary for an orderly human elimination from industry of superannuated or disabled employees, who would continue employment even though they function inefficiently ... . It compensates the employee who as he grows old knows that some compensation for the gradual destruction of his wage earning capacity is being built up'. The Court clarified that gratuity is a retiral benefit of very different kind, as compared to provident fund and pension. It made it clear that there is no overlapping between the three schemes. The concept of gratuity is now being looked at as a compulsory statutory retiral benefit,[198] as gratuity is now payable under the Payment of Gratuity Act 1972. Courts see the PGA as a piece of beneficial legislation that needs to be interpreted liberally. It was enacted with a view to grant benefit to workers, a 'weaker section' in industrial adjudicatory process.[199]

197. *Burhanpur Tapti Mills Ltd v. B.T. Mills Mazdoor Sangh* (1965) 1 LLJ 453.
198. *Lalappa Lingappa v. Laxmi Vishnu Textile Mills*, 1981 Lab. 1C 307 (SC).
199. *M. C. Chamaraju v. Hind Nippon Rural Industrial (P) Ltd*, 2007 LLR 1129 (SC).

Chapter 2. Application of the Act

563. The Payment of Gratuity Act 1972 (PGA) applies to:

(a) every factory, mine, oilfield, plantation, port and railway company,
(b) every shop or establishment within the meaning of any law for the time being, in force in relation to shops or establishments in a State in which ten or more persons are employed, or were employed, on any day of the preceding twelve months.

Section 1(3)(C) of PGA envisages an enabling provision. It empowers the Central Government to extend the provisions of the Act to any other establishment or class of establishments where ten or more employees were employed on any day of the preceding twelve months, as the Central Government may specify in this behalf.

In exercise of the extension powers conferred on the Central Government under section 1(3)(C), it has extended the Act to the following: motor transport establishments, solicitor's offices, local bodies, educational institutions, societies, trusts and circus industry, in which ten or more persons are employed or were employed on any day in the preceding twelve months. It is provided in section 2(3-A) that an establishment to which the Act has become applicable shall continue to be governed by the Act, even if the number of persons employed in it falls below ten.

564. For application of the PGA, the person concerned must be an employee who is employed in an establishment covered by the Act. According to section 2(e), 'employee' means any person (other than an apprentice) who is employed for wages, whether the terms of such employment are express or implied, in any kind of work, manual or otherwise, in or in connection with the work of a factory, mine, oilfield, plantation, port, railway company, shop or other establishment, to which this Act applies, but does not include any such person who holds a post under the Central Government or a State Government and is governed by any other Act or by any rules providing for payment of gratuity;' This is the new definition of the term 'employee' after it was amended by the Payment of Gratuity (Amendment) Act 2009. This is a wider definition compared to the earlier one which was interpreted by the Supreme Court to exclude teachers.[200] In a decided case, a teacher was held by the Supreme Court not to be an employee under the PGA, and therefore not entitled to payment of gratuity under the Act. The Supreme Court desired that the legislature concerned should pass a separate suitable legislation providing for gratuity to teachers.[201] Responding to the Supreme Court's observation, the PGA has been amended by the legislature in 2009. Now the amended definition gives a wider

200. The earlier definition was like what follows: 'Employee refers to any person (other than an apprentice) employed on wages in any covered establishment to do any skilled, semi-skilled, or unskilled, manual, supervisory, technical or clerical work, whether the terms of such employment are expressed or implied and whether or not such person is employed in any managerial or administrative capacity. The definition, however, excludes any person who holds a post under the Central or State Government1 and is governed by any other Act or by any rules providing for payment of gratuity.'

201. *Ahmedabad Pvt. Primary Teachers Assn. v. Administrative Officer*, 2004 LLR 97 (SC).

connotation to the term 'gratuity,' which now will include all employees including teachers. But employees of the Central and State Government continue to be excluded from PGA as they have their own scheme of gratuity.

Another issue for application of the PGA is the salary limit of the employee covered by the PGA. Until recently, persons drawing monthly wages exceeding INR 3,500 were excluded from the purview of the Act. But this ceiling was removed altogether by the Payment of Gratuity (Amendment) Act 1997. So now, all persons who are employees under the Act are entitled to claim gratuity irrespective of the monthly salary that they receive.

Chapter 3. Exemptions

565. Section 5 of the PGA gives powers to the appropriate Government to exempt an establishment, etc. to which the Act applies from the operation of the Act. The Government can do so, if employees in it are in receipt of gratuity or pensionary benefits not less favourable than the benefits conferred under the Act. Similarly, the appropriate Government can also exempt any employee or class of employees who are in receipt of gratuity or pensionary benefits not less favourable than the benefits conferred under the Act.

Chapter 4. Payment of Gratuity

§1. Conditions for Payment

566. Gratuity is payable to an employee in any of the three situations (a) superannuation; or (b) retirement or resignation; or (c) death or disablement due to accident or disease. But, there is a condition that must be fulfilled, for enabling a person to become entitled to gratuity payment – The employee should have completed five years of continuous service. However, the condition of five years is not necessary where the termination of employment of any employee is due to death or disablement. For the purpose of this condition related to disablement, the word disablement refers to such incapacitation that an employee suffers for the work which he was capable of performing before the accident or disease which has resulted in such disablement.

§2. Continuous Service

567. Section 4(1) of the PGA envisages the concept of gratuity being a reward for long, continuous and meritorious service. The emphasis on the term continuous here, is not on continuity of employment but on rendering of continuous service. Section 2A of the PGA defines the term 'continuous service'. A completed year of service is defined to mean uninterrupted service for one year. For this purpose, absence due to sickness, accident, absence without leave (except where an order has been passed treating it as break in service), lay-off, strike, lockout and cessation of work not due to fault of the employee are not treated as interruption. The law thus gives an extended meaning to the term continuous service. The idea is that the worker who has rendered long and meritorious service is not deprived of his right to gratuity by reason of absence of duty due to circumstances beyond his or her control.

An employee is deemed to be in continuous service for a period of one year, if he has actually worked for 190 days when he is employed below the ground in a mine or in an establishment which works for not less than six days in a week, and 240 days in any other case. For this purpose, any period of lay-off, leave with full wages earned in a previous year, absence due to temporary disablement caused by accident arising out of and in the course of employment, and any period of maternity leave shall be deemed to be period of actual work. Thus, the Supreme Court has rightly observed that if otherwise eligible, even a daily wage worker can be entitled to gratuity.[202]

In case of an employee working in a seasonal establishment, continuous service would mean that he or she has actually worked for not less than 75% of the number of days on which the establishment was in operation.

202. *Municipal Corporation of Delhi v. Female Workers (Muster Rolls)*, AIR 2000 SC 1274.

§3. Amount of Gratuity Payable

568. Gratuity is payable to an employee at the rate of fifteen days' wage for every completed year of service or part thereof in excess of six months. Wages here refer to wages last drawn by the employee concerned. In case of piece-rated employee, daily wages shall be computed on the average of the total wages received by him or her for a period of three months immediately preceding the termination of his employment excluding the wages paid for overtime. In case of seasonal establishments employees have been classified into two groups, i.e., (i) those who work throughout the year; and (ii) those who work only during the season. Employees in the former category are entitled to gratuity at the rate of fifteen days' wage for every completed year of service or part thereof in excess of six months. Those falling in the latter category are, however, entitled to receive gratuity at the rate of seven days' wage for each season.

The amount of gratuity payable to an employee shall not exceed INR 20 lakhs.[203] However, an employee can receive greater amount of gratuity under an award, agreement or contract with the employer.

569. The term wages is defined as emoluments payable in cash but excluding bonus, commission, house rent allowance, overtime wages and any other allowance.

570. In the case of monthly rated employees, the fifteen days' wages has to be calculated by dividing the monthly rate of wages last drawn by him by 26 and multiplying the quotient by 15.

571. An employee may become disabled due to an accident or some disease due to which he may not be able to do the work with the same efficiency. Such employee may be employed by the employer on reduced wages. Gratuity in case of such employees, shall be computed in two parts

(a) For the period preceding the disablement, gratuity is calculated on the basis of wages last drawn by the employee at the time of disablement.
(b) For the period subsequent to the disablement, gratuity will be computed on the basis of reduced wages as drawn by him or her at the time of termination of service.

The disabled employee shall be paid the total of the gratuity for these two periods.

572. The PGA provides that gratuity may be forfeited wholly or partly. This Act deals with this issue in two parts. It is provided in section 4(6)(a) that if an employee's services have been terminated for committing any act of wilful omission or

203. This amount has been raised from INR 10 lakh to INR 20 lakh by the Payment of Gratuity (Amendment) Act 2018 which has come into force w.e.f. 29 Mar. 2018.

negligence which has caused any damage or loss to, or destruction of, property of the employer, his or her gratuity shall be forfeited to the extent of the damage.

The second category of forfeiture is dealt with in section 4(6)(b). This section deals with those cases where the services of an employee have been terminated due to the following: (a) for riotous and disorderly conduct or any act of violence on his part; or (b) for any act which constitutes an offence involving moral turpitude, provided that such offence is committed by the employee in the course of employment.

Where the service has not been terminated on any of the above grounds, the employer cannot withhold gratuity due to the employee. It was held by the Kerala High Court[204] that where the employee did not vacate the employer's land, his gratuity could not be forfeited. In another case, the entire gratuity of an employee was adjusted by the employer towards disputed penal rent, it was held that the gratuity was no longer a bounty but a valuable right and the same has to be paid. The penal rent cannot be the subject matter of adjudication of gratuity.[205] Gratuity cannot even be attached. It has been held that the employer is a trustee for the provident fund and the gratuity money of the deceased that was lying with the employer. So long as they are with the employer, there is a protection from attachment.[206]

Likewise, protection has been provided against forfeiture of gratuity. In a decided case, it was held that gratuity cannot be forfeited by the employer on the ground that the employee had used abusive language against the employer that would not amount to moral turpitude.[207] Further, where an employee was allowed to retire from service on reaching the age of superannuation, the mere fact that a criminal case was pending against him at the time of his retirement was not considered to be a justifiable reason to withhold gratuity by the employer.[208] Nor was gratuity allowed to be forfeited where an employee had resigned from service and the same was accepted by the company, as it was not a case of termination of service that could possibly attract employer's right to forfeit gratuity.[209]

§4. Compulsory Insurance

573. Experience shows that gratuity due to employees remains Unpaid in several cases. This is often due to sickness of the industry and the consequent inability of the employer to pay the same for lack of resources. So as to cope with this situation, the PGA was amended in 1987 and section 4-A was inducted in it to provide for compulsory insurance of the employer's liability. The insurance must be done

204. *Travancore Plywood Industry v. Regional JLC*, 1996 II LLJ 14 (Ker.); *see also*: *Ramjilal Chimanlal Sharma v. Elphinstone Spg. & Wvg. Mills Co. Ltd* (1985) 1 LLN 228; and *Binny Ltd v. Appellate Authority* (1984) 2 LLN 439 (Kant.)
205. *Shrirahathi M.A. v. NGEF Ltd Bangalore* 2003 II LLJ 918.
206. *Sathyabama v. M. Palamiswamy*, 2004 LLR 270.
207. *Management of Central Theatre, Coimbatore v. Controlling Gratuity Act, Coimbatore*, 2005 LLR 149 (Mad.).
208. *Gujarat State Food Transport Corpn. v. Devendrabhai Mulvantrai Vaidya*, 2004 LLR 225.
209. *Dunlop India Ltd v. Union of India*, 2003 III LLJ 1125.

with the Life Insurance Corporation of India or any other prescribed insurer. However, the employers of establishments belonging to or under the control of the Central Government or any State Government have been exempted from the provisions related to compulsory insurance.

574. It is also provided that the appropriate Government may exempt an employer from the provisions of the PGA who had already established an approved gratuity fund in respect of his employees and who desires to continue such arrangement; and an employer employing 500 or more persons who establishes an approved gratuity fund in the prescribed manner.

575. For the purpose of effectively implementing section 4-A, every employer is required to register its establishment with the CA in the prescribed manner. Only those employers who have taken insurance as mentioned earlier or have established an approved gratuity fund shall be registered by the CA.

576. In case an employer defaults in the payment of the premium for insurance or in the contribution to an approved gratuity fund, it shall be liable to pay to the CA the amount of gratuity due under the Act including interest, if any, for delayed payment.

§5. Nomination for Gratuity Payment

577. The PGA requires that every employee who has completed one year of service shall make a nomination for the purpose of payment of gratuity in the event of his or her death. In doing so, the employee may distribute the amount of gratuity payable to him or her among more than one nominee. In case an employee has a family at the time of making a nomination, he or she shall make the nomination in favour of one or more members of the family. In such cases a nomination in favour of anybody other than a family member is void. If the employee does not have a family at the time of making a nomination, he or she can make the nomination in the name of any person one likes. However, if he or she subsequently acquires a family, such a nomination shall become invalid. In such a case the employee shall make a nomination in favour of one or more members of his or her family. The employee is free to modify a nomination, after giving a notice to his or her employer. In case the nominee predeceases the employee, the interest of the nominee shall revert to the employee who shall then make a fresh nomination in respect of such interest.

§6. Gratuity: To Whom Payable

578. Gratuity is normally payable to the employee himself. However, in case of death of the employee, it is payable to his or her nominee. If no nomination has been made, the gratuity amount shall be payable to the employee's heirs. In case a nominee or an heir as the case may be is a minor, the share of such a minor shall be deposited with the CA who shall invest the same for the benefit of such minor in a prescribed bank or other financial institution. The amount shall be invested for the period, until the minor attains majority.

Part X. Minimum Income Support

579. There is no central law in India which creates right to minimum income of the types that are known to exist in most developed countries. But, the number of government schemes that are aimed at poverty alleviation either by providing some employment especially in villages or by helping those below the poverty line through social assistance, is increasing every successive year.

580. Since independence, considerable efforts of the State have been devoted towards raising the minimum level of living. The incidence of unemployment in the country is high; and so is the dependency of a large part of the population on agriculture. A good percentage of the population lives below the poverty line and has little access to resources for fulfilling its minimum needs. This has to do, mainly with the non-availability of adequate employment opportunities to them. In such a situation, the focus of social security is bound to shift from the traditional areas of social protection to employment generation programmes and thus raising the living standards of people through state support and subsidies in meeting their minimum needs. The planning process in the country has been mainly concerned with increasing the employment opportunities and designing and administering poverty-alleviation programmes. Even now when the Planning Commission has been wound up by the new NDA government, with the idea that market would adjust as per the economic environment, such schemes have become an important area of focus of every government at the centre as well as State level.

As noted earlier, less than 8% of the working people work in the organized sector so as to ask for its rights with some semblance of effectiveness. Others work in the informal and the unorganized sector as they are self-employed or are casual, contract or agricultural workers. The incidence of under-employment is also very high. The main poverty groups are rural; these are mostly agricultural households and cover about one-third of the rural population. A large number of the poor are SCs and tribal people. Women face severe discrimination in the labour market. Female-headed houses tend to be still poorer. Also, since virtually no system of community assistance exists any more, households having many dependent children and old family members are poorer than others.

Mainly, it is the poor and low caste households that are the sources of supply of unskilled and menial jobs at the shop floor level. On the other hand, comparatively better off classes are source of white-collared, skilled, supervisory and managerial jobs. These two sets of people have had differential access to education and training; so they operate in two different labour markets. The amount of traffic between the two is little. What we discuss in this Part relate mainly with those performing unskilled and manual jobs.

581. These realities have led Indian and other economists especially from the developing countries to consider the traditional Western definitions of social security to be too narrow, for they cover a small fraction of the Indian population. They view social security in poor countries to be part of, and fully integrated with, anti-poverty policies such as employment guarantees and food security, among others.[210]

Their definition of social security seeks to ensure meeting the minimum basic needs of the people including adequate nutrition, clean water, shelter, as well as the traditional areas of social security like protection against disability, illness, unemployment and old age.

582. In the peculiar context of a developing economy like India one of the key social security issues is providing universal basic income (UBI) as a measure to alleviate poverty for people in general. UBI is increasingly more important at a time when life has become harder for people due to new economic realities, increased automation, and the resultant rising unemployment and underemployment. Thus, India needs to juxtapose a neo-welfare system with economic and social security needs of people. The system needs to be made simpler, more robust, flexible, and be freed from red tape and inefficacious administration. The existing welfare schemes need to be streamlined and knit in the overall framework of a well carved-out UBI.

583. Keeping the realities of the developing countries in view, we can talk about some key areas of public action that are being adopted in India in various ways. These action areas as far as possible are evolved to satisfy minimum needs of people, which are aimed to ensure a minimal level of income. Such action areas are social assistance schemes for old and disabled people, employment guarantee schemes, social assistance through welfare funds, minimum wage legislation to industrial and agricultural workers; food security though public distribution system, (PDS) at subsidized rates; and social assistance to poor in general.

---

210. *See*, for example, among others, S. Guhan, 'Social Security Options for Developing Countries', *International Labour Review* 133, no. 1 (1994), Geneva; I.P. Getubig, 'Social Security and the Poor: An Introduction', in *Rethinking Social Security: Reaching Out to the Poor*, ed. I.P. Getubig & S. Schmidt (Kuala Lumpur: Asian and Pacific Development Centre). Also *see* J. Dreze & A. Sen, 'Public Action for Social Security: Foundation and Strategy', and R.S.L. Burgess & N. Stern, 'Social Security in Developing Countries: What, Why, Who, and How?', in *Social Security in Developing Countries*, ed. E. Ahmed et al. (Oxford: Oxford University Press).

Chapter 1. Social Assistance to Elderly Poor and Vulnerable

584. The traditional joint Hindu family system in India has been viewed as a source of considerable security to the old and the infirm. But this system is presently witnessing erosion due to rapid change in the social and economic profile of people. The traditional respect and the attitude of empathy and care for the old are being weakened, due to several reasons. The situation calls for supplementing the traditional support system to the elderly, with methods of social assistance. There is a need to evolve mechanisms to make it possible for the aged to live with dignity, honour and respect within the family fold.

585. Due to longer life expectancy, there is a steady increase in the number as well as proportion of the aged in India as the situation is in other countries. Most of the people in this group are supposedly those with low incomes without much independent means of support, as they do not own any productive assets. The State is obliged to look after the needs of these people.

586. The Old Age Pension (OAP) Scheme is an important social assistance scheme, for ensuring minimum income to this class of people in almost all States and Union Territories. However, the rates of these pensions are extremely low. They fall in the range of INR 200 to INR 2,000 per month and are related to a means test. In the state of Delhi, for example, the rate of OAP is INR 2,000 per month.

587. Gujarat is the only State, which has a maternity benefit scheme for landless women agricultural workers. Each woman is given INR 1,000 in case of child birth to meet maternity expenses by way of social assistance.

588. Different States have not kept the same eligibility criteria for the purpose of targeting this section of the poor. Often, the bureaucracy misuses the criteria and brings its whims and fancies for different motives including gratification. In a good number of cases the local politicians unlawfully intervene in deciding the beneficiaries.

589. Apart from OAP, States also provide for social assistance to widows by way of widow pension. The criteria is different in different States – in some cases any widow is entitled to the benefit, others provide it for those above a certain age, for example 60 years. In Gujarat, the widow assistance is available only for one year. The widow is given skill training during this year. But the benefit is subject to a maximum of two children.[211]

590. Many State Governments have extended the pension benefits to younger disabled persons. This is done either as a part of the OAP or by way of a separate scheme. Different degrees of disability are provided for eligibility. In some cases

211. T.S. Sankaran, 'Social Assistance: Evidence and Policy Issues', in *Social Security for All Indians*, ed. Wouter van Ginneken (Delhi: Oxford University Press, 1998), 71.

minimum age limit has not been provided. Often, there are disputes related to eligibility. In many cases the degree of disablement may not be high. It has been suggested that States should provide the same criteria for determination of disability as has been prescribed in Schedule I of the ECA and the Second Schedule of the ESI Act. A minimum of 70% loss of earning capacity has been suggested for eligibility to disability pension.[212]

591. Since 15 August 1995, the Central Government introduced National Social Assistance Programme (NSAP) which provides selected benefits to the poorest 30% of households. Grants are given to States for a wide range of services. Under this scheme the Central Government provides for 100% financial assistance to the States. The Central assistance is made available to the State/Union Territories (UT) in accordance with the norms, guidelines and conditions laid down by the Central Government. Funds are released directly to the districts in two instalments during a year. The scheme is administered by the social welfare department of the Government of India.

592. The benefits under NSAP include assistance by way of social security to poor households in line with the Directive Principles of State Policy enshrined in Article 41 and 42 of the Indian Constitution. The programme has three components (1) National Old Age Pension Scheme (NOAPS); (2) National Family Benefit Scheme (NFBS); (3) National Maternity Benefit Scheme (NMBS). Mainly, the Programme seeks to extend financial assistance to old persons having little or no regular means of subsistence, to households living below the poverty line, in case of death of the primary breadwinner and to pregnant women from households that are below the poverty line up to the first two live births. The eligibility criteria are poor people, families living BPL, pregnant women and senior citizens.

For availing the benefits under the scheme, the beneficiary must approach the officials at the district level. It is implemented by the District Collector/Deputy Commissioner. So as to make the programme cost effective, at the ground level, the scheme is being implemented by the Panchayats (village councils) and Municipalities. The scheme has validity till 31 December 2011.

593. The amount of benefit in the three types of assistance under NSAP are as follows:

(a) OAP to the very poor of age 65 years under the National Old Age Pension Scheme (NOAPS);
(b) survivor benefit to family at a lump sum of INR 10,000 to poor families who lose their breadwinner in the age group of 18 to 65; and
(c) maternity assistance to women belonging to households below the poverty line under the National Family Benefit Scheme (NFBS), restricted to the birth of first two children at a lump sum of INR 500.

---

212. Government of India, *Report of the National Commission on Rural Labour* (New Delhi: Working Group on Economic and Social Security, 1991).

This national package is intended to bring about a common minimum social assistance framework for poor households in India relating to eligibility, types and scales of benefits. The Central Government's matching assistance can encourage the States that are lagging behind in this regard to perform better.

594. Studies conducted[213] on the effectiveness of the States' social assistance scheme for the old showed that the awareness among the people about the scheme is low. They came to know of the scheme through relatives and friends working in Block Development Offices (BDO). Few cases were found, where the dead were drawing an OAP. Most respondents were satisfied about the administration of the scheme except those from Uttar Pradesh (the largest State of India in terms of population). The respondents lamented the apathy of the authorities and also said that the postman delivering the money asked for commission which they felt compelled to pay.

595. The progress in social security schemes where bureaucracy is intimately involved is reported to be dismal. The cost of administration of these schemes is high, and there are instances of bureaucratic inertia, procrastination and red-tapism. In such a situation, a well-articulated and administered scheme of social assistance like OAP can be quite useful. The Gujarat Scheme for widows, for example, is comparatively progressive for it seeks to impart skill rather than merely conferring bounties. It is heartening to note that the Central Government has become awakened to the need for action in this regard. The Country can build on the NSAP of 1995. This will help to sensitize the State Governments and people in general, and can be a useful method of providing social security in developing countries.

213. T.S. Sankaran, 'Social Assistance: Evidence and Policy Issues', in *Social Security for All Indians,* ed. Wouter van Ginneken (Delhi: Oxford University Press, 1998), 57–76.

Chapter 2. Employment Guarantee Scheme Through Legislation (MNREGA)

596. Unemployment allowance is an inalienable part of social security anywhere; but this is, especially so in the developed world. Most developing countries including India are lagging far behind in this regard. The country has witnessed only sporadic efforts in boosting employment through special programmes. The State action in India in this regard is not of paying unemployment allowance but relates to provision of employment opportunities for the poor. Some fairly developed employment guarantee schemes have been in vogue in the States of Kerala and Maharashtra. The Central Government has also tried to ensure minimum income of families by providing for some limited employment guarantees through development programmes. The Central Government programmes relate to difficult situations such as drought or devastation by natural calamities.

597. Most of the programmes in this regard are the rural public works programme. A series of wage employment programmes were devised by the Central Government in the 1970s and 1980s. Each of these was intended to be an improvement over the earlier one. The most important of the early programmes were the Crash Scheme for Rural Employment (CSRE), the Pilot Rural Employment Project (PREP) and Food for Work Programme (FWP). The JRY was evolved in 1989–1990 to replace the two earlier important employment programmes, i.e., the National Rural Employment Programme (NREP) introduced in 1980 and the Rural Landless Employment Guarantee Programme (RLEGP) introduced in 1983. In what follows, we will also discuss the Mahatma Gandhi National Rural Employment Guarantee Act 2005 (MNREGA), which envisages an employment guarantee scheme with legislative foundation. The working of this law has become one of the main points of developmental debate in the country. In fact, some of these above programmes have merged in the MNREGA scheme.

598. The right to work remained enshrined in the Indian Constitution since 1950, as a directive principle of state policy. It could not be implemented, in terms of job guarantee for Indian citizens for various reasons. The Indian economy was in shambles when the British left. There were many reasons for slow growth in GDP and in employment – population was high; people had low skill and literacy levels; and infrastructure was poor. Besides, public sector was playing a dominant role in industrial development, which resulted in bureaucratization, sluggishness, and lack of customer-centricity. For the first time on 25 August 2005, a piece of legislation guaranteeing jobs was enacted in the form of the National Rural Employment Guarantee Act, 2005 (NREGA). It was done at the initiative of the UPA Government. This was a step towards partially operationalizing the right to work, as a directive principle of state policy. On 2 October 2009 the name of the Act was changed to

Mahatma Gandhi National Rural Employment Guarantee Act 2005 (MNREGA), which seeks to provide a minimum income support through work guarantee to poor people as of right.[214]

599. This Act envisages a job guarantee scheme, which provides a legal guarantee for 100 days of employment in every financial year to adult members of any rural household willing to do public work-related unskilled manual work at the statutory minimum wage of INR 100 per day. This rate has been revised by the Central Government from time to time as per the powers conferred by the MNREGA. In this regard, the Central Government has revised the MNREGA wages for each state as on 15 March 2021. The wages for different states vary from a low of INR 193 per day in Chhattisgarh to a high of INR 315 in Haryana. Thus, the MNREGA seeks to provide some semblance of livelihood security to a large number of unemployed or underemployed people waiting to make their life better through increasing their earnings. It aimed to enhance the purchasing power of unskilled or semi-skilled rural people, who find it difficult to get jobs in the job market. It is immaterial whether or not they fall in the category of BPL. It is believed that, overall around one-third of the stipulated work force in this category is engaged in this scheme.

Every rural household under the scheme is entitled to a Job Card which contains the names and photographs of all adult members in the household. This is intended to help them to apply for and receive work. The Job Card records workers' entitlements under MGNREGA. It contains the updated details of work applied for and received, wages paid, etc. For this reason it is extremely important that an updated Job Card is available with the household at all times.

600. MNREGA directs the State Governments to implement the schemes framed. The Central Government meets the cost of wage payment, three-fourths of material cost and some percentage of administrative cost. State Governments meet the cost of unemployment allowance, one-fourth of material cost and administrative cost. The scheme has an in-built motivation for the State Government, to employ the concerned persons in doing the planned work rather than paying them the unemployment allowance. Since, it is the State Governments which have to pay them the unemployment allowance, they are more likely to offer employment to the concerned workers, as three-fourths of the wages of the workers concerned is mainly paid by the Central Government. The amount of unemployment allowance is decided by the State Government. However, there is a condition for this – It will not be less than one-fourth of the minimum wage for the first thirty days, and not less than half of the minimum wage thereafter. All able and willing workers have to be provided 100 days of employment failing which they have to be given unemployment allowance every financial year.

601. Panchayats (village councils) at districts, intermediate and village levels are the principal authorities for planning and implementation of the MNREGA

214. Dr Jean Drèze, a Belgian born economist, and a professor at the Delhi School of Economics, University of Delhi, has been a major influence in designing this poverty alleviation project.

schemes. The whole process of taking up employment and undertaking the work under the scheme is like this – A willing adult member of the concerned rural household has to submit his or her name, age and address with a photograph to the Gram Panchayat (village council). The panchayat is supposed to verify the household; after verification register her/his name; and issue a job card. This card contains all details about the member enrolled including his/her photo. The person so registered can submit in writing an application for work either to the panchayat or to the programme officer (for at least fourteen days of continuous work). All valid applications have to be accepted by the panchayat/programme officer, and s/he has to be issued a dated receipt of the application. The employment letter is sent to the applicant and has also to be displayed at the office of the panchayat. It is provided that the employment has to be provided within a radius of 5 kilometres. In case, the place of work is above 5 kilometres, transport allowance and 10% extra living allowance will have to be paid. There need to be at least fifty workers to become available, for any new work to start. In case, employment cannot be provided under the scheme within fifteen days of receipt of the application, the applicant will be paid the unemployment allowance.

602. The Act prohibits any discrimination between male and female workers. They are also paid the same wages. And, it is not just workers below the poverty line who can apply for employment, but others who are above it can also do so.

603. The NRGEA (later on named MNREGA) scheme became functional with effect from 2 February 2006 in 200 districts in the country. Later on, it was expanded to cover another 130 districts in the financial year 2007–2008. Eventually, with effect from 1 April 2008 it covered 593 districts in India. The outlay for the scheme was INR 11,000 crores in 2006–2007; after that it has been rising quite steeply. For the financial year 2021–2022 the Central Government's outlay for this scheme was INR 73,000 crores. Today, it is operating in all 644 districts of the country. This figure speaks of the enormity of this national exercise, which is reflective of the extent of the problem of poverty and lack of meaningful employment opportunity in the country.

604. It must be admitted that MGNREGA helps in achieving many objectives – economic as well as social. Apart from rural employment and income generation by the poor, it fosters rural development and perhaps environmental development as well. Besides, when men and women are paid the same wages, it internalizes some degree of feeling of equality between the sexes. It also enables democratic and participative working among people as they design the work to be performed and are not forced by the bureaucracy about the projects to be started. The Act provides that works must be targeted towards some specific rural development activities. These may include water conservation and harvesting, afforestation, rural connectivity, flood control and protection such as construction and repair of embankments, digging of new tanks/ponds, percolation tanks and construction of small check dams, etc. The employed are given work such as land digging, levelling, tree plantation, among others, which eventually are necessary for carrying out the project concerned.

605. In view of the enormity of the unemployment problem in India, it is without doubt that MNREGA is a path breaking legislation. It envisages a rights-based approach framework that has created a paradigm shift in looking at the employment generation programme. Besides the economic objective of employment generation, it is an instrument of inclusive growth. A significant area of impact of MNREGA is internalizing respect for paying minimum wages to working people which will reduce exploitation in society as a value. It will also reduce migration to help fight problems in cities. It positively impacts empowerment of rural poor besides increasing their purchasing power. It also has potential for fighting the menace of terrorism. It has recently been observed that the market wages are lower in many areas compared to the MNREGA scheme rates; and also that employers are finding it difficult to get workers in the villages at the market rate. This will certainly help the market rates to rise and prevent exploitation of the vulnerable sections in the society.

606. Some of the critical areas that need continued focus in MNREGA are spreading greater awareness among the prospective workers; enhancing involvement of local people in the decision processes; greater vigilance to see that the system is not misused; and transparency to ensure prevention of use of funds; and accountability for the work done, proper use of funds and serving the stated objectives. There is considerable scope for training awareness generation among the programme officers and the panchayat members. Universities and management institutions can be asked to prepare case studies for training the concerned functionaries and for devising general lessons for management in view of Indian socio-political realties.

607. There is need for continued support to the scheme. University and business schools may be involved and asked to encourage their students to adopt a village each for development work and visit the village as part of their curriculum. The experiment can also be useful in devising implication for social protection strategies in rural context as well as promoting better rural governance with which social protection is intimately connected.

Chapter 3. Social Assistance Through Welfare Funds

608. The provision of social security to employees in the unorganized sector is a daunting task. More than 90% workers are working in the informal or unorganized sector. They generally suffer from low earnings, lack of stability and durability of employment including its migratory nature in many cases, frequent changes in the employer and nature of employment. It has been found very difficult or even impossible to extend to them the benefits of a contribution-oriented or employers' liability-oriented social security scheme which are enjoyed by the workers in the organized sector.

609. India has coined a unique method of providing social security to workers employed in certain specified employments. This is done, by way of administering social assistance for the beneficiaries from out of the welfare funds created by levying cess on the goods produced by the establishments covered or exports made of goods produced in such establishments. These funds are used to provide fulfilment of certain minimum needs of people employed in such establishments. Usually, they are employed in highly vulnerable positions in the unorganized sector. It has been found very difficult to protect this class of people through usual labour legislation. Towards this goal, separate legislations have been enacted by Parliament. Five welfare funds have been set up to be administered by the Ministry of Labour, Government of India. These welfare funds have been set up for workers in mica mines; limestone and dolomite mines; iron ore, manganese ore and chrome ore mines; *beedi* workers and cine workers. Of course, these workers are only a small minority of the total workforce in the country in the unorganized sector. The agricultural labour in the country is nearly, totally unorganized and is also not subjected to any meaningful social protection. Likewise, the other categories of unorganized workers, who are mostly non-factory workers, employed in small establishments do not enjoy any meaningful social protection. Efforts are on, to expand the welfare fund approach to cover more categories and sub-categories of work.

610. The Central Government scheme of welfare funds is outside the framework of the specific employer and employee relationship. The resources are raised by the Central Government on a non-contribution basis and the delivery of welfare services is normally done without linkage to individual worker's contribution, real or notional. Apart from the welfare funds set up by the Central Government, various State Governments have made similar provision of welfare funds for different types of workers. There exist, for example, more than sixteen welfare schemes in Tamil Nadu for construction workers, truck drivers, footwear workers, handloom and silk weaving workers, and other categories of informal workers. But the most comprehensive welfare schemes have been set up by the Kerala state, which is also the highest in the human development index in India. Its schemes cover a large number of informal sector occupational groups. The difference in this model is that it is not a social assistance scheme, but is contributory in nature, and therefore is a kind of social insurance. The contributions are made by employers, employees and State Government. Different schemes have different types of schemes. Some of the prominent benefits under these welfare schemes include: provident fund, gratuity, retirement benefit, disability allowances, funeral expenses, pension scheme, education and medical care, maternity benefits, unemployment benefits, and special schemes benefits. Most other states in the country have provided for only minimal welfare benefits compared to those provided by Kerala.

The welfare funds follow a sectoral approach, and are in addition to many poverty-alleviation and employment generation programmes run by the Central and State Governments like MNREGA, IRDP, JRY, etc.

In this Chapter, we shall discuss the benefits provided under various welfare funds.[215] These welfare funds have been set up under the following Acts of Parliament for the welfare of workers concerned. These Acts are the Mica Mines Labour Welfare Fund Act 1946; the Limestone and Dolomite Mines Labour Welfare Fund Act 1972; the Iron Ore, Manganese Ore and Chrome Ore Mines Labour Welfare Fund Act 1976; the Beedi Workers' Welfare Fund Act 1976 and the Cine Workers' Welfare Fund Act 1981.

611. For the purpose of administering welfare assistance through the Welfare Fund Organization (WFO), the country is divided in to 9 regions. This arrangement facilitates the extension of welfare measures under different welfare funds. There are regional welfare commissioners who are cess commissioners for the purpose of collecting cess, under The Limestone and Dolomite Mines Labour Welfare Fund Act, 1972 and The Iron Ore, Manganese Ore and Chrome Ore Mines Labour Welfare Fund Act, 1976 for ore used in domestic consumption. The LWO is headed by DGLW. He is assisted by Welfare Commissioner (headquarter), who supervises the functioning of the offices of regional welfare commissioners.

612. In order to give effect to the objectives laid down in the above Acts, the WFO has formulated various welfare schemes. These schemes are in the field of public health and sanitation, medical facilities and the prevention of disease; water supply and facilities for washing; educational facilities; housing and recreational facilities including standards of living, family welfare, including family planning education and services; medical facilities; transportation to and from place of work (for mine workers only); and such other welfare measures and facilities as may be prescribed by the government.

---

215. The above Acts provide that the Central Government may apply the welfare fund, among others, to meet the expenditure incurred in connection with measures and facilities of the following types:

(i) Defraying the cost of measures for the benefit of such persons, directed towards the provision and improvement of public health and sanitation, medical facilities and the prevention of disease; water supply and facilities for washing; educational facilities; housing and recreational facilities including standards of living, nutrition and amelioration of social conditions; family welfare, including family planning, education and services; transportation to and from place of work (for mine workers only) and such other facilities as may be prescribed.

(ii) To grant loan or subsidy to a State Government, a local authority or an employer, in aid of any scheme approved by the Central Government for the purpose connected with the welfare of workers engaged in the beedi/cine/non-coal mine sector.

613. The expected number of workers who are benefiting from the welfare funds is 4.9 million in case of *beedi* industry; 73,650 in case of limestone and dolomite mines and iron ore, manganese ore and chrome ore mines and 68,000 in case of cine industry.

614. To fully appreciate the rationale of introducing a social assistance scheme through the welfare fund we may note down the conditions of working and employment in *beedi* industry by way of an example. In general, the economic and health conditions of *beedi* workers are pathetic. An overwhelming majority of *beedi* workers are home workers. They live in conditions of extreme poverty and are paid very low wages. They are scattered over a wide area. They suffer from malnutrition and other health problems. Their children work along with them and therefore do not get even primary education. Their housing conditions are bad. Hardly any access to medical facilities is available to them, nor can they afford to go to private medical practitioners. Employers mostly make arrangements to supply them raw materials at home, where they roll *beedis* and make bundles to supply them to their employers. The employer-employee relationship, however, remains disputed in most cases. Therefore, for applying the protection to *beedi* workers under the welfare funds, it is not necessary to establish the existence of employment relationship.

Nevertheless, the identification of these workers is necessary for effectively extending benefits under the welfare scheme. For this purpose, the Regional Commissioner's office concerned makes arrangement to issue identity cards to the *beedi* workers. Similarly, especially mine and cine workers work under very difficult conditions and face somewhat similar problems. Hence, the introduction of welfare funds for workers in these establishments.

The Central Ministry of Labour & Employment has also initiated action for rehabilitating the beedi workers with a view to providing them an alternative source of employment. This is due to the apprehension among Beedi manufacturers and workers that employment of workers in beedi industry may get reduced due to the anti-Tobacco campaign of the government.

615. Eligibility for getting assistance – Earlier there were eligibility income ceiling limit for the workers who could get the welfare benefit under Limestone & Dolomite Mines, Labour Welfare Fund and Iron Ore Mines, Manganese Ore Mines & Chrome Ore Mines Labour Welfare Fund. Since 2008–2009 this wage ceiling has been removed. All mine workers including manual, unskilled, skilled, highly skilled, clerical are entitled to avail benefits under various welfare schemes.[216] But for eligibility of some of the benefits under different welfare fund schemes, some conditions still exist.

§1. Financial Assistance for Housing Facilities

616. The LWO has attached highest priority to the programme for construction of housing for *beedi* and mine workers under various Welfare Funds Acts enacted

216. *Annual Report, Ministry of Labour 2008-09* (New Delhi: Government of India), 72.

for these sections of society. Some of the key features of the Revised Integrated Housing scheme (RIHS) are as follows: Earlier, the RIHS 2007 envisaged housing subsidy of INR 40,000 per tenement per worker, which was released by the DGLW on 50:50 basis, in two equal instalments. Recently, a revamped housing scheme has been introduced from December 2016. This envisages a subsidy of INR 150,000 per beneficiary household. RIHS 2016 is applicable to the workers engaged in Beedi/ Iron Ore Mines, Manganese Ore & Chrome Ore Mines /Limestone Ore Mines, Dolomite Ore Mines/Mica Mines and Cine Industries, registered with the LWO. In the scheme, subsidy of INR 150,000 is released in three instalments on 25:60:15 ratio (first is given in advance, second is released on reaching the lintel level, and the third after the receipt of the inspection report that the construction of houses has been completed in all respect).

§2. Group Insurance Schemes

617. In case *beedi* and cine workers in the age group of 18 to 60 years are not subscribers of Employees Provident Fund scheme, they are covered under a group insurance scheme. The benefits under the scheme are as under:

- Natural Death INR 10,000
- Accidental Death INR 25,000
- Partial Disability INR 12,500 (Partial disability insurance is not applicable for Cine Workers)
- Total Disability INR 25,000.

§3. Funeral Expenses of *Beedi*/Cine/Mine Workers

618. There is a provision of providing INR 1,500 to the family members of the deceased *beedi*/cine/mine worker for meeting the funeral expenses.

§4. Wedding Expenses

619. There is a provision of providing financial assistance to a widow/widower of *beedi*/cine/mine worker for meeting the wedding expenses of their daughters. In this regard, a sum of INR 5,000 is payable on each occasion of the marriage of their first two daughters.

§5. Educational Facilities

620. Another priority area under assistance from labour welfare funds is education for workers' children. There is also a scheme for providing midday meal scheme for the children of mica-mine workers. With a view to further encourage educational activities among children of *beedi*, mine and cine workers, the following schemes are in operation: Scholarship scheme for children studying from Class I to IV is INR 250 for boys as well girls; for children studying in V to VIII is INR 940 for girls and INR 500 for boys; for Class IX it is INR 1,140 for girls and INR 700 for boys; for children studying in Class X is INR 1,840 for girls and INR 1,400 for boys; for those in Class XI and XII it is INR 2,440 for girls and INR 2,000 for boys; for ITI students it is INR 10,000 for girls as well as boys; for non-professional degree courses/postgraduate courses; two-three year diploma courses and BBA/BCA & PGDCA it is INR 3,000 for girls as well as boys; and for professional degree courses i.e. BE/BTech /MBBS/BAMS/BUMS/BSc (agriculture) and MCA/MBA it is INR 15,000.

§6. Recreational Facilities

621. The LWO also provides for various recreational, educational and cultural facilities through development of multipurpose institutes (DMPI) and welfare centres. These facilities include education of children and adults, sports and games for adults and children, motivation of workers, midday meals for children and training for female dependants of miners in tailoring and embroidery. For organizing sports/games, social and cultural activities for mine workers and their families there are provisions for assistance in making purchase of sports gear; organizing sports/games/tournaments activities by the department; provision for celebration of three national festivals; provision for celebration of seven social functions; purchase of colour and black television sets and dish antenna to be placed at workers colony.

There is a scheme for setting up of Community Centre in Beedi Workers Housing Colony, having a minimum of fifty houses. The State Government should submit the plan and estimate for construction of Community Hall. An amount of INR 1 lakh is released on completion of construction of the community centre.

§7. Water Supply

622. A scheme for financial assistance for implementing water supply in mica, iron ore, manganese ore, chrome ore, limestone and dolomite mines is in operation. Under this, the Central Government provides financial assistance not exceeding 75% of the estimated cost of approved water supply schemes. Similarly, a separate scheme is in operation for sinking of wells in the mining areas.

Chapter 4. Welfare Fund for the Building and Other Construction Workers

623. The largest segment of workers in the unorganized sector are the construction workers. As per the latest estimates there are 5.02 crore building and construction workers in India. As per the latest estimates in the beginning of 2018 the number of construction and building workers registered under BOCWA was 28,615,785. This category of workers has not had much social protection, despite the existence of two laws for them nearly fifteen years ago. The two pieces of legislation that were enacted for them are The BOCWA; and BOCWWCA. Also, so as to clear procedural hurdles to make them operational, the Building and Other Construction Workers (RECS) Central Rules, 1998 were notified by the Central Government on 19 November 1998. There is provision for setting up welfare fund under this Act, though it does not come under the DGLW like the welfare funds discussed in the previous chapter of this section.

624. BOCWA is applicable to every establishment employing ten or more workers, in any building or other construction work, the project cost of which is more than INR 10 lakhs. The objective of BOCWA is to be 'an act to regulate the employment and conditions of service of building and other construction workers and to provide for their safety, health and welfare measures and for other matters connected therewith or incidental thereto'. Among others, this Act envisages constitution of Central and the State Advisory Committees to advise the appropriate Governments on matters arising out of administration of this Act. The Act also provides for constitution of Welfare Boards by the State Governments to give direction in matters of welfare of workers employed in construction activities. There is provision also for registration of beneficiaries under the Fund and provision to them of identity cards, etc.

625. The substantive provisions of these two Acts relate to regulation of the following: employment and conditions of service; health, safety and welfare measures for the construction workers; setting up a Welfare Fund at the State level to be financed by contribution made by beneficiaries; levy of cess on all construction works at rates between 1% and 2% of the construction cost incurred by an employer.[217] The higher judiciary in the country has supported the beneficent objective of the BOCWA. In a recent case,[218] the Supreme Court held that the establishments/premises registered under the Factories Act 1948 employing construction workers in the construction of factory premises were not excluded from the application of the BOCW Act in terms of an exclusion clause of the BOCW Act. The Court gave primacy to the 'superior purpose' envisaged in the BOCW Act and the Welfare Cess Act, as their purpose is the welfare of the unorganized labour class involved in construction activity.

---

217. The Central Government has presently notified the cess @1%. Most State Governments have also notified the same rate.
218. *Lanco Anpara Power Limited v. State of Uttar Pradesh & Ors* (2016) 10 SCALE 99).

626. The Fund so collected can be used for providing financial assistance to the workers and their families in case of accident, old age pension, housing loans, payment of insurance premia, children's education, medical and maternity benefits, etc. Most of the State Governments and Union Territories have also constituted State Welfare Boards. The Government of Tamil Nadu has been implementing its own Act. An amount of approximately INR 62,363 crores (cumulative) has been collected as Cess by the State Governments and Union Territories so far and an amount of approximately INR 22,365 crores (cumulative) has been spent on the Welfare Schemes for Building and Other Construction workers by the State Governments and the Union Territories.[219]

627. The reason for the slow or the non-existent progress in implementing the BOCWA is the nature of the construction industry, and the lack of a comprehensive scheme of social security in the country of which this category of workers can also become a part. The constructions sites are scattered all over the country, and the people employed in them mostly do casual work. They are migratory in nature. These features of the industry make the implementation of the Act difficult. Even the trade unions have not taken too serious interest in their implementation, due to lack of sufficient pressure from below; mainly due to highly casual nature of the job of the workers concerned.

Interestingly, the Supreme Court of India has intervened in the matter and has been directing the status of implementation of these two Acts consequent to a writ petition concerning the case of *M/s National Campaign Committee, C.L. (NCCL)* v. *Union of India and Others*. Further, as per the directions of the court, the Central Government constituted a committee under the chairmanship of labour secretary to monitor the implementation of the directions issued under the Act, specifically with reference to the utilization of Cess fund for welfare schemes. The monitoring committee has been holding regular meetings with secretaries of labour department of states.

219. *Annual Report, Ministry of Labour 2020-21* (New Delhi: Government of India).

Chapter 5. Minimum Wage

628. The Central Legislature enacted the Minimum Wages Act 1948 (MWA), which is applicable throughout the territory of India to some select employments. It was enacted to secure welfare of workers by providing a minimum limit of wages in these employments.

The MWA provides for fixation by the Central or the State Government, as the case may be, minimum wages for employments detailed in the Schedule to the Act. The minimum wages may be fixed by the Central Government for employments that are carried on by or under the authority of the Central Government, or by a railway administration or in relation to mine, oil field or major port or any corporation established by a Central Act. For other employments mentioned in the Schedule of the Act, the State Government concerned is authorized to fix and revise the minimum wages.

629. The employments mentioned in the Schedule are those where sweated labour is most prevalent or where there is a high degree of possibility of exploitation of labour. It is provided that more categories of employments can be added under the Act. A general extension power has been conferred on the Central as well as State Governments in their respective jurisdictions, to apply the Act to other employments where it is considered appropriate. Apart from industrial employment, the Schedule also includes 'employment in agriculture, that is to say, any form of farming including the cultivation and tillage of the soil, dairy farming, the production, cultivation, growing and harvesting of any agricultural or horticulture commodity, the raising of live stock ...'.

630. The legislature intended to apply the MWA to those industries or localities in which wages paid to the workers in the light of subsistence level are inadequate. It is acknowledged that in developing countries labour may offer itself on starvation wages. Hence the need for a law like the MWA.

631. The MWA envisages that the minimum wage rates must ensure not only the mere physical needs of the worker which would keep him just above starvation. Rather, apart from ensuring subsistence for the worker and his family, the minimum wage must also preserve his efficiency as a workman. Thus, it has been held by the SC that the minimum wage must provide some measure of educational and medical requirements and amenities.[220]

632. In another case, it has been held by the Supreme Court that in prescribing the minimum wage rates, the capacity of the employer need not be considered, as the State assumes that every employer must pay the minimum wages for the

220. *Hydro (Engineers) P. Ltd v. Workmen*, AIR 1969 SC 182.

employee's labour.[221] In later decisions, the apex Court has even held that non-payment of minimum wage will amount to employment of forced labour which is prohibited by Article 23 of the Constitution.[222]

633. The expression minimum wage has not been defined in the Act, perhaps, because it may not be possible to lay down a uniform minimum wage for all regions and all employments throughout the country. Varying and different conditions prevail from industry to industry and from one part of the country to another. The judiciary has been considerably guided by notions of social justice[223] in matters related to fixation and revision of minimum wages.

634. The fixation of minimum wages in India has been guided by five norms which were accepted by the Tripartite Committee of the Indian Labour Conference (ILC) held in (1957). These five norms are

(i) In calculating the minimum wage, the standard working class family should be taken to consist of three consumption units for one earner.
(ii) The minimum food requirements should be calculated on the basis of a net intake of calories, as recommended by Dr Aykroyd for an average Indian adult of moderate activity.
(iii) The clothing requirements should be estimated at per capita consumption of 18 yards per annum which would give for the average workers' family of four, a total of 72 yards.
(iv) So far as housing is concerned, the rent corresponding to the minimum area provided for under Government Industrial Housing Scheme should be taken into consideration in fixing the minimum wage.

Fuel, lighting and other 'miscellaneous' items of expenditure should constitute, 20% of the total minimum wage.

635. Studies have reported that the enforcement of the MWA in India is quite poor. In many States, the rates fixed are even below the current rates of wages. Also, still large sections of agricultural labour have not yet been brought within the ambit of the Act in several States. Even where the Act has been implemented, the machinery for the fixation and enforcement of minimum wages is not uniform. In some States the Revenue Department implements the Act for the agricultural labour, in others the labour department is the enforcement agency. In many cases, it is quite difficult to locate the employer especially in case of home-based workers. Even the prosecutions for non-payment of minimum wages are often not successful. The penalties prescribed are so insufficient that a simple economic calculation encourages

221. *Crown Aluminium Works v. Their Workmen*, AIR 1958 SC 30.
222. *Peoples' Union of Democratic Rights v. Union of India (Asiad Case),* 1982, II LLJ 454 (SC).
223. *Workmen of Reptakos Brett &Co Ltd v. Management* (1992), I LLJ 340 (SC).

violation of the law, rather than its compliance.[224] Especially for the agricultural labour, the Act is believed to be a dead letter in most States. In most cases minimum wages for agricultural labour are not revised for long. In fact, there is a strong argument for suspending the operation of the MWA in rural areas. The key reason is that at the peak of the agriculture season, labour can dictate its own terms and actual wages will tend to be much higher.

636. In order to ensure a greater degree of effectiveness of the minimum wage legislation across the length and breadth of the country, a thinking is presently going on in the government circles to make some amendments in the MWA. There are a large number of workers in the country who work as casual or daily wagers or in contract employments or in other forms of labour in the unorganized sector. The thinking is about allowing each job to be brought within the ambit of the MWA, and not just those presently listed by the Centre and the States as per the scheme of the MWA. It is being thought that every worker should be paid the higher of the two – lowest wage fixed for an unskilled worker or the National Floor Level Minimum Wage for any employment other than that covered in the Schedule. On the basis of increase in the Consumer Price Index, the Central Government has fixed the National Floor Level Minimum Wages of INR 178 per day with effect from 1 June 2019.

At present, the MWA provides that both the Centre and States have the power to notify any job in the Schedule of the MWA only when the number of employees in that job is 1,000 or more. Then only, minimum wages in that employment can be fixed. Otherwise, workers in that employment will be left to the operation of the market forces. For the purpose of minimum wage fixation, there are forty-five jobs identified in the Centre's agricultural and non-agricultural lists while states have identified as high as 1,709.[225] However, it is to be seen that this thinking is put into operation by bringing in changes in the MWA on this pattern.

224. *See*, Rani Advani & Debi S. Saini, 'The Constitutional Vision of Development, Unorganized Labour, and Accessibility to Justice System', in *Labour Law, Work and Development,* ed. Debi S. Saini (New Delhi: Westwill Publishing Company, 1995).

225. *Annual Report, Ministry of Labour 2017-18* (New Delhi: Government of India), 69.

Chapter 6. Food Security Through the PDS

637. India has a very wide network of PDS through which essential food items are supplied to the public at subsidized rates, which are usually less than the market rate. Through this network essential items like wheat, rice, sugar, kerosene, edible oils and soft coke began to be supplied. The main purpose of the PDS was to provide a price support programme for the consumer during the period of food shortage of the 1960s. It was thus meant to be an instrument of price stabilization so that especially poor and deprived people do not become a victim of price spiral in matters of their food requirement

638. As on 29 July 2020 there was a network of more than 5.37 lakh fair price shops (FPS) that are distributing essential commodities to the families covered under PDS. The PDS system in India is believed to be the largest network of distributing food items of its kind in the world. India had also been running some anti-poverty programmes where food was distributed for work to unemployed poor people, who are asked to contribute to doing some public works. Overall, PDS, till 1992, was a general entitlement scheme for all consumers without any specific target.

639. The PDS aims at transferring income to the poor via fair price shops and control price shops, and thus reducing their insecurities in life. But it was discovered through research that the cost of transferring INR 1 was INR 5.37, which included costs of both the Central and State Governments. Some people therefore suggested cash payment to the poor, through electronic transfers. But given the low level of illiteracy in the country, and possibility of fraudulent manipulations, this was not found quite suitable in the Indian conditions though advocates of this method are increasing.

640. With effect June 1992, the Revamped Public Distribution System (RPDS) was launched in 1,775 blocks throughout the country. Later on, from 1 April 2000, PDS ceased to be a general entitlement scheme as income tax payees were excluded from the list of beneficiaries of the PDS for sugar. This reflected the Government's intention of confining the PDS as a vehicle of social security to the needy only.

641. Until recently, the PDS provided entitlement to all consumers without any special focus on the poor, which gave way to the targeted PDS (TPDS) initiative, which was introduced in June 1997. TPDS envisaged issuing 10 kg of foodgrains per month to the poverty group household at lower prices. The issue price for this 10 kg foodgrain was 40% of the economic cost of the foodgrains. For the rest, the issue price was expected to be 80% of the economic cost. This system of TPDS had been introduced, after the steep hike in PDS prices immediately after the liberalization of the economy. This had worsened the living conditions of the poor.

642. In furtherance of the government's objective of TPDS, a revolutionary step taken by the UPA government in the area of providing food security to people was the passage of the National Food Security Act, 2013 (NFSA). This Act was notified on 10 September 2013. It envisages provision of food and nutritional security of right quantity of quality food at affordable prices so that they can live a dignified life. This Act was devised on the proactive initiative of the development economist Jean Drèze, who in support of it observed: '... the Bill is a form of investment in human capital. It will bring some security in people's lives and make it easier for them to meet their basic needs, protect their health, educate their children, and take risks'.

All states and union territories have been covered under the Act, which provides coverage to 81.35 crore persons. Thus about two-thirds of the population receives food grains at very highly subsidized rates. There is no linkage of the coverage of this scheme to the poverty estimates. This includes about 75% of the country's rural population and 50% of the urban population. These households are entitled to receive food grains at the rate of 5 kg per person per month. The issue price is far below the cost of acquisition of the food grains at the issue prices of INR 3.00, INR 2.00 and INR 1.00 kg for rice, wheat and coarse grains respectively. This is a happy development and at attempt to revive welfare in the era of globalization, which otherwise is coming under strain globally.

643. There is no doubt that the PDS system has been able to avert famines and acute food scarcities. But it has not really succeeded in providing food needed for an active and healthy life to its people. The goal of balanced diet is far from realization. The PDS which was envisaged as the key mechanism in the Government's food security system has not achieved the desired results. It was observed by the Ninth Five Year Plan (1997–2002) document that 'In spite of mounting food subsidies, evaluation studies indicated that supply of subsidized food grains through the PDS has not resulted in improvement in household level food security. Self-sufficiency of food grains at national level and availability of food grains at affordable cost at local level had not got translated into household level food security for the poor.'[226]

644. Even as NFSA is an excellent development, there have always been problems in implementation of government schemes such as this. In a recent case the Supreme Court of India showed its concern when it found that even after four years of its enactment the NFSA was not being implemented properly. It observed that its implementation was pathetic, food commissions envisaged under the Act had not been set up by many State Governments who had the Act on the 'back-burner'. One of the questions that is debated is whether a scheme like the PDS is an effective medium to help the needy.

226. Planning Commission, Ninth Five Year Plan (1997–2002), Vol. II, p. 529.

Chapter 7. The Legislation for Meeting the Basic Social Protection Needs of the Unorganized Sector Workers

645. Since most workers in India are employed in the unorganized and often informal sector, there are serious problems in introducing social insurance programmes for them. In a large number of cases, it is difficult to identify the employer. Unlike organized sector workers whose main concern is social security, unorganized sectors workers need employment security, income security, and social security simultaneously. Therefore, their needs are often different from the regular workers in the organized sectors. Interestingly, the meaning of the term 'unorganized sector workers' is itself problematic. A committee of the Indian Labour Conference that examined the draft of the USSWA suggested the inclusion of the following workers as organized sector workers: home-based, wage workers, migrant workers and self-employed workers.

646. Endorsing the need to protect the unorganized sector workers, NCL-II suggested enacting an umbrella legislation for unorganized sector workers, which meets their variegated needs. The Commission identified these needs as follows: The social security measures for the unorganized workers should include health care, maternity and early child care, provident fund benefits, amenities, benefits including housing, drinking water, sanitation, compensation for employment injury, retirement and post-retirement benefits, cover in case of loss of earning or the capacity to earn schemes. The capacity to earn schemes could either run independently or in association with government, welfare bodies, NGOs and social organizations. These schemes could aim at upgradation of skills and the education of workers and elimination of child labour, forced labour, and unfair labour relations and practices.[227]

647. Since the submission of the report of the National Commission on Labour-II (NCL-II), a thinking was going around for enacting an 'umbrella legislation to envisage some minimum protection to unorganized labour'.[228] These workers have remained out of the protection of the existing labour laws, most of which apply mainly to the 'organized sector'. In its first tenure the UPA Government appointed in 2004 the National Commission for Enterprises in the Unorganised Sector (NCEUS),[229] headed by the noted economist, Professor Arjun Sengupta. After taking into account the recommendations of NCL-II and the NCEUS, a bill was introduced in Indian Parliament, which was eventually passed as the Unorganized Sector Workers' Social Security Bill, 2008. This bill received the assent of the President of India on 23 December 2008 and has now become an Act. This Act titled The UWSSA has not been brought into force yet.

---

227. Government of India, *Report of the National Commission on Labour-II* (New Delhi: Ministry of Labour, 2002), vol. I & II.
228. Government of India, *Report of the National Commission on Labour-II* (New Delhi: Ministry of Labour, 2002), vol. I & II.
229. NCEUS, Comprehensive Legislation for Minimum Conditions of Work and Social Security for Unorganized Workers, New Delhi, July 2007.

648. The USWSSA is being seen as a historic Act as it seeks to confer some semblance of social security to unorganized workers in the country. The Government is preparing itself to create the structure for putting it into effect. USWSSA provides that the government would periodically notify schemes intending to benefit those who are covered by it. These schemes may relate to life and disability cover, health and maternity benefits, old age protection and any other benefit as may be determined by the Central Government. Under this Act, some insurance schemes may be brought, that may involve collecting some money from the workers covered and are likely to be operated by insurance companies. Of course, the Central and State Governments may subsidize the contributions payable. Under one such scheme, i.e. RSBY, the Centre and the States had been sharing the burden in the ratio of 75:25. This scheme has now given way to the Ayushman Bharat–National Health Protection Mission.

649. The Act creates multiple 'Social Security Advisory Boards' both at the Centre and State levels, as the think tank to facilitate its implementation. These Boards have the powers to recommend, advice, review, and monitor various aspects of the working of the Act. It is provided that the Central Board must consist of at least thirty-one members and the State Boards shall have twenty-eight members. It must, however, be remembered that the real powers remain with the Central Government that may give directions to these Boards or to the State Governments, in matters relating to the implementation of this legislation. These Boards are quite large as well.

650. There is a provision for the unorganized sector workers above fourteen years to register themselves and receive a 'smart' identity card. The 'smart' cards contain each holder's biometric information such as fingerprints; these particulars could help in containing fraud. Smart cards proved to be quite useful in implementation of the Rashtriya Swasthya Bima Yojana (RSBY) which is a health insurance scheme for the BPL families, and had been admired for its initial success. With this base work in view, the Government started taking steps towards implementing the spirit of the USWSSA. RSBY has now merged with ABY, also called PM-JAY.

651. USWSSA provides that the State Governments may design their own schemes related to provident fund, employment injury benefit, housing, education, skill upgradation, funeral assistance and old age homes.

652. For quite some time this remained somewhat symbolic. It is for the workers' organizations and the best friends of labour to build on these basics of workers' rights and eventually attract the attention of the Government towards a legal structure that facilitates realization of some semblance of dignified existence for people working in the unorganized sector. How far the provisions of USWWA are realizable would depend on the working class unity, the health of the economy, and the political will of the government

653. There are some issues of concern in the way this Act has been framed. The Act is applicable only to a small section of unorganized labourers whose income limit is expected to be notified by the Government. There is every possibility that the subsequent notification by the Government will include such parameters that might have the effect of excluding a good number of unorganized workers, from the applicability of this law and the schemes framed under it. The Act also does not make any provision for any penalties to punish those employers who violate it.

654. At this point in time, from an analysis and overall reading of all the positive and negative aspects underlined in the Act, it seems that this Legislation will be able to fill the void that has been there, ever since the country attained Independence. The implementation mechanisms laid down in the Act seem to be quite good and can be successfully implemented at all levels in case there is proper coordination between the Centre and the States. The Act may encounter some problems and hurdles in future related to implementation. At the same time, it should be admitted that the Act should be commended as a comprehensive attempt to meet the minimum basic needs of the people employed in the unorganized sector.

Part XI. Enforcement of Protection

655. Both the Central and State Governments have created labour administration framework in their respective jurisdictions for enforcing the protection envisaged by the labour and social security laws. Administering labour laws and social security administration are by and large looked at as a composite issue in India. Almost all labour and social security laws of major significance in the country have been enacted by the Central Legislature. But, so far as administration of these laws is concerned, both the Central and State Governments play major roles in their capacity of appropriate Government. Broadly, the Central Government involves itself in participation in international conferences, implementing ILO conventions and recommendations, labour welfare and labour relations in mines, major ports and oil fields and railways and for promoting labour and social security research. State Governments have the bulk of responsibility for labour law implementation. For the purpose of administering a social security law, both Central and State Governments have been conferred specific jurisdictions.

656. The ESI Act and the EPF Act envisage statutory bodies as key administrative organs. These bodies have tripartite representations at the top level for ensuring a greater degree of effectiveness. All the three parties, i.e., employers, employees and Government Officials are represented in the governance structure of these bodies. This type of tripartism in administration has been contemplated only in these two social security laws. The institutional framework of the ESIC does reflect some degree of autonomy in its functioning, even as the autonomy is considerably diluted by the fact that its Chairman is the Central Labour Minister. Therefore, there are several areas where social security exigencies are overawed by the political expediency exercised through the interference of politicians and Government bureaucrats. In case of provident fund, the autonomy to the EPF organization is merely symbolic. It is virtually run like a Government Department. Several key decisions are taken by the Government's Ministry of Finance and the Ministry of Labour. This is so, perhaps, because these two institutions handle huge sums of money, mostly invested in Government securities. But, since variegated benefits are administered by especially the ESIC, the need for autonomy becomes obvious from the view point of efficacious administration.

657. It is important that the administration of social security scheme is based on a totally different approach from that of administration of Government departments. The employees working in the social security schemes have to be trained differently than other Government Officials, as they deal with distribution of social protection benefits. These people have to be more humane than those involved in other types of administration. Under the social security framework, the administrators concerned deal with the sick, injured, old, women in maternity, the invalid, the unemployed and the distressed survivors of the deceased. Therefore, it is necessary that the delivery of service to the injured person is inexpensive and efficient. If one wishes to realize these goals, the strengthening of bureaucratization of the mechanism and greater Government control certainly proves counterproductive. This would necessitate conferring greater autonomy on the tripartite body concerned, so as to develop administrative vision based on the needs of efficiency and cost-effectiveness. Therefore, there is an urgent need to soften the control of Government ministries on the tripartite boards/corporations envisaged under the Indian system. The ESIC and EPF Organization must be answerable to the elected Parliament directly and not through the Labour Ministry.

658. Several agencies, organizations and departments are busy in administration of social security. This hampers the objective of simplification. Ideally, there should be a single office at the national level with offices at regional, district and local levels from where the concerned schemes and benefits can be administered. The IP can be issued a permanent Social Security Number which can be used throughout the country, by resorting to computerization. The beneficiary can also be provided with permanent identity card and pass book containing the details of the employed person and his or her family members. These cards and pass books may also contain the benefits provided and methods through which the benefits can be secured.

659. The key link in the administrative hierarchy of the social security legislation is the inspectorate. It is also the chief arm of the labour department. It is necessary that proper exercise of inspection powers takes place so that the employers do not escape their liability under the Act. The problem of inefficient administration of the social security legislation is largely related to the recruitment and training of the inspectorate as also the structuring of the government labour departments which oversee the social security administration.

660. While the need for inspection machinery cannot be exaggerated, lately there is a general move of the Government towards freeing industry from the inspector *raj*. This is to promote marketization and liberalization as the chief economic philosophy of development. Therefore, attempts are being made towards viewing social security and labour laws as self-enforcing laws, requiring minimum of supervision. For success of this, we need better education and understanding of the employers as well as workers and more efficacious training of the inspectorate. Excessive interference by the inspectorate unrelated to the exigencies of the working of the industry may prove to be self-defeating. There was one good development is the amendment to the ESI Act in 2010, i.e., the post of Insurance Inspector is redesignated as Social Security Officer. The idea underlying this change is to give to them the role of facilitator rather than of mere inspector. It is perhaps for the first time, that the word social security is officially used by a legislation in India. This might be of symbolic importance to begin with, but should be seen as a good beginning towards change of attitudes. The ESI Amendment Act 2010 also provides that

DG of the ESIC shall be Chairman of MBC to improve quality of medical benefits. This strengthens control of the DG; earlier this post was with the medical profession.

Any measures for promoting the effectiveness of the social security administration must take into account the problems and susceptibilities of all the three actors. Also important in this regard is the administrative structuring of the protection system. We will be analysing these in reference to the three main types of the social security laws that we have in India, i.e., employees' state insurance law; the laws relating to provident fund and pension schemes and the laws contemplating unilateral liability of employers. In this part, by enforcement we are mainly concerned with the exercise of executive powers by the inspectorate and similar administrative mechanisms. Provisions related to the exercise of quasi-judicial powers and procedures of making claims have been dealt with in the Part XII titled 'Claims and Adjudication'.

Chapter 1. The Structure of the Social Protection Enforcement

§1. Enforcement Authorities

661. The concept of appropriate Government is very important, in knowing the administrative mechanism of a law for its enforcement. Certain laws like the ECA are enforced only by the State Governments, even as this law was enacted by the Central Legislature. Others have divided the responsibility of administration between the Central and the State Governments. Thus, the Central Government is the appropriate Government in some employments and industries and the State Governments in relation to the others. This is so, for example, under the PGA. Apart from exercising the administrative responsibility, the appropriate Government also appoints the quasi-judicial body envisaged under a specific social security law to adjudicate claims and contentions of the parties under that law. Governments usually delegate their powers to officers concerned and authority envisaged, if any. The powers delegated to the aforesaid authority are subject to the conditions that may be specified in the notification delegating such powers.

662. The appropriate Governments have created certain key offices under various pieces of social protection legislation, to provide enforcement mechanism. Primarily, this mechanism consists of the inspectorate which is envisaged by most such laws. The inspectors or SSOs visit sites of the establishment and see whether the law concerned is being properly enforced or not. They also prepare cases for filing prosecution proceedings against those persons who violate the provisions of a law. Apart from them some other agencies could also be involved in labour administration. For example, the ESI local office is an important agency in enforcing the ESI Act. It mainly distributes cash benefits to the IP. Likewise, assistant PF Commissioners play a very important role in the administration of the EPF Act.

We may consider the structure of the enforcement authorities under three heads: (i) enforcement mechanism under the ESI Act; (ii) enforcement mechanism under the EPF Act; and (iii) enforcement mechanisms under the employer liability schemes.

I. The ESI Scheme

663. The ESI Act provides for the appointment of staff to assist the ESIC in administering this law. As we noted in an earlier part, the ESIC has been empowered to set up Regional Boards, Local Committees, Regional and Local MBCs and delegate powers to them as may be envisaged in the ESI Regulations. All States where the ESI Act is in operation have constituted a Regional Board which supervises the administration of the ESIC Scheme by the State Government. A Regional Director has been appointed in each State, to supervise the work of various local offices of the ESIC in the State.

664. Also, there is a medical board in each State to decide the degree of disablement in case of accidents after a case is referred to it. There is a local committee for each station whose secretary is the manager of the local ESIC office. The local committee meets periodically and suggests appropriate action in different cases.

665. The work of inspecting the working of the ESI scheme is carried out by the inspectors who, as we noted above, are now rechristened as social security officers. The power of inspection has been conferred by Regulation 102 of ESI Regulations on other officers as well. They include the DG, the Insurance Commissioner, a Deputy Insurance Commissioner, a Regional Director, a Deputy Regional Director, an Assistant Insurance Commissioner, an Assistant Regional Director and a Local Office Manager. In addition to these, the DG of the ESIC can also confer on any employee the powers of a social security officer (SSO). The SSOs have been conferred the power to require any principal or immediate employer to furnish to him all information that he may consider necessary, for the purpose of enforcing the provisions of the Act. They also have the power to enter any office, establishment or factory occupied by the principal or immediate employer and examine accounts, books and documents that are considered necessary for inspection. An SSO can also examine any person in regard to whom he has reasonable cause to believe to be an employee. It is provided by the ESI Regulations 1950 that every principal employer shall maintain a bound inspection book and shall be responsible for its production, when demanded by the inspector.

The SSO shall send notes of irregularities and illegalities discovered at the time of inspection to the principal employer who shall enter the note in the inspection book. Also, a good thing is amendment in ESIA through ESI (Amendment) Act 2009, which envisages streamlining of the procedure for determination of contribution to avoid harassment of employers; for, the Inspectors now do not have the power to inspect the books of accounts of the establishment beyond five years which till the date of amendment was unlimited period.

666. Where an SSO or any other official of the ESIC is prevented by the principal or immediate employer in exercising his functions as per section 45-A of the Act, the ESIC can on its own motion determine the amount of contribution payable, in respect of employees of that factory or establishment. But the ESIC has to give to the immediate or the principal employer a reasonable opportunity of being heard.[230] It has been held that the inability to pay contribution is not relevant,[231] and it cannot be pleaded as a ground against liability imposed by the Act.

667. The SSOs of the ESIC have the power to launch prosecution proceedings for violation of the Act after obtaining sanction from the officer concerned in the Court of Magistrate Class I. However, any misuse of their powers is sought to be minimized by the recent amendment Act of 2009. It seeks to streamline the procedure for determination of contribution, so as to avoid harassment of employers as

230. The proviso to subs. (1) of s. 45-A requiring the ESIC to give the right of hearing has been inserted by the 1989 amendment. Earlier, there was no unanimity among various High Courts on the question of affording opportunity before determining the amount of contribution under s. 45-A. The proviso has made the affording of the hearing opportunity obligatory.

231. *South India Viscose Cooperative Stores Ltd v. Regional Director*, ESIC (1986), II LLJ 149 (Mad.).

these SSOs now do not have powers to inspect the books of accounts of the establishment beyond five years, as under present system of unlimited period.

668. The ESI Act provides for the setting up of an independent recovery machinery on the pattern of the Income Tax Act. The amendment Act of 1989 introduced, among others, sections 45-C to 45-I. The ESIC should exercise the recovery proceedings within a reasonable period of the contributions falling due, as is the case under the EPF Act.[232]

Any contribution payable under the ESI Act may be recovered as an arrear of land revenue. Where an amount is in arrear, the authorized officer may issue to the recovery officer a certificate under his signature specifying the amount of arrears.

The authorized officer means the DG, Insurance Commissioner, Joint Insurance Commissioner or Regional Director. A recovery officer means an officer of the Central Government or the ESIC who has been nominated to exercise powers of a recovery officer. The recovery officer shall proceed to recover the amount by one or more of the following modes, namely (a) attachment and sale of the movable or immovable property; (b) arrest and detention in prison; and (c) appointing a receiver for the movable or immovable property.

669. It is inferable from the provision of section 45-E of the ESIA that the issue of a certificate by the authorized officer to the recovery officer is unchallengeable. Neither the principal nor the immediate employer is allowed to dispute the correctness of the amount, and no objection to the certificate so issued on any other ground shall be entertained by the recovery officer. However, the authorized officer has the power to withdraw the certificate, by sending an intimation to the recovery officer.

670. Even when a certificate has been issued to the recovery officer to recover any amount, the authorized officer may grant time for the payment of the amount. Thereupon, the recovery officer shall await the recovery of that part of the amount of the certificate which pertains to the said reduction for the period for which the appeal or other proceedings remain pending.

671. Notwithstanding the issue of a certificate to the recovery officer, the DG or any other officer authorized by the ESIC may recover the amount by any one or more of the modes provided in section 45-G.

II. The EPF Organization

672. As noted earlier, the CPFC is the chief executive of the EPF Organization. Besides, for every State a regional PF Commissioner and other officers have been appointed to assist the CPFC in discharging his duties.

232. *Hyderabad Race Club v. ESIC* (1998), III LLJ 877 (Suppl.); *Regional PFC v. K.T. Rolling Mills* (1995), I LLJ 882(SC).

673. For the enforcement of the EPF Act, the appropriate Government has been empowered to appoint inspectors and to assign to them limits within which they will function. They enjoy the usual inspectorial powers including seeking furnishing of information from the employer, entering and searching any premises, requiring account books and registers, examining employers or any contractors from whom any amount is recoverable, making copies of abstracts and seizing registers and other documents.

674. Usually, there are two types of default on the part of the employer under the EPFA, i.e., non-payment of contribution and non-submission of returns. Employers have been obliged to file monthly as well as annual returns to the regional PF Commissioner. The department can prosecute those who violate these requirements. The inspector concerned scrutinizes the records and if he detects any default or discrepancies, he recommends prosecution. On his recommendation the Regional PF Commissioner sanctions prosecution. In this regard, every inspector has been given the power of an assistant public prosecutor. He files prosecution petition in the court of a Magistrate Class I.

675. For detecting violation of the EPF Act and the schemes framed there under, inspectors can inquire into the correctness of the information furnished; ascertain compliance of the EPF Act and schemes framed there under; ascertain the applicability of the Act and the schemes to an establishment and determine the conditions subject to which exemption was granted under section 17.[233]

676. The inspector also pursues the prosecution cases filed by him until they are finally disposed of. However, it has been observed that his functions should not be considered as merely regulatory; he performs promotional functions as well.[234] In this regard, he is expected to educate the employers and employees covered under the Act and also help correcting incomplete and defective submission of PF returns.

677. The recovery procedure as envisaged by the EPF Act is quite similar to that provided under the ESI Act and the Income Tax Act. Provisions related to amendment of the certificate, stay of proceedings and other modes of recovery find place in the recovery procedure provided under the EPF Act as well. The 1988 amendment to the Act has smoothened the recovery process. It provides for setting up of an independent recovery machinery. The powers of and procedure followed by the recovery officers, authorized officers and the inspectors under the Act are the same as in the ESI Act. The authorized officers under the EPF Act have been defined to be the CPFC, Additional Provident Fund Commissioner, Deputy Provident Fund Commissioner, Regional Provident Fund Commissioner or any other officer authorized by the Central Government. Recovery officer is defined to be any officer of the Central Government or the BOT constituted under the EPF Act who may be

233. This section gives power to the appropriate Government to exempt any establishment from the provisions of the EPF Act which provides for provident fund benefits to its employees that are not less favourable than those provided under the Act.
234. *28th Annual Report (1980–81)* (New Delhi: the EPF Organisation Government of India), 68.

authorized by the Central Government to exercise the powers of a recovery officer, under the Act. The Assistant PF Commissioners have been notified as recovery officers. The recovery officers have the power of a civil court while trying a suit for the purpose of receiving evidence, administering oath, enforcing the attendance of witness and compelling the production of documents.

III. Employers' Liability Schemes

678. The Central and State Governments in India have created Labour Department in their respective jurisdictions, which functions under the overall leadership of the Labour Minister concerned. Especially, the creation of employers' unilateral responsibility to provide many types of social protection like the ECA and MBA requires increasing intervention and responsibility on the part of the Government and its agencies like the labour department. The key role of labour department includes application of basic labour standards through a system of inspection. The social security laws envisaging employer's liability have conferred discretion and latitude to the officials entrusted with the enforcement of the Acts concerned, for the idea is to arm them to efficaciously deliver the protection envisaged by a specific legislation. It may not be possible to lay down minute rules and guidelines for each situation. Such discretionary powers, for example, can be noted in the case of the ECA and the MBA. We can consider the enforcement mechanism of different laws in this category.

A. Employees' Compensation Law

679. There is no provision for the appointment of any inspector under the ECA. Perhaps, the reason for this is that there is no field responsibility involved in the enforcement of the Act. The employer's responsibility to pay compensation is contingent on an employee meeting with an accident resulting in injury arising out of out of and in the course of employment. It is not like the ESI Act or the EPF Act where the employer's responsibility is of persistent and continuing nature. Under both these laws, the employers have to deduct employees' contribution every month and have to deposit the same along with their own contribution with the ESIC or the EPF Organization, as the case may be. Under the ECA, in a way, the employer himself performs the enforcement role.

For example, after the employer receives a claim application, he can settle the claim with the employee. The employers have been obliged to maintain a notice book in the prescribed form at the premises where employees are employed. This notice book has to be readily accessible at all reasonable times to any person acting bona fide on behalf of the injured employee. An entry in this book would be considered to be sufficient notice of the accident to the employer.

680. Interestingly, the Commissioner under the ECA discharges a trinity of functions, i.e., administrative, advisory and quasi-judicial. The ECA manifestly emphasizes only his quasi-judicial functions. A close reading of the Act and the rules framed under it, however, would reveal that he enjoys administrative powers as well. The quasi-judicial role of the Commissioner has been discussed in Part XII titled 'Claims and Adjudication'. Usually, all pieces of labour and social security legislation provide separate functionaries who exercise administrative and quasi-judicial powers. The ECA is a distinct exception, where both sets of powers are vested in the Commissioner. In this part, we will confine to his other two roles.

681. In exercise of their administrative powers, Commissioners have been conferred power to require from any employer submission of any statement regarding fatal accidents. The employer has to submit the statement within a period of thirty days from the receipt of the notice. The statement must contain the circumstances in which death of an employee was caused and whether the employer is liable to pay compensation for the death. If the employer accepts the liability fully or partially, the Commissioner is the administrative authority to receive the compensation from the employer. If the employer disowns his responsibility, the Commissioner is obliged to make necessary inquiry. At this point, he exercises his advisory role, when he is expected to inform any dependants of the deceased workman that it is open to them to make a claim. After receiving the claim application, he exercises his adjudicatory powers to decide the case.

682. Another administrative power exercised by the employer relates to the registration of agreements between the employer and the employee concerned as required under section 28 of the ECA. The memorandum of agreement about payment of compensation has to be submitted to the Commissioner. He registers it, if he feels that it is fair and genuine. He may refuse to register an agreement if the sum of compensation is inadequate or the agreement is not genuine.

683. The Commissioner has even been conferred the recovery powers as provided by section 31 of the Act. This is a quasi-administrative function. It is provided that for this purpose the Commissioner shall be deemed to be a public officer within the meaning of the Revenue Recovery Act 1890.[235] He has the power to recover any amount payable by any person under the ECA, whether under an agreement for payment of compensation or otherwise. He can himself start the recovery proceedings without having been moved by the employee or his dependant to do so. He may even request the Collector concerned to collect the arrears of compensation.

684. The enforcement mechanism of the ECA is a unique arrangement. It was based on the American model where the Commissioner was expected to exercise variegated powers, so as to safeguard the interests of the injured or deceased workman and to do justice dispensation efficaciously. It may, however, be noted that the performance of this arrangement is far below the expectations, and a large number of cases of industrial accidents go unreported. Also, many times the powers of Commissioner are vested by some State Governments in any judicial officer of the civil

235. *Century Flour Mills Shikarpur v. Amir Buksh*, AIR 1937 Sind 6.

judiciary by way of additional charge. In such cases, they merely perform the adjudicatory part of their duties. The administrative and advisory powers get relegated in the oblivion. The employees may feel that such legal provisions did not even exist. For example, this is what is happening in the State of Gujarat.[236] There even unions have not demanded conferring of administrative and advisory roles to some other officials. This takes away the spirit of the Commissioner system as it was originally envisaged.

B. Maternity Benefit Law

685. The MBA 1961 is administered both by the Central and the State Governments in their respective jurisdiction. The Central Government is responsible for administering the Act in mines and circuses, and the State Governments are responsible for its administration in factories, plantations and other establishments, whether owned privately or by Central or State Governments. The State Governments also have the power to extend the applicability of the Act to any other establishment or class of establishments, after the prior approval of the Central Government. The Central Government is empowered to give necessary directions for proper execution of the provisions of the Act which the State Government shall have to comply.

686. The inspectorate is the key authority in the enforcement of this Act. The inspector under the MBA enjoys more powers than those usually enjoyed by the inspectors under other labour and social security laws. They have the usual administrative powers in regard to entry into premises concerned and examining any registers and records, examination of persons believed to be employees, requiring the employer to give information needed, and making copies of any registers and records.

Interestingly, the inspector under this Act is also the quasi-judicial authority for adjudicating the claim of the woman workers under this Act, and also for dealing with their complaints regarding dismissal or discharge made by the employer on account of the absence of a woman worker as per the provisions of the Act. These two provisions taken together reflect a very important role conferred on the inspectors.

687. Inspectors under this Act may also file complaints regarding the commission of an offence under the Act in any court of competent jurisdiction. This is an important administrative power enjoyed by them.

236. Debi S. Saini, *Redressal of Labour Grievances, Claims and Disputes* (New Delhi: Oxford & IBH, 1994), 158.

C. Gratuity Law

688. The Payment of Gratuity Act 1972 (PGA) is administered both by the Central Government and the State Governments. The Central Government is the appropriate Government in relation to establishments belonging to or under the control of the Central Government; or establishments having branches in more than one State; or a factory belonging to or under the control of the Central Government or a major port, mine, oilfield or railway company. In other cases, the State Government is the appropriate Government and has to administer this law. The appropriate Government is authorized to exempt any employee or class of employees to whom this Act applies from the operation of the provisions of this Act if the Government feels that such employees are in receipt of gratuity or pensionary benefits not less favourable than those conferred by the PGA. The power to exempt is an administrative power.

689. The key responsibility of administration conferred by the PGA is on the CA. In cases where the Central Government is the appropriate Government, Assistant Labour Commissioners (ALCs) have been appointed as CA and Regional LCs as Appellate Authority.

In case of State Governments, the officials on which these powers have been conferred vary from State to State. The CA exercises mainly quasi-judicial powers but some administrative powers as well. The CA accepts the deposit of gratuity from the employer in case of a dispute, i.e., the sum which the employer admits to be payable by him. The CA also issues a certificate to the Collector, to recover the gratuity for the benefit of the aggrieved person.

690. The CA is also authorized by section 11 of the PGA to file within fifteen days, from receiving an authorization from the appropriate Government a complaint to the Magistrate concerned to try an offence against an employer who has not paid the amount of gratuity.

691. Mostly, the administrative work involved in supervising the working of the PGA is done by the inspectors. They are appointed by the appropriate Government usually for a definite area. They enjoy the usual inspectorial powers as are conferred by other laws on social security.

D. Provisions of Unemployment Benefit under IDA

692. The IDA is administered both by the Central Government and the State Governments. The Central Government is the appropriate government in relation to industrial disputes concerning any industry carried on by or under the authority of the Central Government or by a railway company or in relation to several public corporations specified in the IDA. In relation to other industries, State Governments administer the IDA in their respective jurisdictions.

693. Interestingly, there is no provision of appointment of inspectors under the IDA nor of any other officers exercising such powers. Conciliation officers exercise such powers related to processing of disputes. But the labour departments both in the Central and the State spheres have residuary powers to administer the IDA. In most states, Labour Officers or Labour Enforcement Officers (LEOs) act as Conciliation Officers. But the IDA does not talk either of any Labour Officer or any Labour Inspector. However, they exercise significant powers related to the administration of the Act including the provisions of Chapters V-A and V-B.

694. The appropriate Government exercises its administrative authority in deciding whether an industrial establishment is of a seasonal character or whether work is performed in it only intermittently. It has the 'final' say in the matter. The appropriate Government has made rules, for the administration of the Act. In case of retrenchment under section 25-F of the IDA, the authority specified by the appropriate Government receives prescribed notice from the employer. It also receives the sixty days' notice that is required to be given by the employer, in case of closure of an undertaking.

695. The appropriate Government grants or refuses to grant permission for lay-off, retrenchment and closure under Chapter V-B of the IDA. Its decisions in this regard are binding for all parties. In case of violation of any provision of the IDA the wrongdoer can be prosecuted, under section 29 of the Act. Section 34 provides that the prosecution cannot be done without the permission of the appropriate Government. For such prosecution, the sanction is given by the Ministry of Labour.

696. In the Central sphere, the LEO can file prosecution proceedings before a Magistrate Class I, depending upon the place at which the breach has taken place. The Commissionerate has been authorized to process the file for obtaining the permission for closure, retrenchment and lay-off, etc. under the IDA. After that the files are sent to the Central Government.

697. At the State level, the administrative arrangements differ from State to State. In Gujarat, for example, the Labour Commissioner (LC) is the authority for sanctioning prosecution of defaulters under many labour laws, though not all. It is he who is authorized to sanction prosecution of private parties for breach of awards and settlements under section 29 of the IDA. First of all, the prosecution work is initiated at the regional level, and then the file is sent to the LC for his sanction. There, prosecution in case of industries owned or controlled by the State Government, only the State Government can sanction prosecution. The LC is also the specified authority under section 25-O, which talks about permission for closure.

§2. Distinguishing Features of Enforcement Mechanism

698. A reading of the provisions relating to the enforcement machinery for social security legislation shows some common patterns regarding the entrusting of powers to different levels of officers, which can be noted in the following.

699. Wherever field investigation is called for, different pieces of social security legislation have provided for the appointment of inspectors, e.g., the EPF Act. An inspector or officer superior to him have inspection powers, under the Act concerned. They enjoy usual inspectorial powers.

700. Wherever the work of recovery of a claim or work involving higher responsibility is to be entrusted, senior officers like the Regional LC in the Central sphere or the LC in the State sphere have been designated as the competent authority.

701. In cases where an appeal over the decision of the CA has been provided, heads of the organization are designated as Appellate Authority.

702. Some social protection laws provide for the settlement of claims. In such cases, regional LC (Central) or Deputy LC (State) has been given powers to investigate claims and issue the required certificate of the amount to be recovered by the Collector. These officers have been given powers of Civil Courts for investigating the claims made.

703. The administration of some laws requires advising from the Central Government or the State Government. This necessitates knowledge of local conditions. For this purpose, constitution of tripartite Advisory Boards at the Centre or State level has been provided for. Usually, the Central Government has the power to supersede the advisory boards in case it is not able to perform its functions or misuses its powers. In some laws, advisory committees or councils have been constituted to advise the Government on matters relating to the administration of the Act.

704. The violation of the provisions of the Acts concerned constitutes an offence, which is punishable with imprisonment or with fine or both. But, cognizance is not taken by competent courts except with the previous permission of appropriate Government or the head of the organization. In some cases, an inspector files a complaint.

705. Various social protection laws have authorized the 'Appropriate Government', to appoint authorities to exercise specific powers. In exercise of these powers, the appropriate Governments have by notification or otherwise designated officers in labour department or appointed full-time officers to exercise powers conferred under the respective Acts. The authority of these officers has to be activated for availing the benefits under the Act.

Chapter 2. Administrative and Technical Problems

706. It is generally felt that the working of most social security schemes in India does not reflect achievement of satisfactory standards of efficiency. Inefficiency is noticeable in nearly all areas of working, including registration of employers and workers, collecting the contributions, maintaining books and records, determining benefits and claims and disbursement of cash benefits. Perhaps, the most serious of the problems from the point of view of the IP relate to the administration of the health care scheme.

The nature and complexity of the problems facing the Indian social security system have a direct impact on the efficacy of the ESI scheme in protecting its beneficiaries. We shall discuss some of the problems which lie at the root of the ESI's operation and which eventually affect the development of social security. Thus, we shall examine various administrative difficulties that are encountered. They are – bureaucratic attitude and lack of proper training of personnel, excessive control and illusory autonomy, difficulties in collecting contribution, lack of computerization and difficulties in medical care administration.

§1. Problems

I. Attitudinal Problems and Lack of Training

707. The ESI administration is generally short of trained and experienced personnel. It encounters difficulties in achieving satisfactory standards of efficiency in some basic tasks such as registration of the employers and the employees, collecting contributions, maintaining records and deciding level of benefits. Already, workers have to face negative attitude of employers towards their problems. They also find that the administration of the ESI Scheme is full of red-tapism. A complex set of forms have to be filled up, for availing the benefits. Perhaps more dissatisfied with the administrative procedures are the employers. They contend that they have to face the problem of excessive paper work in preparing and filing detailed monthly returns. This involves considerable cost. Employees' representatives are also quite critical of high administrative costs as well as cost involved in running the ESI scheme. Thus, there is need for training of the staff and the introduction of less bureaucratic methods of working to ensure transparency and efficiency. Especially, there is a shortage of computer skills among the existing staff most of whom are not computer savvy. It is absolutely necessary that the staff is trained in modern techniques of management. The staff has also to be better trained in financial management. Trained people are needed both at the managerial and subordinate levels with knowledge of computer techniques. They should be able to advise the users, manage the files and determine the rights of the claimants. This requires training. The ILO should be involved in training of personnel, since it possesses rich experience of providing consultancy for similar problems in different cultural settings.

708. There is no real professional training centre to train people. In actuality, there is also lack of experts in social security to provide training. Very few people are available. Presently, the training provided is also not quite satisfactory; it appears sporadic. There is need for systematic training in organizational behaviour and problem solving. It is also necessary to evolve training programmes in human resource management (HRM) including motivation, performance management, diversity management, leadership, organizational culture, employee involvement, team working, employee engagement, strategic alignment of human resource interventions to business goals, and conflict resolution. The ESIC officers are seen working with a bureaucratic mind set which adversely affects the image of the ESI Scheme.

709. The whole attitude of the concerned functionaries is likely to change, if the need for social security is given due importance. The subject of social security and protection should be compulsorily taught in secondary schools, as part of courses on social sciences. This will change the attitude of those working in the social security agencies. Effort should also be made to popularize a wider concept of social security, as per the problems of Indian people. It has also been suggested that there should be a continuous education programme regarding the social security benefits. This will help in raising the awareness of the beneficiaries about their rights, obligations and methods of securing their entitlements.[237]

II. Collection of Contributions

710. One of the major administrative problems faced by the social security agencies is the collection of contributions. It is the employer who has to collect the employees' contributions and deposit them along with its own contribution with the ESIC or the EPFO, as the case may be. In a large number of cases, the employers fail to make regular payments or to make payment within the deadline even as there are penalties for late payment. Another malpractice that is widely known to be in vogue is falsification of records by the employers relating to wages and the number of employees. It is the inspectorial staff which carries out the supervision of employers. The lack of proper training of the administrative staff as well as its overload lead to the problem remaining as it is. It is necessary that the procedures and systems are reorganized, collection system is improved and a closer supervision of employers is ensured.

III. The Problem of Excessive Governmental Regulation

711. Keeping in view the way Government and related institutions have worked over the years, there is no doubt that we need to 'reinvent government'. By this is meant developing a new model of public administration, which can be called entrepreneurial Government. This model should seek to enhance competition between service providers, undermine bureaucratic power, increase people's power, enhance

237. 'Social Security and National Development – Report of A National Seminar in India', New Delhi, 19–30 Sep. 1977, 91.

community control and focus on goals rather than rules and regulations. There is a general need to overhaul the structure and profile of bureaucracy and give greater role to technocrats and experts. We need to rely more on experts, subject specialists, technocrats and professionals in our policy making. Also, we need to recognize the due importance of market forces and the need for the resultant efficiency considerations. Many countries in the developed world have been moving to this model. For example, the British Government has succeeded in compelling the local governments to infuse a competitive spirit in their working patterns. It has been emphasizing contract arrangements, in training and undermining Government sponsored training programme. Drastic changes have been introduced in the National Health Service (NHS). Hospitals and health authorities find themselves in new roles as 'purchasers' and 'suppliers' of health care. The law is encouraging major NHS hospitals to restructure themselves as private companies so as to have autonomy in employment of staff, negotiating wages and conditions of employment.

712. As noted earlier, the Indian social security system gives tremendous control to the Central Government and the Ministry of Labour, which is responsible for a great deal of inefficiency in the working of the social security mechanism. The objectivity of the enforcement machinery has become highly suspect. There is an urgent, need for diluting Government control and granting autonomy to the tripartite agencies managing the social security institutions. If beneficiaries can be involved in the enforcement of laws,[238] with due safeguards, the performance of the social security framework is bound to improve.

IV. Administration of Medical Benefit

713. The administration of the medical benefit represents a unique experiment of providing health care to the IP, through cooperation between the Union Government (through the ESIC) and the State Governments. The ESI Act, though a central law, places the responsibility of medical care, under the scheme, on the State Governments. When the ESIC decides to extend the ESI Scheme to a new geographical area or new classes of workers, it has to ensure completion of medical arrangements in that location. It is the State Government which is responsible, for the arrangements for medical care in the State. State Governments, however, sometimes find it difficult to extend the scheme due to several reasons. One of the key reasons is the financial burden by way of their share in the cost of medical care. Another limitation is the lack of arrangements required to provide necessary medical facilities of prescribed standard. The State Government's share of medical care has been reduced from one-third (as originally contemplated) to one-fourth and later to one-eighth. The ESIC bears the responsibility of seven-eighth of the expenditure, on medical care for those covered under the ESIA and their family members.

238. 'Social Security and National Development – Report of A National Seminar in India', New Delhi, 19–30 Sep. 1977, 90.

714. The MBC advises the ESIC about the extent or the standard of medical care. Every State Government is represented on this statutory body. Broadly, the MBC lays down the contents of the medical care to be provided, the services to be provided, norms for establishing hospitals and dispensaries including staffing, equipment and other facilities. The implementation of these standards, however, is often a problem with many State Governments due to their financial limitations and manpower resources. That is why, the cost of medical care per capita differs from State to State. The ESIC has laid down norms for benefits and also fixed a ceiling of expenditure on medical care to be applied uniformly all over the country. This has helped in containing the cost of medical care.

§2. Attempts Towards Better Administration

I. Making the Inspectorate Customer-Friendly

715. In order to secure the willing cooperation of the employers in making the ESI Scheme a success, it is necessary that they should not face undue harassment by the inspectorate. In this regard, the ESIC headquarter has issued a set of new guidelines to its field officers. These guidelines are aimed at doing away with some avoidable harassment of employers, in the process of inspection. The guidelines direct the inspector concerned to shun any prejudice and vindictive attitude, during inspection of employers' records. They should also avoid their tendency to include in the report items of doubtful nature, which could be settled by discussing the matter with the employer. It has recently changed the designation of inspectors to social security officer (SSO). But mere change in the designation will not be of much help unless mind-set of the officers concerned changes. These SSOs have also to ensure that the irregularities noticed at the time of inspection are communicated to the employer on the spot and the same are entered in the inspection book by the employer in the presence of the inspector.

716. It is often noticed that the employer and the officer concerned differ on the amount of wages on which contributions are payable. In such cases, the inspectors were until now reporting to the regional officer the total ledger balances. It is now provided that the SSO shall segregate the wage element while reporting the amount to the regional officer.

717. Sometimes, the employer makes a representation to the regional officer for reverification of records on grounds of an alleged *mala fide* on the part of the inspector. In such cases, the new guidelines provide that the Regional Director shall not get the records reverified by the same SSO but by a different one, preferably a team of two SSOs.

II. Need to Focus on Better Technology and Behavioural Skills

718. The ESIS is one of the important schemes, the success of which will be determined by the future of social security in India. In a country of India's size, an agency like the ESIC has to use modern techniques of data processing, so as to effectively grapple with the problems. Computerization helps in facilitating the administrative tasks imposed on the ESIC. It not only helps in providing more efficient service to the contributors but also reduces general management costs. Even in other spheres of provision of public services, computerization has become an integral part of modern management across the country.

719. The process of computerization was initiated in the ESIC in 1990 at a small scale which was confined to a few local offices, one dispensary and the central medical store at Delhi. Later on software was developed in 1992 for registration of IP, inventory control of drugs and dressings, OPD registration and for maintenance of exit and re-entry records. Following this an EDP Centre was also established at Delhi regional office on an experimental basis in 1993 and software developed was made operational immediately thereafter.

720. In 1998, the National Informatics Centre Service Institute (NICSI) and ESIC entered into an agreement whereby the ESIC computerization project was entrusted to the former, on a turn-key basis. In the past ten years or so, ESIC has further upgraded itself on that front. ESIC has implemented an IT enablement plan/ ERP Solutions in ESIC in a time bound manner, as per study/suggestions made by experts concerned. It has also speeded up computerization and e-governance through ERP.

721. Perhaps as much or even more important is the change of mind-sets of the ESI employees including that of the hospital and dispensary staff with whom the employees interact while taking their services. There is general feeling of apathy among the staff which is not customer-centric, and treats the covered IP in the usual bureaucratic manner. That is why even trade unions have been asking the managements for being excluded from the ESI coverage. Instead, they ask for empanelment of private hospitals that have a better image of customer service. Better techniques of attitude testing be resorted to so that ESIC undertakes strategic recruitment – something that needs much to be desired. Some areas of public-private partnership may also be thought of.

Part XII. Claims and Adjudication

722. It is important to understand as to what is meant by social security claims and their adjudication. Social security and related entitlements involve rights of people intended to be protected; these rights emanate from the laws and schemes of the State. In India, these rights can be located in three sets of legislation – social insurance law (i.e., the ESI Act); laws imposing unilateral liability on the employer for protecting its/his employees against specific contingencies (ECA, PGA, MBA and IDA) and laws providing for contributory provident fund and pension schemes which are set up through the joint contributions of the employer and the employees. All the three sets of legislation envisage different types of adjudicatory bodies – that are known as quasi-judicial bodies in India – for resolving related disputes.

723. By and large, ordinary lower courts have no jurisdiction in matters of most labour and social security laws; for almost each such law creates its own adjudicatory body. Sometimes, the State Government concerned authorizes an adjudicator to decide disputes under various labour and social security laws. For example, in the State of Haryana, a conciliation officer under the IDA has been vested, among others, with the power of – a 'commissioner' under the ECA; 'authority' under the Payment of Wages Act 1936; 'CA' under the Payment of Gratuity Act 1972, etc.

724. Most disputes in all the above categories of social security laws relate to non-payment of employees'/workers' claims. In the case of social insurance law (i.e., the ESI Act), such disputes are against the social security agency (i.e., the ESI Corporation). In the case of provident fund, they are usually against the Regional Provident Fund Commissioner who exercises administrative powers. In case of employers' liability legislations, these disputes mostly relate to non-payment of the benefit by the employer concerned. In this part, we shall be considering matters relating to employee claims and their adjudication under all three forms of social security legislation in the country.

Chapter 1. The Employees' Insurance Court

§1. Jurisdiction and Powers of EI Court

725. Section 74 of the ESI Act contemplates the constitution of Employees' Insurance Courts (EIC) for specified local areas. A quasi-judicial body, as per most other pieces of labour and social security legislation consists of one person only. However, an EI court can consist of more than one person – the exact number has not been specified in the ESIA. Unlike the Commissioner in the ECA, who can be a non-judicial person, a judge of an EI court can be only a person who has been a judicial officer or a legal practitioner for five years or more.

726. In practice, no separate EI courts are usually set up. Existing civil or labour courts are conferred jurisdiction of EI courts in addition to their normal duties. The rationale of creation of separate courts was to ensure that the matters are decided expeditiously, with less legalistic procedures. In actuality, the time taken in the disposal of many cases in ordinary civil courts is too long. One reason for this is heavy workload of civil courts. Especially, in areas where adjudicatory workload is heavy there is a need for setting up of full-time EI courts. As far as practicable, a full-time EI court may be set up for a group of neighbouring centres or visiting courts can be constituted.[239]

727. Section 75(1) of the ESI Act specifies the questions or disputes that an EI court can decide. These relate to the following: whether a person is an employee; average daily wages of an employee; rate of contribution payable in respect of an employee or sets of employees; the person who is the principal employer; rights of a beneficiary; duration of any benefit; disputes related to review of dependants' benefits, etc. Section 75(2) of the ESIA specifies the claims which an EI court can decide. These relate to recovery of contribution from principal employer; claim by principal employer to recover contribution from any immediate employer; benefits admissible, etc.

The above stated matters, questions and claims shall be decided by the EI court subject to section 2-A of the ESI Act. It says that while deciding any question on disablement if the decision of a medical board or a medical appeal tribunal has not been obtained, the EI court shall direct the ESI Corporation to do so. It has been held that the dispute as to whether an establishment is a factory or not must be decided by the EI court.[240]

728. The ESI Act has barred the jurisdiction of civil courts, in matters that fall in the jurisdiction of an EI court. The idea underlying such prohibition is that where the liability is created by a statute, an aggrieved party must pursue the special remedy provided by it and must be discouraged to get the redressal of his grievance in a civil court. However, a suit in a civil court can still be instituted to question the

239. 'Report of the ESI Review Committee', 1982, 14.
240. *ESIC v. R.P. Gundu* (1983) Lab. IC 1634.

order of the tribunal created by a statute, even if its order is expressly or impliedly made final, if the said tribunal abuses its powers or does not act under the Act but acts contrary to its provisions.[241]

§2. Institution and Commencement of Proceedings

729. It is provided that all proceedings related to the ESI Act shall be instituted in the EI court appointed for the local area concerned. If an EI court feels that a matter can be more conveniently dealt with by any other EI court, it may order transfer of that matter to that EI court.

730. Proceedings before an EI court shall start with an application by the aggrieved person concerned. Every such application shall be made within a period of three years, from the date on which the cause of action arose. In certain cases such as (i) claim for benefit for IP; or (ii) a claim for dependants' benefit by the dependants of the IP, the application should be made within a period of twelve months. The EI court may allow a claim, after this date on reasonable grounds.

In case of a claim by the ESI Corporation for recovering contributions from the principal employer the application cannot be made after the expiry of five years from the last day of the period to which the claim relates.

§3. Powers and the Procedures of the EI Court

731. The EI courts have been conferred all the powers of a civil court for summoning and enforcing the attendance of a witness, compelling the discovery and production of documents, administering oath and recording evidence. The EI court, like most other quasi-judicial bodies, is not subject to the civil procedure. It shall follow such procedure as is prescribed by the rules made by the State Government.

732. Orders of the EI court are enforceable as if they are decrees passed in a suit by a civil court.

733. A party may be represented before the EI court by a legal practitioner or by an officer of a registered trade union or any other person, with the permission of the EI court.

§4. Reference and Appeal to the High Court

734. An EI court can submit any question of law for the decision of the High Court concerned. If it does so, it shall decide the question pending before it, in accordance with such decision of the High Court delivered in this regard.

---

241. *Firm Radha Krishna v. Ludhiana Municipality*, AIR 1963 SC 547.

735. Appeals against orders of an EI Court may lie to the High Court concerned when the order of the EI court involves a substantial question of law. The period of limitation for appeal under this section is sixty days. However, when the question is whether certain facts give rise to legal right of liability, the interference shall involve a question of law. Whether a tannery in dispute was a factory or not was held to be a question of law.[242] A jurisdictional fact can be questioned in an appeal.[243] Whether the employee sustained injury out of and in the course of his employment is purely a question of fact.[244]

---

242. *East Asiatic Co. v. ESI Corporation*, 1960 Lab. IC 1296 (Del.). Also *see*: *Sudershan Weaving Factory v. ESIC* (1990) I LLN 931 (P&H).
243. *Kalpana Kala Kendra v. ESIC*, 1985 Lab. IC 763.
244. *ESI Corpn v. Parmeswaran Pillai*, 1977 Lab. IC 194.

Chapter 2. Adjudication System for Occupational Accidents and Diseases

§1. Claims

736. Claims for compensation under the ECA may broadly fall into three categories

(i) uncontested claims;
(ii) claims involving disputed cases related to injury; and
(iii) fatal cases.

737. The ECA provides that the employer and the employee may mutually agree to settle a claim in certain cases. But this law expects the commissioner to act as the watchdog of fairness. Under section 28 of the ECA, any agreement with the employee to accept a lump sum payment must be registered with the commissioner. He has the powers to refuse to register an agreement and make order to that effect if he feels that the agreement has been arrived by way of fraud, undue influence or some other improper means.

738. First of all, the injured employee has to give to the employer a notice of accident. If the employee desires to claim a compensation under the Act, he has to offer himself for medical examination by a qualified medical practitioner. He may be examined at the premises of the employer if the employer offers to have him examined. The employer may also send the medical practitioner to the employee's residence or to some place in the vicinity. If an employee refuses to submit himself to a medical examination or objects such examination, his right to compensation gets suspended during the period of such refusal or objection. Section 6 of the ECA provides that if the disablement is temporary, the employer will be liable to pay compensation in the form of half-monthly payments directly to the employee. The Commissioner is authorized to review the continuation of half-monthly payments either on the application of the employer or the worker. For this purpose, a certificate from a medical practitioner must be submitted.

739. If parties are unable to agree on the compensation amount, the employee must make an application to the Commissioner for his decision. The Commissioner exercises his adjudicatory power to determine the employee's claim. In other words, the Commissioner intervenes only if the parties do not reach an agreement. The application may be made by the person himself, a legal practitioner on his behalf, an official of an insurance company, an inspector appointed under the Factories Act or the Mines Act or any person with the permission of the Commissioner.

740. The time-limit for making an application by an employee is two years from the date of the occurrence of the accident. In cases of death, the application should be made within two years from the date of death. If the compensation claim is on account of contracting of a disease, the computation of time-limit begins from the first day from which the employee was continuously absent as a result of the disease.

741. Any memorandum of agreement made between the parties for a lump sum compensation has to be sent to the Commissioner, whose duty is to satisfy himself about the genuineness of the agreement. When satisfied, he should record it in a register. Failure to send an agreement to the Commissioner for registration attracts penalty on the employer under the provisions of section 29 of the ECA.

742. In case of a fatal accident, the employer has been obliged to send a report of the accident to the Commissioner. The Commissioner may also get the report of such an accident from some other source. Then the Commissioner may send to the employer a notice requiring him to state the circumstances attending the death of the employee. He should ask the employer whether he is prepared to deposit the compensation payable under the Act in relation to the said death. The employer shall submit such a statement within thirty days from the receipt of the notice.

743. When an injury suffered by an employee results in death, the amount of compensation cannot be paid by the employer directly to the employee's dependants. It has to be deposited by the employer with the Commissioner. No payment by an employer directly to the dependants shall be deemed, to be a payment of the compensation. He can, however, give an advance to any dependant on account of compensation of an amount equal to three months' wages of the deceased employee. While making the final payment of the compensation, the Commissioner is entitled to adjust this amount. If the Commissioner thinks that the sum of compensation for an employee's death that the employer has deposited with him is insufficient, he may call upon the employer to show cause to this effect and then make an award after adjudicating the claim. For this purpose, the Commissioner has to fix a date for hearing the parties. This will involve giving notice to the parties in this regard. On receiving the deposit of the compensation amount, the Commissioner serves a notice to each dependant of the workman calling them to appear before him. Then, the Commissioner distributes the compensation amount among them in such a manner as he thinks fit. If any lump sum deposit with the Commissioner is payable to a workman or a person under a legal disability (e.g., a minor), the Commissioner may direct that the sum should be invested or otherwise dealt with for her/his benefit.

§2. ADJUDICATION

744. Adjudication powers under the ECA vest in the Commissioner, who is appointed by the State Government for a specific area. In some States, an ALC or labour officer has been given the power of a Commissioner under ECA. In such cases, Commissioners may not be law graduates. In other States the powers of a Commissioner under the ECA are vested in a civil judge, who is always a judicial officer. Very recently, the WCA (Amendment) Act 2009 has provided the qualification for a person who can be appointed as a commissioner under the ECA. Earlier, the appointing authority had a lot of discretion in the matter. Presently, it can be any person who is or has been a member of a State Judicial Service for a period of not less than five years or is or has been for not less than five years an advocate or a pleader or is or has been a Gazetted Officer for not less than five years having educational qualifications and experience in personnel management, human resource development and industrial relations. He may be appointed for such area as may be specified in the notification.[245]

745. The Commissioner is authorized to decide any/all questions pertaining to the liability of an employer to pay compensation, i.e., the amount of distribution, distribution of compensation, etc. He can also decide whether the person injured is an employee or not, and also the nature and extent of disablement.

746. Since the Commissioner exercises quasi-judicial powers while determining the claim, the ECA has conferred on him the power of a civil court for taking evidence on oath, enforcing the attendance of any witness and compelling the production of documents and material objects.

747. A claim application to the Commissioner is made in the prescribed form. It will contain a statement of circumstances in which the accident has taken place and the exact claim that the applicant makes. The date on which notice was served on the opposite party should also be given. The application should state the steps he took to secure a settlement and also why it was not possible to settle the dispute. The questions to be determined by the Commissioner should be made out. If the applicant is illiterate or for any other reason is unable to furnish the required information in writing, the application shall, if the applicant so desires, be prepared under the direction of the Commissioner. Thus, a Commissioner under the ECA has also been conferred advisory role.

748. The ECA provides that the Commissioner may appoint one or more persons who have special knowledge of the problems arising in the case to assist him in his enquiry. It has been held that the function of such an assessor is to help the Commissioner in appraising the evidence.

749. So far as the recording of evidence is concerned, the Commissioner shall make a brief memorandum of the substance of the evidence of every witness as he proceeds to examine the witness. Such a memorandum shall be written and signed by the Commissioner with his own hand. If the Commissioner is prevented from making such a memorandum, he shall record the reason of his inability to do so. In that case, the memorandum will be made through his dictation, which he shall sign. But the evidence of a medical witness is required to be taken down word for word.

---

245. *See* s. 20 (1) of the ECA as amended by the WCA (Amendment) Act 2009.

750. The Commissioner will make an award after hearing the parties, recording their evidence and hearing and appraising the arguments of both the sides. The Commissioner is empowered to award more compensation than was claimed by the claimant, since the Act is a beneficent legislation.[246] The Commissioner can award costs against the unsuccessful party. But in case he does not pass such an order he must give its reasons in writing. He can award interest under section 4-A (3) of the ECA at the statutory rate from the date of the accident.[247] Since ECA is a beneficent legislation, the judiciary has ruled that the earning capacity and disability have to be understood in a pragmatic way. So, when an injury was mentioned in Part I or Part II of the Schedule of the Act and the doctor had certified it to be a case of 60% disability, the court justified the commissioner's decision in holding that it was a case of 100% loss of earning capacity.[248]

751. The 2010 amendment to the ECA has charged the Commissioner to dispose of the matter relating to compensation under the ECA within a period of three months from the date of reference and intimate the decision in respect thereof within the said period to the employee. This is a welcome development so as to provide expeditious relief to the beneficiaries. Earlier, there have been several cases of delays, which prove to be frustrating for affected persons who are already in distress due to the death or disability of the employee concerned.

§3. Distribution of Compensation

752. When the employer admits his liability for payment of compensation in a case, the employer shall deposit the sum admitted with the Commissioner.

753. The employer is obliged to deposit the compensation with the Commissioner, and not make the payment directly, in two cases: (i) in case of death; and (ii) in case a lump sum compensation is payable to a woman or a person under a legal disability (say, a minor). After the compensation amount has been deposited, the Commissioner must issue a notice asking the dependants to appear before him for determining as to who are the dependants of the deceased, under the Act and in what proportion the compensation will be apportioned among the dependants. In case, the Commissioner is satisfied that no dependants exist he shall refund the balance of money back to the employer. This shows that the compensation envisaged by the ECA is merely a social protection and not a part of the estate of the diseased.

754. The Compensation amount deposited in respect of the death of an employee shall be apportioned among the dependants of the deceased employee or any of them in such a proportion as the Commissioner thinks fit. It is not like the situation in the ESI Act, where the share of each dependant is specified in the Act.

---

246. *B. Srikanth Reddy v. K. Mahesh* 2005 LLR 30 (AP).
247. *Div. Manager, New India Assurance Co. Ltd v. S. B. Singh* 2003 Lab. IC 598 (Ori.). Also *see, Ved Prakash Garg v. Premi Devi* (1997) 8 SCC1 14.
248. *New India assurance Co. Ltd v. K Yadaih* 2005 LLR 821 (AP).

The ECA expects the Commissioner to act as a well-wisher and counsellor of the injured employee and the dependants of the deceased employee. It is for this reason that such discretionary powers have been conferred on him.

I. Investments of Compensation

755. In case the lump sum amount of compensation deposited with the Commissioner is payable to a woman or a person under legal disability, such sum may be invested or otherwise dealt with for the benefit of the women concerned or such legally disabled person in a manner that the Commissioner directs. In case a half-monthly payment is payable to any person under a legal disability, the Commissioner may order that the payment may be made during the disability to any dependant of the employee or to any other person whom the Commissioner thinks suitable.

756. In some cases, the Commissioner may be satisfied that some beneficiary children are being neglected by their parents or that there is a change in the circumstances of any dependant. If he is satisfied that this requires a change in his earlier order as to distribution or investment, he may do so. But if his new order prejudicially affects any person, he shall give him an opportunity of show cause.

§4. Civil Courts Barred

757. Civil courts have been barred by section 19(2) of the ECA to settle or decide any question which under the Act is required to be settled or decided by a Commissioner. They have also been barred to enforce any liability incurred under the Act. It has been held, however, that section 19(2) does not oust the jurisdiction of the Civil Court to try a suit for compensation for death of a workman.[249] In respect of a claim of a Central Government employee under the ECA, the Central Government Tribunal has concurrent jurisdiction with the employees' compensation Commissioner.[250]

§5. Appeals

758. The proceedings under the Act are subjected to the appellate power of the High Court of the State concerned. Also, if any question of law arises in an application before the Commissioner, he may refer it to the High Court concerned for its decision. The Commissioner shall then decide that matter in conformity with such decision. An appeal shall lie to the High Court from the following orders of the Commissioner:

---

249. *Minerals & Chemicals v. Thevan* (1991) 2 Cur. LR 834 (Ker.).
250. *Union of India v. Sarup Chand Singla* (1989) 9 ATC 167 (Chand.).

(i) an order awarding compensation;
(ii) an order awarding interest or penalty under section 4-A of the ECA;
(iii) an order refusing to allow redemption of half-monthly payments;
(iv) an order related to distribution of compensation among dependants of a deceased employee; and
(v) an order refusing to register a memorandum of agreement.

759. As per section 30 of the ECA, appeals are allowed to the High Court only when a substantial question of law is involved in the appeal, and when the amount in dispute in the appeal is not less than INR 10,000. Also, no appeal is allowed when the parties have agreed to abide by the decision of the Commissioner. In case the employer decides to appeal against the Commissioner's order awarding compensation, against him, he cannot do so unless the appeal application is accompanied by a certificate from the Commissioner. This certificate should state that the appellant has deposited with him the amount payable under the order being appealed against. It has been held that a substantial question of law is involved in a finding of a Commissioner when it is not based on evidence or is arrived at by ignoring a material piece of evidence or misreading an evidence.[251] But under section 30 of ECA, the High Court cannot reappraise a pure finding of fact.

251. *Managing Director, O.R.T. Co. Ltd v. S. Rama Mohan Rao* (1988) I LLJ 200 (Ori.).

Chapter 3. Claims for Provident Funds and Pensions

760. As noted earlier the main legislation for provident funds and pensions for working people in the formal sector (excluding the Central and State Government employees) is the EPF Act 1952. It envisages framing of three schemes – the Provident Fund Scheme, the EPS and the Deposit-linked Insurance Scheme (DLIS). The EPF organization is administered by the BOT. Its chief executive is the Provident Fund Commissioner, also called the Chief Provident Fund Commissioner.

761. The EPF Act obliges the Provident Fund Commissioner to administer the provisions of this legislation. Apart from being the administrative head of the EPF Organization, he discharges quasi-judicial functions as envisaged under section 7A(2) of the Act. The quasi-judicial power under this section can also be exercised by Additional Central PF Commissioners, any Deputy PF Commissioners, any Regional PF Commissioners or any Assistant PF Commissioners. They exercise their adjudicatory powers, in case a dispute arises about the applicability of the EPF Act to an establishment or for determining the amount due from an employer under any provisions of the Act or any of the schemes administered under the EPF Act.

762. For adjudicating the dispute, the official concerned has to conduct such inquiry as he may deem fit. For this purpose, he enjoys the usual powers under the Civil Procedure Code 1908 (CPC) in matters of enforcing attendance of any person, seeking discovery and protection of documents, receiving evidence on affidavits and issuing commissions for examination of witnesses. The officer is empowered to conduct ex parte enquiry if the concerned employer, employee or any other person required to attend the inquiry fails to do so. Where the order is passed against an employer ex parte, he may within three months from the date of communication of such order, apply to the officer concerned for setting aside the order. In case he satisfies the officer that the show cause notice was not duly served or that he was prevented by any sufficient cause from appearing in the inquiry proceedings, the officer can set aside the ex parte order and proceed with a fresh enquiry.

763. In case the party aggrieved by an order of the officer concerned under section 7A, does not prefer to file an appeal before the appellate authority, he can apply for review of that order to the officer who had passed the order. The application for review may be made when the applicant discovers any new and important matter or evidence that was not in his knowledge or could not be produced by him when the order was made or feels that there is a mistake or error apparent on the face of the record. The officer can also review his order on his own motion if he feels it necessary.

764. The EPF law provides for reopening the officer's order determining an amount payable by an employer when he feels that any amount to be determined has escaped his notice. This can be done where he feels that there was an omission or failure on the part of the employer to make available any document or report or information. This redetermination can be made within a period of five years from the date of communication of the order passed. But any such redetermination can be made only after the employer is given a reasonable opportunity of representing his case.

765. If any employer makes a default in the payment of any contribution under the Act, the CPFC or any other officer authorized by the Central Government is empowered to levy and recover damages from such employer. But the damages shall not exceed the amount of arrears. The employer must be given an opportunity to present his case. Even though the authority has the discretion to levy damages but his order should disclose that the case of the aggrieved person has been properly considered.[252]

766. The EPF Act was amended in 1988 to provide for the constitution of one or more Appellate Tribunals to be known as EPF Appellate Tribunal. An Appellate Tribunal consists of one person only. It can be manned by only a judge of a High Court or a District Judge. An appeal to an Appellate Tribunal may be preferred by any person who is aggrieved by any notification or order issued by the Central Government or any authority. The order or notification may relate to any of the following:

(i) application of the provisions to establishments employing less than twenty persons;
(ii) application of the provisions to establishments with the approval of the employers and employees under section 1(4);
(iii) order passed by the Provident Fund Commissioner;
(iv) order passed on review;
(v) order on reassessment of escaped amount; or
(vi) order passing damages.

The appeal by an employer cannot be entertained unless he has deposited with the Tribunal 75% of the amount due from him that has been determined by an officer. The period of limitation for filing the appeal is provided in the EPF Appellate Tribunal (Procedure) Rules 1997, and is sixty days from the date of the notification or the order which is being appealed against. Section 7D of the EPF Act was added later on, which provides that the industrial tribunal constituted by the Central Government as per provisions of the IDA shall be the Tribunal for the purpose of EPF Act from the date of commencement of the Finance Act, 2017. The industrial tribunal is now authorized to exercise the jurisdiction, powers and authority conferred on it by the EPF Act. The place of the appeal shall be filed by the appellant with the tribunal within whose jurisdiction the appellant resides; or the cause of action has arisen; or respondent against whom relief is sought ordinarily resides.

252. *Siemens Engineering Mfg. Co. v. Union of India*, AIR 1976 SC 1785.

Chapter 4. Gratuity Claims and Adjudication

§1. Claims

767. A person who has become eligible for the receipt of gratuity under the Payment of Gratuity Act 1972 (PGA) has to apply to the employer in the prescribed form, within one year from the date on which the gratuity becomes payable.

768. As soon as the gratuity becomes payable to an employee, section 7(1) of the Act imposes an obligation on the employer that he should determine the amount payable (whether or not the employee makes the application). Then, he should give a notice to this effect to the person to whom the gratuity amount is to be paid. In this notice, the employer has to specify the amount of gratuity and fix the date of payment, which shall not exceed thirty days from the date of the receipt of the application. If the employer finds that the claim of the employee is not admissible, he should still give a notice specifying the reasons as to why the claim is not being considered as admissible. In either case, a copy of such notice is required to be given to the 'CA' under the Act for adjudication of gratuity disputes.

769. If there is any dispute over the amount of gratuity payable, or over the admissibility of any claim, the employer shall deposit with the CA such amount that he admits to be payable by him.

770. Where there is a dispute as to the amount of the gratuity, the claimant may make an application to the CA. Such an application has to be made by the claimant within ninety days.

§2. Adjudication

I. Appeal

771. The quasi-judicial function of adjudicating the disputes related to determination and payment of gratuity is performed by the 'CA' which is appointed by the appropriate Government under section 3 of the PGA. The Authority is responsible for the administration of the Act. In this regard, it adjudicates the dispute and also exercises recovery powers. In a sense both administrative and quasi-judicial powers are vested in the CA. Usually, the labour officers concerned are conferred the power of CA for deciding gratuity disputes. The PGA envisages an Appellate Authority which hears appeal from the decision of the CA. Usually, deputy LC in various states has been conferred the powers of the Appellate Authority under the PGA.

772. When the CA receives an application for deciding a gratuity dispute, it shall make a due inquiry and give the parties to the dispute a reasonable opportunity of being heard before determining the matter in dispute. Based on this determination, the Authority will direct the employer to pay the amount accordingly. If the Authority violates the *audi altrem partem* (i.e., hear the other party) rule of natural justice, its order is liable to be quashed. For the purpose of conducting the inquiry under section 7(4) of the PGA, the CA enjoys the powers vested in a civil court under the Code of Civil Procedure 1908 (CPC) with regard to enforcing parties' attendance, discovery and production of documents, receiving evidence on affidavits and issuing commissions for the examination of the witness concerned.

773. Section 7(7) of the PGA confers a right of appeal on persons aggrieved by the order of the CA. The appeal can be made to the Appellate Authority. The aggrieved party must prefer the appeal within sixty days from the date of the receipt of the order. But the Appellate Authority can condone the delay beyond sixty days if it is satisfied that the appellant was prevented by sufficient cause from filing the appeal within sixty days.

774. The employer's appeal shall not be admitted unless at the time of preferring the appeal he produces a certificate of the CA. This certificate should state that the appellant has deposited with him an amount equal to the amount of gratuity required to be deposited as per the authority's determination. This provision curbs the tendency of excessive litigation on the part of employees.

§3. Recovery of Gratuity

775. The CA has also been conferred recovery powers vis-à-vis the employer if he does not pay the gratuity determined. But it cannot do so on its own, but only on an application from the employee. When the employer does not pay the gratuity amount within the prescribed time and the employee makes an application, the CA can issue a certificate for that amount to the Collector, who shall recover the same as arrears of land revenue and pay the amount to the person entitled. The recovery can be made together with compound interest on the amount at the rate specified by the Central Government. Interest will be payable from the date of expiry of the prescribed time. But before doing so, the Appellate Authority has to give an opportunity of showing cause against the issue of such certificate. Also, the amount of interest shall in no case exceed the amount of gratuity payable.

776. The recovery powers in the PGA are so structured that the Act has been described as a self-contained Code[253] covering all essential features of a scheme for payment of gratuity. This also implicitly excludes recourse to any other statute for payment of gratuity. The idea underlying this law is to safeguard the employee's interest against any unnecessary harassment by the employer and to restrain the employer from denying the gratuity to the employee.

253. *State of Punjab v. Labour Court, Jullandur* [1981] I LLJ 354 (SC).

Chapter 5. Claiming Maternity Benefit

777. A woman entitled to claim maternity benefit under the MBA 1961 may give notice in writing to her employer stating that she or her nominee should be paid the maternity benefit. In this notice she should also undertake that she will not work in any establishment during the period for which she receives the maternity benefit.

778. In case of a woman who is pregnant the notice shall state the date from which she will be absent from work. However, it appears that the law does not take this requirement very seriously. Perhaps the law-makers were aware that if strictly enforced, this provision will prove harsh especially to a large number of illiterate and semi-literate women beneficiaries under the Act. That is why section 6(3) of the Act states that, any woman who has not given this notice when she was pregnant, may give it after delivery.

779. On receipt of the notice, the employer shall permit such woman to absent herself from the establishment during the period for which she will receive the maternity benefit.

780. Section 6(5) of the Act lays down that the amount of maternity benefit for the period preceding the date of expected delivery is payable in advance on production of proof by the woman worker that she is pregnant. The amount due for the subsequent period shall be paid within forty-eight hours of production of the proof of delivery of a child. The relaxation of the requirement of notice on the part of the woman concerned goes a step further. She is not disqualified for the payment of maternity benefit if she has not given the notice. It is provided that in such cases the inspector under the Act, either on his own motion or on an application made by the woman, is empowered to order the payment of such benefit to her.

781. The practice of exploitation of women workers during pregnancy is known to be quite widespread in India. On coming to know of pregnancy, employers often try to remove them from service on frivolous grounds. Section 12 of the MBA prohibits dismissal or discharge of a woman worker during or on account of such absence. Employers are also prohibited even to vary their service conditions to their disadvantage during the absence. It is provided by section 12(2)(b) that any woman should not be deprived of maternity benefit or medical bonus or be dismissed or discharged in the circumstances mentioned above. If so, she may, within sixty days from the day on which order of deprivation or discharge/dismissal is communicated to her, appeal to the prescribed authority. The decision of such authority on her application shall be final. The powers of the prescribed authority mentioned above have been vested in the inspector appointed under the MBA in most States.

782. Inspectors under the MBA are important functionaries in the enforcement of this law. Though their main functions are administrative, they have also been entrusted with quasi-judicial functions under section 17 of the Act. This section authorizes the inspector to direct the payment due to a woman under the Act. It states that if the maternity benefit payable to the woman worker is improperly withheld, she may make a complaint to the inspector to this effect. Complaint can also be made if her employer has dismissed or discharged her during or on account of her absence from work in accordance with the provisions of the Act. On receipt of the complaint or even on his own motion, the inspector may make an inquiry into the matter. If he is satisfied that the payment was wrongfully withheld, he may order payment to be made. In case of discharge or dismissal of the woman worker violating section 12, the inspector is authorized to pass such orders as are just and proper according to the circumstances of the case.

783. An appeal over the decision of the inspector lies to the prescribed authority within a period of thirty days from the date on which such decision is communicated. For example, in Gujarat State the 'Chief Inspector of Factories' has been designated as the prescribed authority in this regard.[254] In case an appeal is preferred, the decision of the prescribed authority is final.

784. Any amount payable under the section is recoverable by the collector of the district concerned in the same manner as an arrear of land revenue are recovered.

254. Debi S. Saini, *Redressal of Labour Grievances, Claims and Disputes* (New Delhi: Oxford & IBH, 1994), 83.

Chapter 6. Claiming Lay-Off, Retrenchment and Closure Compensation

785. The IDA mainly contains a conciliation-adjudication-arbitration model of industrial disputes resolution. It envisages three types of adjudicatory bodies for deciding interest and rights disputes – industrial tribunals, labour courts and national tribunals. While labour courts can decide only rights disputes, the other two can decide both rights and interest disputes. A dispute can be adjudicated only after it is referred to the adjudicatory body concerned by the appropriate Government. There is one class of cases where the dispute need not be referred to an adjudicatory body by the Government; in such a case the parties concerned can approach the labour court directly. They are called cases involving recovery of money due under settlement or award or provisions of Chapter V-A or V-B of the IDA. This provision is made in section 33C of the IDA.

786. In case the money is due to a workman under a settlement, award or Chapter V-A or V-B of the IDA, an application has to be made to the appropriate Government for recovery of money due to the worker. This application can be made as follows: (a) by the workman himself; or (b) by any person authorized by him; or (c) in case of his death by his assignee or heirs. In case the Government is satisfied that any money is so due, it is incumbent on it to issue a certificate for that amount to the collector who will proceed to recover the money in the same manner as an arrear of land revenue. Thus, it implies that the appropriate Government will naturally act as the 'Certificate holder'[255] for the recovery of the claim by the workman. For such cases, Regional LCs (Central) or Deputy LCs (State) have been given powers to investigate claims and issue certificates of the amounts to be recovered by the collector. These officers have been given powers of civil courts for the purposes of investigating claims.[256]

Normally, the time limit for making such an application is one year from the date on which the money became due. The time may, however, be relaxed by the Government if it is satisfied that the applicant had sufficient cause for not making the application within one year.

787. If the benefit due to a workman has not been calculated or there is any dispute about the amount of money or benefit to be commuted, he can apply to the labour court under section 33C (2) of the IDA for calculation of the benefit, and then apply under section 33C (1) for its recovery. Thus, in case of a dispute, a worker can approach the labour court to compute the exact amount of compensation for lay-off, retrenchment or closure as the case may be. Interestingly, there is no time limit prescribed in the IDA for activating the labour court under section 33C (2), however belated the application may be. If a claim is valid, it must be entertained whatever the delay. By an amendment of the IDA in 1982, the labour court is now given three months for making its decisions on a matter under section 33C (2). However,

255. *Lily Biscuits Co. (P) Ltd v. Board of Revenue, West Bengal* (1965) 11 FLR 335.
256. Debi S. Saini, *Redressal of Labour Grievances, Claims and Disputes* (New Delhi: Oxford & IBH, 1994), 152.

the time limit may be extended if necessary. In actuality, it is rarely so that the case is decided within the prescribed time limit.

788. It may be mentioned that section 33C does not cover disputes which come under section 10, that is, disputes which are referred by the appropriate Government for adjudication. Rather, it provides for the enforcement and execution of only an existing right or claim of the workman derived from an award or settlement.

A proceeding under section 33C (2) is in the nature of an execution proceeding; and therefore, this does not involve a right of plaintiff to relief and the corresponding liabilities of the defendant, i.e., whether the defendant is at all liable or not. It has been held that the workman cannot put forward a claim in an application under section 33C (2) in respect of a matter not based on an existing right.[257] Thus, a claim against a successor in business cannot be decided under section 33C (2).[258]

789. For the purpose of computing the money value of a benefit, the labour court can appoint a commissioner. The commissioner shall submit a report after taking necessary evidence. If so, the labour court shall determine the amount after considering the report of the commissioner and other circumstances.

790. The labour court shall forward its decision under section 33C(2) to the appropriate Government, and any amount found due by the labour court may be recovered in the manner provided in section 33C(1).

257. *Central Inland Water Transport Corpn Ltd v. Workmen* (1974) 4 SCC 696; *Punjab Beverages (P) Ltd v. Suresh Chand* (1975) 2 SCC 144.

258. National Labour Law Association, The Indian Labour Code (Draft) 1994, Fredrich Ebert Stiftung, New Delhi, 1994, 125. However, no action has been taken by the Government on enacting any such National Labour Code.

Part XIII. General Conclusions

791. So far as non-employee common workforce in the country is concerned, a large part of it constitutes the informal sector, agriculturists or those who are self-employed in small vocations. In such circumstances, the provision of social security through social insurance becomes a complex issue. The electoral exigencies of political parties have to necessarily focus on some kind of state-sponsored social assistance. This is done with a view to pleasing and empowering this section of population through various popular or poverty-alleviation schemes. Most such schemes have been organized in an ad hoc manner, and not as part of a comprehensive scheme of social security framework.

One such scheme has been launched by the NDA government which came into force in 2014, which involves an insurance cover for people, among others. As most people in the above category are living in poverty or exclusion, they have never had any bank account. The government devised a scheme of financial inclusion for such people. It launched a nationwide Pradhan Mantri Jan Dhan Yojana (PMJDY). Some of the stated objectives of the scheme are providing access to financial services including banking, savings, remittance, credit, insurance, and pension to all.

An account under this scheme can be opened with any bank branch. There is no stipulation of maintaining a minimum bank balance in the account under this scheme; it can even have a zero balance. Every accountholder under the scheme gets an accidental insurance cover of INR 1 lakh and a life cover of INR 30,000, which is payable on the death of the beneficiary person. One covered account holder per household is entitled to avail of overdraft facility up to a sum of INR 5,000. The scheme enables any transfer of benefit by the government directly to the bank. Accountholders can also get direct access to any pension scheme of the government.

792. The Prime Minister Suraksha Bima Yojana (PMSBY) has another scheme for common people launched by the NDA government. It is a government-backed accident insurance scheme for common people. It was launched by Prime Minister Narendra Modi on 8 May 2015. The scheme is available to people in the age group of 18 and 70 years having bank accounts. Annual premium of INR 12 exclusive of taxes is payable for each of the covered person. The government has exempted levy of GST on premiums payable under this scheme. The accident insurance scheme is being offered through banks and is administered by public sector general insurance companies. The benefits payable under the scheme are INR 2 lakhs in case of death or total permanent disability, and 1 lakh in case of partial permanent disability. This scheme has been linked to bank accounts opened under PMJDY. Ten crore people had enrolled under this scheme by the end of 2017. As on that date a total of 9,705 claims had been disbursed against 12,975 claims received.

793. If one looks at the structure and working of the Indian social protection system and the value choices of the State in terms of the objects of the protection and the contingencies covered one can notice many problems. These problems are partly attributable to the limitations of a developing country including limited resources of the State, with nearly a sizeable section of the population officially living below the poverty line. But equally important is the bureaucratic inefficiency which is true of most public services in the country. However, some States like Kerala have shown a better performance in administering social protection. The problems are attitudinal, systemic as well as administrative.

Looking at some of the recent state initiatives in this regard, one can notice that over the years a still greater degree of importance is being given to various social assistance schemes so as to mitigate the woes of common people in general and especially the poor. There is scope for innovating policies in consonance with people's needs, so as to effectively reach social benefits to a larger section of the population. For example, there is need for innovation in tackling the problems of large masses of farmers in the country, a large number among whom have committed suicide due to a high sense of economic insecurity for various reasons. Most of the 58% of the working people, whose occupation is agriculture (very small farmers), often find themselves in heavy debts due to poverty and crop failure. Governments at Centre and State levels have often waived farm loans taken by them from public sector banks. Experts believe this to be a poor option which results in many anomalies. There is a strong need to innovate about ways in which state assistance can provide effective economic security to farmers in such situations.

Of course, the country has its fiscal constraints; still there is a lot of scope for innovation in this regard which can help making the system more effective. Very recently, there appears a silver lining in this regard. In the state of Sikkim, the ruling Sikkim Democratic Front, which has to again go for elections in 2019, has promised UBI to the people in the state within three years and has included it in election manifesto. The country already have a cash transfer scheme by state agencies at the central and some State Government levels in some matters especially old age pension for poor senior citizens. With the Aadhaar card becoming a popular method of checking genuineness credentials direct cash transfer could be a useful medium to alleviate poverty.

Chapter 1. Working of the Formal Social Security Framework

794. The formal social security framework in India caters to the needs of a very small section of the working population. Since long a debate has been going on whether to improve the existing schemes or to extend them to other sections of employees including self-employed people. It is important to summarize the key problems in the framework of social security provisions in India in the formal sector.

§1. Problems Involved

795. The pith and substance of social security benefits in India is administered by the ESI Corporation, so as to realize the goals of the ESI Act 1948. This Act provides not just health care facilities through dispensaries and hospitals, but also cash benefits such as sickness, maternity, dependent and occupational-injury benefits through its local offices. The Act is made applicable area-wise. Its extension depends on the infrastructure of medical facilities available in the States concerned for providing medical benefit. This benefit is mostly administered by the State Governments on behalf of the ESIC. Lack of suitable infrastructure for efficient administration of medical facilities is the single most important factor which has hindered the extension of the ESI scheme. . Only a small percentage of the total workforce in the country is covered under this scheme. The huge informal sector is completely out of its ambit. Academics and evaluators of the scheme have pointed out various shortcomings in its working. These include restrictive coverage and eligibility, poor quality of medical care, lack of professionalism in administration of ESI dispensaries and hospitals, corruption among the staff, high cost and delays and malpractices in the disbursal of cash benefits. These problems need to be attended to by making systemic changes.

796. The EPF Act provides for provident fund three main types of protection to the employees covered – accumulation of PF contribution as a kind of saving, pension and deposit-linked insurance benefits. The country has separate laws for coal mine workers, plantation workers and those working as seamen. The EPF Act 1952 applies to industries employing twenty or more persons. Still a large number of establishments remain uncovered due to, among others, inefficiency, indifference and corruption in the inspectorate. Apart from that, there are several areas of its working which require attention including delays in disbursement of benefits, low rate of return on investments, and large arrears from employers. The separate law on gratuity, which should technically fall in the broad category of retirement benefits, is a unilateral liability of the employers. It involves considerable problems of enforcement.

797. There are four major social protection laws which create unilateral liability on the part of employers in the contingencies related to occupational accidents; maternity; gratuity, on retirement or death, etc. and unemployment caused by lay-off, retrenchment and closure. The laws involved are ECA, MBA, PGA and IDA.

Despite the formal protection, a large number of occupational accidents go unreported. Employers somehow try to evade their responsibility due to ignorance of the people covered or through collusion with labour bureaucracy. There are other problems related to delays, bureaucratic inefficiency and corruption in the administration of these laws. The multiplicity of labour and social security laws also makes things complex.

§2. Possible Solutions

798. The problems involved in the working of the formal laws on social security are systemic as well as administrative (and attitudinal). One can possibly think of some broad lines of solutions.

799. Since the most severe criticism of the ESI Scheme is about the administration of medical facilities, this issue requires the greatest focus of the reform agenda. There is a case for separating the administration of medical benefit and cash benefits. Most of the resources of the ESI Corporation are spent on the medical benefit. A National Social Security Authority of India (NSSAI), as proposed by the National Labour Law Association,[259] in its proposed Indian Labour Code, may be created to take care of administering all cash benefits including unemployment benefits. Insurance based on contributions with this authority could be made mandatory. The number of persons employed for coverage under this law may be brought down to five or more from the present ten.

The setting up of a National Institute of Social Security for training the staff of the EPF Organization at New Delhi is a welcome development. This institute can be used for training the staff of the proposed NSSAI, when established. Computerization of the administrative work will help reduce cost, which will eventually lead to increasing the quality of services provided by the NSSAI. There is need to give considerable thinking to the provision of medical benefit. It has been opined that the hospitals of ESI should be handed over to the State Governments.[260]

Exploring the possibility of comprehensive medical insurance through the involvement of private insurance companies can be thought of. A separate agency administering health benefits including provisions of medical care can be created.

800. In order to ensure an acceptable level of quality of medical services, the structure, funding and services to be provided by the proposed national agency for administering health care should be decided on the criteria of efficiency, quality and cost. There is a definite case of involving the private sector to evolve a viable scheme of PPP in this regard.

---

259. National Labour Law Association, The Indian Labour Code (Draft) 1994, Fredrich Ebert Stiftung, New Delhi, 1994, 125. However, no action has been taken by the Government on enacting any such National Labour Code.

260. S. Guhan, 'Towards a Comprehensive Social Security Policy', in *Social Security for all Indians*, ed. Wouter van Ginneken (New Delhi: Oxford University Press, 1998), 163.

Chapter 2. Towards Integrated Social Security

801. Countries at the global level have adopted unitary as well as pluralist models of social security. A variety of schemes and institutions exist to serve the goals of social protection at the global level. Countries like the United Kingdom and Australia have moved towards a single institution being given the responsibility of social security administration. In many countries which have adopted pluralist models, several organizations are involved in the exercise.

802. A study of the working of the Indian social security system would show that the Indian model still remains in a pluralist framework. Several laws provide for imposing unilateral responsibility on employers for protection of their employees against various contingencies. Most of these schemes and institutions have been created by intervention of the Central (Federal) Government.

803. Any progressive scheme of social security must so articulate its framework that the employers' unilateral liability legislation gives way to general social insurance scheme(s). This helps to promote better chances of implementation and is more equitable as well. Also, there is a need to decrease the number of agencies involved in the exercise so as to avoid duplication of benefits and problems relating to coordination of the work of these agencies. Two key social insurance laws in India are the ESI Act and the EPF Act, which are administered by the ESI Corporation and the EPF Organization respectively. The former deals basically with issues related to health care and earning-capacity related contingencies. The EPF Act deals mainly with issues related with old age and post-retirement situations.

804. Experts have felt an urgent need to provide for an integrated social security framework creating one or more agencies under an overall administrative framework with clear cut policy and operational aims. The key rationale for advocating institutional integration is twofold: (i) preventing duplication of benefits; and (ii) reducing the administrative cost in collection of contributions, payment of benefits, performing of inspectorial functions and other overheads. For example, there is overlapping of survivors' benefits payable under the ESI scheme with survivors' pension payable as per the pension scheme framed under the EPF Act. Likewise, a worker who becomes disabled due to occupational injury gets disability pension under the WCA or the ESI Act and also invalidity pension under the EPS. In case a merger of the two organizations is affected, one of the benefits can be adjusted when a person becomes entitled to receive the benefits under these two schemes. This would be a better way of rationalizing the social security protection.

805. Several attempts have been made towards suggesting an integration of the social security schemes. The earliest attempt was the constitution of a study group by the Ministry of Labour, Government of India. The study group gave four major suggestions: (i) a single agency should first assume administrative responsibility for the ESI Act, EPF Act, Coal Mines Provident Fund and Bonus Schemes Act and Assam Tea Plantations Provident Fund Scheme Act; (ii) improving the level of cash benefits and standard of medical care including hospital facilities; (iii) converting the EPF scheme into a pension-cum-gratuity scheme; and (iv) substantial enhancing of employer's contribution both under the ESI scheme and the EPF scheme. The Study Group opined that the integration should be done to fulfil the aims of achieving substantial economy in expenditure and enhanced convenience to the parties. However, amidst various objections mainly from the employees it was decided to shelve the integration proposal. In 1963, the ESIS Review Committee devoted itself at length on the creation of a single social security scheme. It suggested administrative merger of the two schemes and taking steps to convert provident fund into a pension-cum-gratuity scheme. It felt that a pension scheme would involve a large number of beneficiaries all over the country and a large network of local and sub-local pay offices. It also opined that the local offices created under the ESI scheme could be utilized for this purpose. It was felt needless to set up two sets of local offices under the two schemes. The committee also suggested one composite contribution payable by the employers and the employees. However, it opined that two separate accounts could be maintained – one for short-term benefits and the other for benefits of long-term nature. The National Commission on Labour 1969 (NCL) also agreed with and endorsed the proposals of the ESIS Review Committee. It hoped that with marginal increase in the rates of contribution, India could eventually move to a single comprehensive social security agency. Later on, in its 123rd report, the Estimates Committee of Parliament (1970) emphasized the integration of social security schemes not just for administrative reasons but for achieving the objective of rationalization of benefits and equalization charges. Pursuant to these, a blueprint of integrated schemes was drawn by Dr N.N. Chattrejee,[261] a personnel management expert, in 1972. Later on, Dr R.K.A. Subrahmanya,[262] a well-known social security expert in India also drew a blueprint on somewhat similar lines in 1985. A still more comprehensive draft of an integrated social security model came from the National Labour Law Association in 1994, where such a model has been intended to become part of a much broader project of providing a single Indian Labour Code (Draft).[263] This code, among others, sought to merge major Indian labour laws into a simpler but more comprehensive bill of labour entitlements.

806. Out of the several suggestions made towards integration, the proposal by the National Labour Law Association (NLLA) needs to be given careful consideration. This proposal envisaged a National Social Security Authority of India (NSSAI), in whose consultation was recommended to be drawn appropriate schemes of social security. The proposed NSSAI was expected to be responsible for administering all the schemes. It also envisaged the Social Security Fund of India or of a State to be administered by the Central Board of Social Security or a State Board of Social Security. It suggested collection of a sizeable contribution from

261. Professor N.N. Chatterjee, *Blueprint for the Integrated Social Security Organization and Scheme*, vol. I & II (New Delhi: Ministry of Labour and Rehabilitation, 1972).
262. R.K.A. Subrahmanya, *Social Security Perspective of Coming Decades* (New Delhi: Council of Indian Employees, 1985).
263. The Indian Labour Code (1994) (Draft) National Labour Law Association (New Delhi: Friedrich Ebert Stiftung, 1994).

employers not exceeding 30% of the monthly wage bill. In addition to the usual benefits available under the existing schemes, the Code also advocated providing invalidity benefit, terminal benefit, unemployment benefit, old age benefit, insurance benefit and guarantee of payment of wages in the event of failure of the employers to pay the wages due to permanent closure or insolvency of establishments. The Code also provided for establishment of one or more welfare funds for providing social security to the classes of employees/persons who are not covered by the proposed social security schemes. It suggested that the appropriate government may make one or more supplementary schemes for the benefit of self-employed persons as well, after consulting the Central or State Board of Social Security.

807. Despite a long history of nearly thirty-five years of attempts towards integrating the social security schemes in India, no concrete attempt has actually taken place at the level of the legislature till the new NDA government came to power. The issue, therefore, remained a mere academic debate. With the adoption of the globalization programme of the Government of India through the New Economic Policy of 1991, its desire to intervene in labour matters has further gone down. Post-NEP governments are grappling with different shades of problems, even as provision of social safety net is a very important part of the globalization programme. Presently, one of the most important goals of the Government is inviting more foreign direct investment by reducing labour cost and otherwise facilitate setting up of industries by MNCs. Social security, especially in the organized sector, is now low on the Government agenda. This has suppressed the reform process in social security integration, as Governments do not want to legislate anything that hikes the cost of production, howsoever it may be otherwise justified. As discussed in chapter 4 of this part, a significant development towards reconceptualization of social security in the country is the proposed social security code in March 2018, which is still debated among social partners.

808. In terms of coverage there is one good development that happened through the enactment of the ESI (Amendment) Bill 2009. Several changes were made in the working of the ESIA including the extension of the Act to those getting a salary of INR 15,000 per month. This coverage limit for ESIA has later on been raised to INR 21,000. Among others, a new Chapter V-A was added which made it possible for ESIC to extend medical care to non-IP against payment of user charges. This was done to facilitate provision of medical care to the BPL families and other unorganized sector workers. These amendments ensured coverage of more workers under the ESI Scheme in the organized sector. This amendment also led to the ESIC participating in schemes such as RSBY was framed for BPL people. Later on more such schemes were enacted after the passage of the UWSSA. These amendments were also seen as efforts towards bringing the provisions of the Act in tune with the changing circumstances. In a way, this did prove to be a step towards integration and expansion.

Chapter 3. Is Building a National Consensus on Reconceptualization of Social Security Feasible?

809. The Indian system of social security is based on the Western model which is essentially relevant to industrially advanced countries. The Western model seeks to provide relief to the needy in case of specific contingencies. Unlike the developing countries like India, these economies have not witnessed an alarming incidence of chronic poverty, as also steep inequalities caused by globalization that India is witnessing at present. The contingent poverty in the advanced world would relate to interruption in regular income due to specific uncertain happenings, known as contingencies in social security jargon. These societies evolved social insurance as the key mechanism of tackling these contingencies. A large part of the workforce in the advanced economic world works in the organized sector, where social security schemes can be implemented by deducting contributions from salaries. The needs of these countries have not necessitated considering means-tested social assistance as a serious alternative to the social insurance model. On the other hand, a country like India realizes the limitations of contributions-based social security. That is why, we have schemes envisaging unilateral liability of the employer continuing since long. India's special problems also justify the adoption of welfare funds and welfare spending as social assistance measures to workers in the unorganized sector. Yet its social security policy lacks a comprehensive vision about the future of India and of various vulnerable groups constituting it.[264] With their modernistic and colonial mindsets, developing countries like India have tried to ape Western models without much critical debates.

810. For several good reasons, a developing country like India finds itself supporting a strange kind of social protection, focusing only on the organized sector – meaning semi-Government institutions and other public and private enterprises using power and employing ten or more persons and those not using power but employing twenty or more persons. The country has to recognize its peculiar profile in making choice of appropriate social security instruments. This will help it appreciate the need to move beyond the western model.

811. Only less than 8% of the Indian working population is employed in the organized Sector; which includes unorganized workers working in the organized sector. The number of people living below the official poverty line is still high. Most working people are self-employed in various agriculture or industry-related vocations or are contract/casual workers. The terms on which this section of people work are far below the minimum acceptable standards of employment which can reflect even a semblance of dignified work-life. Their needs are different from those of the similarly placed workers in the developed world.

Social scientists have therefore felt the need to redefine social security in the context of the peculiar social protection requirements of the developing countries. For

264. Debi S. Saini, 'Some Issues in the Working of Social Security Laws', *Indian Journal of Labour Economics* 48, no. 4 (2005).

example, it is argued that in view of the above mentioned susceptibilities of developing countries, social security should be fully integrated with the anti-poverty policies such as employment guarantees and food security;[265] should focus on adequate nutrition, shelter, health care and clean water supply as well as the usual contingencies[266] and should explore the use of social means to prevent deprivation and vulnerability to deprivation.[267] Ginneken's[268] definition of social security arises from a number of basic risks and needs. Thus, it is important that we look at social security in the Indian context towards attacking chronic as well as contingent poverty through an appropriate set of measures for income support and income maintenance.

812. Focusing mainly on the formal sector especially in developing countries in India, the social security model is also not quite just and fair, because it fails to help the neglected 92% working people. It also leads to widening the gap between the rich and the poor. The formal sector worker is an organized interest group with some political power to shape governments' policy, which is not the case with informal sector workers. Therefore, we need to rethink the alternative ways of meeting the social security needs of all sections of society. That is why, even issues such as provision of a suitable vocational training framework are considered as an important issue of social security.[269]

813. The social security policy in the context of a country like India should focus on basic minimum needs like primary education, food security and primary health. It should also emphasize poverty-alleviation measures of land and asset redistribution. Contingency-related social protection should become a part of the overall anti-poverty approach. For example, India has evolved employment generation programmes such as JRY, the Integrated Rural Development Programme (IRDP), and employment programmes like MNREGA. We have also developed useful programmes like Integrated Child Development Scheme (ICDS). More recently, the government has been compelled to initiate health insurance schemes like Ayushman Bharat Yojna. But we also need focus on prevention of sickness through better primary health care rather than sickness benefit alone. These preventive schemes, of course, are not the whole answer to social security questions, but they can be complementary. Preventive measures cannot be a total substitute to contingencies-related needs.

---

265. S. Guhan, 'Social Security Options for Developing Countries', *International Labour Review* 133, no. 1 (1994), Geneva.
266. I.P. Getubig, 'Social Security and the Poor: An Introduction', in *Rethinking Social Security: Reaching Out to the Poor*, ed. I.P. Getubig & S. Schmidt (Kuala Lumpur: Asian and Pacific Development Centre, 1992).
267. J. Dreze & A. Sen, 'Public Action For Social Security: Foundation and Strategy', in *Social Security in Developing Countries*, ed. E. Ahmed et al. (Delhi: Oxford University Press, 1991).
268. Wouter van Ginneken (ed.), *Social Security for All Indians* (Delhi: Oxford University Press, 1998).
269. Debi S. Saini, 'Imperatives of Globalization and Vocational Training Framework in India', *Prajnan – Journal of the National Institute of Bank Management* XXXIV, no. 3 (2005); and Debi S. Saini, 'HRD Through Vocational Training: The Indian Model', *Indian Journal of Industrial Relations* 40, no. 4 (2005).

814. A good number of social and economic security needs of Indian people emanates from the fact that a larger part of Indian population lives in rural areas, and employment in agriculture is whopping 42% of working people. In most developed countries it is only between 1% and 5% of the total working population. Since the scope for raising productivity in agriculture is little, output in agriculture in India is just one-third of per worker GDP at the national level. These facts add to the dimensions and complexity of social and economic security needs of people in the country. So as to confront this reality, governments at the Central and State levels have been providing social assistance through a number of welfare measures and subsidies for farmers and rural households. It is estimated that Indian farmers receive subsidies of INR 2.2 trillion per year. Their subsidy list, among others, includes areas such as fertilizer, power, crop insurance, seeds, credit, and irrigation. Also, Central and State subsidies on food grains covers nearly three-fourths of the entire rural population in the country. Besides, MNREGA scheme offers 100 days' employment guarantee in a year to one adult to each rural household, which is a situation of manufacturing employment with focus on paying wages to those having the guarantee than on getting any specified public work done.

This explains the nature of social security dimension of people in general, which is quite identical with poverty alleviation and assisting people in general in that regard. Thus, welfare spending by the state and its agencies towards improving people's lives becomes an important dimension of social security in an emerging economy like India.

815. Bureaucratic inertia and indifference is another issue that needs to be focused on in any discussion on the social security system in India. The incidence of bureaucratic corruption in publicly administered schemes including social protection interventions is known to be high in the country, though it is getting reduced with the lowering of the power of the bureaucracy in the globalizing dispensation. Thus, there is a strong case for making the social assistance and anti-poverty programmes efficient and meaningful. The cost of administering these schemes too has to be brought within affordable limits. Like most other public agencies, social security administrative agencies lack innovativeness and accountability. They resist change more than is the case with other segments of society. We may need to involve NGOs and local authority in ensuring better administration of social security to help operationalize the wider definition of social security. For example, Self-Employed Women's Association (SEWA) has done commendable work in this regard under the able leadership of Ms Elaben Bhat.[270] Especially after the seventy-third and seventy-fourth constitutional amendments, the political scenario in India

---

270. Ela Bhatt, *We Are Poor But So Many* (Delhi: Oxford University Press, 2006); Debi S. Saini, 'Community-based Forms of Social Security in the Unorganized Sector: Can the Indian Approach be Replicated', *Zeitschrift fur auslandisches and internationales Sozialrecht* (ZIAS) (*Review of Foreign and International Social Law* 22, no. 1 (2008) published in German as also in English by the Max Planck Institute for Foreign and International Social Law, Munich, Germany); and Debi S. Saini, 'Securing Working Class Rights for Informal Sector Workers in India: Case Study of Self-Employed Women's Association', *Indian Journal of Labour Economics* 50, no. 4 (2007).

is changing fairly rapidly.[271] *Panchayats* (People's Councils) and local bodies are being activated in cooperative administration. Their cooperation in social security administration can help reap the benefits of decentralization.

816. Ayushman Bharat Yojana (ABY) or PM-JAY as it is also called, is a welcome step in making available a more comprehensive health protection to poor people in general, but given the unimpressive record of the success of such schemes, time only will tell how far it meets the health needs of targeted section of the Indian society. As large as more than 70% of the Indian workforce belongs to the category of self-employed, casual or contract workers. Given the inefficiency of public agencies in meeting their needs, we need to innovate new models of public-private partnership including involving insurance companies in this regard. There is also good scope for developing a private market in regard to life, health and disability insurance so as to supplement social insurance.

817. The Indian State sees the writings on the wall that are resulting from the new sets on inequalities emerging due to the pursuit on neo-liberal policies. When the inequalities between different sections of society become steeper and even frightening, it has to take steps to address the resultant problems. That is what seems to be happening now. We can thus witness state coming for the first time since independence with some new ideas like employment guarantee, health insurance for the poor families, waiving of farmers' loans, and social security for the unorganized sector workers through the enactment of UWSSA. Till very recently, the bureaucratic mind-sets were cautioning about such ideas being too burdensome on the state exchequer. The stock market and capitalist lobbies show steep reaction to such measures. These initiatives are mainly in the category of social assistance rather than social insurance, though there is some element of insurance as well in some of them. This shows the difficulties and needs differences between the haves and the poor classes. With the economic difference between classes becoming steeper any idea of uniform conceptualization of social security will become more and more difficult. India's social security discourse therefore will continue to reflect this kind of duality.

818. At the time of its establishment, the ESIC set up a vision of reaching almost the entire Indian population. It has so far covered less than 10% population. With the recent hike in the coverage limit to employees getting up to INR 21,000 per month, this percentage is likely to go up. But at the same time, we need to keep in mind the hostility that is developing among trade unions and the common employees against being included in the ESIS rather than somewhat more attractive group insurance schemes. Employees now know the pursuit of higher incidence of customer's satisfaction that private hospitals are keeping in mind in the chaotically competitive world. They wish to become beneficiaries of these emerging realities. So instead of arguing for an integrated social security framework, the discourse is

271. Debi S. Saini, 'Law and Social Development in India', paper presented at the International Dialogue on Law and Social Development organized by Parliamentary Commission on Social Development (Mexico City, Mexico, 24–26 Nov. 1999).

likely to move towards a duality, unless we take some urgent steps to make the working of ESIC acceptable by the employees in general.

819. While the ESIC is running more than 150 hospitals across the country, there continues to be dissatisfaction over their infrastructure and services being provided by them. Also, the procedural formalities involved in availing the services from them are not customer-friendly. The bureaucracy has not bothered to look into these issues. The staff in some of the ESI managed hospitals does not reflect technical and behavioural competence in handling emerging situations. Private insurance companies, although may be more expensive, they customize their products as per the needs of the customer, and thus become sought after by the clients. Therefore, more and more progressive companies prefer to tie up with them so as to keep their employees in spirits of motivation. This throws a big challenge to the ESIC to stem the rot and improve performance and address the concerns of the employers and their employees. However, if we separate the medical facilities from other needs for old age economic security, the need for unification is stronger so that we are able to avoid duplication of some of the services and the resultant anomalies.

Chapter 4. The Social Security Code (SCC): An Attempt Towards Integration and Simplification

820. Interestingly, the Indian Parliament passed three Labour Codes (out of four codes) by amalgamating existing central labour laws with a view to simplify and rationalize the rules. These Codes received the President's consent on 28 September 2020. They are: the Code for Social Security, 2020; the Occupational Safety, Health and Working Conditions Code, 2020; and the Industrial Relations Code, 2020. The fourth code, the Code on Wages, 2019, was passed by the Parliament and received the President's consent in 2019. These codes are, however, not yet enforceable. Even when they are made applicable, time will tell whether this new initiative can indeed help in expanding the social security coverage in the country as also in a simplified and effective way.

821. The SSC seeks to rationalize and consolidate different statutes on social security and make social security delivery easier in terms of understanding its framework and its implementation. Under the Code the existing EPFO and ESIC are envisaged to get converted into fund managers.

822. The coverage of contingencies provided for in the code relate to: health, old-age, disability, retirement, unemployment and maternity benefits. The existing pieces of social security legislation including the schemes framed under the Unorganised Workers Social Security Act 2008 have been subsumed in the code. The scheme provides that it would be wholly financed by the government for people below the poverty line, and would be contributory for others. In the first phase, all workers will get minimum benefits. Other benefits would be added gradually later on.

823. The definition of 'employee' is very wide. It covers permanent workers, casual workers, fixed-term workers, piece-rate/commission-rated workers, informal workers, home-based workers, domestic workers and seasonal workers. All workers would not get covered straight away. Those who have been excluded from the protection presently would be included gradually. .

824. The beneficiaries of the scheme will be divided into four groups. In the first group are those living below the poverty line. They cannot be expected to contribute to social security on their own; so the same would be paid by the government on their behalf. The second group comprises workers in the unorganized sector. They might be capable of partially contributing to it but they need assistance from the government. In the third group will fall people who are self-sufficient and can fund their social security with or without help from their employers. The fourth group comprises financially comfortable people; they can support themselves for risks covered under the scheme.

825. The government claims that SSC would benefit about 50 crore workers. A three-tier administrative structure is envisaged for operationalizing the SSC. At the top is the National Social Security Council, which will be headed by the Prime Minister. Below that would be the Central Board of Social Security at the Central level; and there would be state boards at the State level too. Greater expectations are being attributed to the State Governments to enforce the scheme and realise its goals.

826. An establishment is the one that employs one or more workers. The National Council has been authorized to determine the minimum period of work that entitles a person to be classified as worker under the code.

827. One of the most attractive parts of the SSC is that it envisages enabling public-private partnership (PPP) in administering the social security system in the country. This is especially important as the role of government entities in delivery of health care and other services has been far from satisfactory. In this regard, it talks of licensing of intermediate agencies. The services of these agencies could be used in the fields of, among others, fund management, service delivery, benefit disbursement, and record keeping. The Central and State boards are being empowered to exercise control over these agencies with a view to protecting the interest of subscribers.

828. One of the key benefits of the SSC is a wider coverage of even self-employed people in the health scheme. Presently, workers not covered by the ESIC receive benefits like medical attention through government's primary health centres, dispensaries and hospitals; they do so as members of public. But these health care providers are not working satisfactorily, leading to public disappointment about their service delivery. Despite promises of making the system better, there is virtually no progress in improving the quality of care provided. Contributions from employers, welfare funds, and government assistance are expected to lead to more effective functioning of these entities.

829. The code seeks to incentivize coverage of workers in the course of works contract, which will help prevention of tax avoidance/evasion. The employer has been made liable for covering his employees in the social security system. The person awarding the works contract is being made accountable to make a fixed deduction from the payment made for the work contract, and deposit it in the Social Security Fund.

Selected Bibliography

Books and Commentaries

Ahmed, E., et al. *Social Security in Developing Countries*. Oxford: Oxford University Press, 1991.

Bagchee, S. 'Employment Guarantee Scheme in Maharashtra'. *Economic & Political Weekly*. XIX, no. 37, 1 September 1984.

Beveridge, W. *Social Insurance and Allied Services*. London: HMSO, 1942.

Bhatnagar, Deepak. *State and Labour Welfare in India: An Appraisal of the ESI Scheme*. New Delhi: Deep & Deep, 1985.

Dandekar, Kumudini, *The Elderly in India*. New Delhi: Sage, 1996.

Dev, Mahendra S. 'Social Security in the Unorganized Sector: Lessons from the Experiences of Kerala and Tamil Nadu States'. *The Indian Journal of Labour Economics* 37, no. 4 (October–December, 1994).

Dreze, J. & A. Sen. *Hunger and Public Action*. Oxford: Oxford University Press, 1989.

George, Alex. 'Hospitalization Insurance'. *Economic & Political Weekly*, 15 March 1997.

Getubig, I.P. & S. Schmidt (eds). *Rethinking Social Security: Reaching Out to the Poor*. Kuala Lumpur (Malaysia): Asia and Pacific Development Centre, 1992.

Ginneken, Wouter van (ed.). *Social Security for All Indians*. Delhi: Oxford University Press, 1998.

Guhan, S. 'Social Security Options for Developing Countries'. *International Labour Review* 133, no. 1 (1994).

Gupta, B.P. (ed.). *Digest of Important Labour Judgements 1981–85*. New Delhi: PHD Chambers of Commerce and Industry, 1986.

Gupta, N.H. *Social Security Legislation for Labour in India*. New Delhi: Deep & Deep, 1986.

Gupta, R.C. *NGO Experiences in Social Security*. New Delhi: Friedrich Ebert Stiftung, 1994.

Hirway, Indira (ed.). *Denial of Maternity Benefit to Women Workers in India*. New Delhi: Oxford & IBH, 1986.

ILO. 'Social Security and National Development – Report of a National Seminar in India'. New Delhi, 19–30 September 1977.

Johri, C.K. 'India – Labour Law and Industrial Relations'. *International Encyclopaedia of Laws*. The Netherlands: Kluwer, 1998, Part II, Ch. 4.

Selected Bibliography

Krishnamurty, V. 'A Social Security Model for India: The Kerala Model', in *Social Security in India*, ed. R.K.A. Subrahmanya & S.K. Wadhawan. Friedrich Ebert Stiftung and Social Security Association of India, 1994.

Malhotra, O.P. *The Law of Industrial Disputes*, vols 1 & 2. New Delhi: Universal Book Traders, 2004.

Malik, P.L. *Handbook of Labour and Industrial Law*, 5th edn. Lucknow: Eastern Book Company, 2018.

Mathew, Babu. 'A Brief Note on Labour Legislation in India'. *Asian Labour Update* Issue No. 46 (January to March 2004).

Mathew, Thomas. 'Medical Insurance for All'. *Economic and Political Weekly*, 15 February 1997.

Mongia, J.N. (ed.). *Readings in Indian Labour and Social Welfare*. Delhi: Atma Ram & Sons, 1980.

National Labour Law Association (NLLA). *Simplification, Rationalization and Consolidation of Labour Laws and Social Security*. New Delhi: NLLA, 1993.

Patel, B.B. *Social Security for Unorganized Labour*. New Delhi: Oxford & IBH, 1993.

Saini, Debi S. 'Political and Legal Framework and Hurdles', In Budhwar, P. and Verma, A. (Eds.), ***Doing Business in India***, London: Routledge, 2018.

Saini, Debi S. 'Community-Based Forms of Social Security in the Unorganized Sector: Can the Indian Approach Be Replicated', *Zeitschrift fur auslandisches and internationales Sozialrecht* (ZIAS) (International Journal on International and Foreign Law published in German as also in English from Germany) 22 no. 1–2 (2008).

Saini, Debi S. 'Securing Working Class Rights for Informal Sector Workers in India: Case Study of Self-Employed Women's Association'. *Indian Journal of Labour Economics* 50, no. 4 (2007).

Saini, Debi S. 'Some Issues in the Working of Social Security Laws'. *Indian Journal of Labour Economics* 48, no. 4 (2005).

Saini, Debi S. 'HRD Through Vocational Training: The Indian Model'. *Indian Journal of Industrial Relations* 40, no. 4 (2005).

Saini, Debi S. 'Imperatives of Globalization and Vocational Training Framework in India'. *Prajnan – Journal of the National Institute of Bank Management* XXXIV, no. 3 (2005).

Saini, Debi S. 'Law and Social Development in India'. Paper presented at an International Workshop on Law and Social Development, organized by the Legislature's Commission on Social Development (Mexico, 24–26 November 1999).

Saini, Debi S. 'Labour Legislation and Social Justice: Rhetoric and Reality'. In *Economic and Political Weekly* – Special issue on Review of Labour, vol. XXXIV, no. 39 25 September–1 October 1999.

Saini, Debi S. (ed.), *Labour Law, Work and Development*. New Delhi: Westvill Publishers, 1995.

Saini Debi S. *Redressal of Labour Grievances, Claims and Disputes*. New Delhi: Oxford & IBH, 1994.

Saini, Debi S. 'Towards Securing Social Protection for Industrial workers with special reference to the working of the Employees' State Insurance Act, 1948', LLM Dissertation, Unpublished, Faculty of Law, University of Delhi, Delhi, 1979.

Saini, Debi S. & Pawan Budhwar. 'Managing the Human Resource in Indian SMEs: The Impact of Indigenous Realities on Effectiveness', *Journal of World Business* 43, no. 4 (2008).

Sankaran, T.S., R.K.A. Subrahmanya & S.K. Wadhawan (eds). *Development of Social Security Programme in Developing Countries*. New Delhi: Friedrich Ebert Stiftung and Social Security Association of India, 1994.

Sankaran, T.S., R.K.A. Subrahmanya & S.K. Wadhawan (eds), *Social Security in Developing Countries*. New Delhi: Har-Anand Publication, 1994.

Sarma, A.M. *Aspects of Labour Welfare and Social Security*. Bombay: Himalaya Publishing Co., 1981.

Singh, Parduman. *Social Security in Asia and Pacific: A comparative study*. New Delhi: Friedrich Ebert Stiftung and Social Security Association of India, 1992.

Singh, Parduman. *Social Security System in Developing Countries: Asia, Africa & South America*. New Delhi: Friedrich Ebert Stiftung, 1997.

Srivastava, S.C. *Social Security and Labour Laws*. Lucknow: Eastern Book Company, 1985.

Social Security Association of India, National Commission for Women, Friedrich Ebert Stiftung (eds). *Social Security for Women*. New Delhi, 1994.

Subrahmanya, R.K.A. *Evolution and Status of Social Security Systems in India*. New Delhi: Social Security Association of India & Friedrich Ebert Stiftung, 1995.

Subrahmanya, R.K.A. *Social Security: A Critical Survey*. Delhi: B.R. Publications, 1998.

Subrahmanya, R.K.A (ed.). *Social Security in India: Extension of Social Security Schemes*. New Delhi: Friedrich Ebert Stiftung and Social Security Association of India, 1995.

Subrahmanya, R.K.A. (ed.). *Social Security for Women*. New Delhi: Friedrich Ebert Stiftung and Social Security Association of India, 1995.

Subrahmanya, R.K.A. 'Social Protection Schemes of LIC and GIC for Workers in the Urban Informal Sector', paper produced for ILO (New Delhi, 1994, Mimeo).

Suhrith, Parthasarathy & A.K. Visalakshi. 'The Unorganized Sector Workers' Social Security Bill: Defending the Support-Led Security Approach'. *Labour Law Journal* III (2007).

Varandani, G. *Social Security for Industrial Workers in India*. Delhi: Deep & Deep, 1987.

Wadhawan, S.K. *Social Security for Workers in the Informal Sector in India*. Geneva: ILO, 1989.

Periodicals

Labour and Industrial Cases
Labour Law Reporter
Labour Law Journal
Indian Journal of Labour Economics
Journal of the Indian Law Institute
International Labour Review
Indian Journal of Labour Economics
International Social Security Review

Selected Bibliography

Reports

All India Trade Union Congress (AITUC). *Report of the AITUC-ILO Workshop on Social Security for Workers*. New Delhi, 1997.

Chatterjee, Bhudev. *Journey from my Provident Fund to Our Pension Scheme*. New Delhi: EPF Organization, 1996.

Employees' State Insurance Corporation (ESIC). Annual Report, 2016-17, New Delhi, 2017.

EPF Organization. *Reports of the Employees' Provident Fund Organization*. New Delhi.

Gopalan, Sarla & Mira Shiva. *National Profile on Women, Health and Development–Country Profile: India*. New Delhi: Voluntary Health Association of India and World Health Organization, 2000.

Government of India. *Annual Report 2017-18*. New Delhi: Ministry of Labour, 2018.

Government of India. *Blueprint for the Integrated Social Security Organization and Scheme*, vol. I and II by Professor N.N. Chatterjee, Ministry of Labour and Rehabilitation. New Delhi, 1972.

Government of India. *Report on Health Insurance for Industrial Workers*. New Delhi, 1944 (B.P. Adarkar Committee Report).

Government of India. *Report of the National Commission on Labour* (2nd). Ministry Labour, New Delhi, 2002, vol. I and II.

Government of India. *Report of the National Commission on Labour.* Government of India, Ministry of Labour, New Delhi, 1969.

Government of India. *Employees' State Insurance Corporation (ESIC) – Annual Report 1999–2000*. Ministry of Labour, New Delhi, 1999.

Government of India. *Economic Survey 2017-18*. Ministry of Finance, New Delhi, 2000.

Government of India. *Report of the ESIS Review Committee.* Ministry of Labour, New Delhi, 1966.

Government of India. *Report of the ESIS Review Committee*. Ministry of Labour, New Delhi, 1982.

Government of India. *Report of the Working Group on Social Security*. New Delhi: Economic Administration Reforms Commission, 1984.

Government of India. *Report of the EPF Review Committee* (Ramanujam Committee). New Delhi, 1982.

Government of India. *Report of the National Commission on Rural Labour*. New Delhi: Ministry of Labour, 1991.

Government of India. *National Social Assistance Programme (NSAP) Guidelines*. New Delhi: Ministry of Rural Areas and Employment, 1995.

National Commission on Enterprises in Unorganized Sector (NCEUS). *Skill Formation and Employment Assurance in the Unorganised Sector*. New Delhi, April 2009.

NCEUS. *A Report on Technology Upgradation for Enterprises in the Unorganised Sector*. New Delhi, April 2009.

NCEUS. *Report on Conditions of Work and Promotion of Livelihood in the Unorganized Sector*. New Delhi: National Commission for Enterprises in the Unorganized Sector, August 2007.

NCEUS. *Financing of Enterprises in the Unorganised Sector & Creation of a National Fund for the Unorganised Sector (NAFUS)*. New Delhi, November 2007.

NCEUS. *Comprehensive Legislation for Minimum Conditions of Work and Social Security for Unorganised Workers*. New Delhi, July 2007.

NCEUS. *Social Security for Unorganised Workers*. New Delhi, May 2006.

National Institute of Public Finance and Policy. *Appraisal of Provident Fund and Allied Schemes – Opinion Survey Among Subscribers*. New Delhi, 1986.

National Labour Law Association (NLLA). *Indian Labour Code*. New Delhi: National Labour Law Association, 1994.

Prasad, A. & K.V. Prasad. *Home-working in India: A Review*. National Labour Institute, New Delhi, unpublished document. Saiyadain, Mirza S., Arun Monappa & Meena Mahulkar. *Employees' State Insurance Scheme: An Evaluative Study*. Centre for Regional Management Studies, Indian Institute of Management, Ahmedabad, 1980.

Sankaran, T.S. *Working of Statutory Welfare Funds in the Mining Sector in India*. New Delhi, mimeo.

Schmidt, Michael. *Crisis of Social Policy – Impact on Social Security System*. New Delhi: Social Security Association of India and Friedrich Ebert Stiftung, 1993 Mimeo.

Shariff, Abusaleh. *Employees' State Insurance Scheme in Gujarat: Key Results of a Survey*. Gujarat Institute of Development Research, Gota, Ahmedabad, 1994.

Subrahmanya, R.K.A. *Social Security Perspective of Coming Decades*. New Delhi: Council of Indian Employers, 1985.

UNDP. *Human Development Report 1994*. New York: Oxford University Press, 1994.

Venkata-Ratnam, C.S. *Health Care for Industrial Employees in Large Public and Private Sector firms in India*. New Delhi: International Management Institute (IMI), Mimeo.

Selected Bibliography

Table of Indian Statutes, Schemes and Regulations

The Ayushman Bharat Yojana (ABY)
The Beedi Workers' Welfare Cess Act 1976
The Beedi Workers' Welfare Cess Rules 1977
The Beedi Workers' Welfare Fund Rules 1978
The Beedi Workers' Welfare Fund Act 1976
The Bonded Labour System (Abolition) Act 1976
The Building and Construction Workers (Regulation of Conditions of Service) Act 1996
The Building and Other Construction Workers' Welfare Cess Act 1996
The Cine Workers' Welfare Fund Act 1981
The Coal Mines Provident Fund and Bonus Scheme Act 1948
The Code for Social Security, 2020
The Code on Wages 2019
The Consumer Protection Act, 1985
The Employees' Compensation Act 1923
The Employees' Compensation Rules 1924
The Employees' State Insurance Act 1948
The Employees' State Insurance (Central) Rules 1950
The Employees' State Insurance (General) Regulations 1950
The Employees' Provident Fund and Miscellaneous Provisions Act 1952
The Employees' Provident Fund Scheme 1952
The Employees' Provident Fund Appellate Tribunal (Procedure) Rules 1997
The Employees' Deposit-Linked Insurance Scheme 1976
The Employees' Pension Scheme 1995
The Employment Assurance Scheme
The Food for Work Programme The Indira Awas Yojana
The Integrated Rural Development Programme
The Industrial Disputes Act 1947
The Industrial Disputes (Central) Rules 1947
The Industrial Relations Code 2020
The Iron Ore, Manganese Ore and Chrome Ore Mines Labour Welfare Fund Act 1976
The Jawahar Rojgar Yojana
The Limestone and Dolomite Mines Labour Welfare Fund Act 1972
The Minimum Wages Act 1948

Table of Indian Statutes, Schemes and Regulations

The Maternity Benefit Act 1961
The Maternity Benefit (Mines and Circus) Rules 1963
The Mica Mines Labour Welfare Fund Act 1946
The National Family Benefit Scheme
The National Maternity Benefit Scheme
The National Old Age Pension Scheme
The National Rural Employment Programme
The National Rural Landless Employment Guarantee Programme
The National Social Assistance Scheme
The Occupational Safety, Health and Working Conditions Code 2020
The Payment of Gratuity Act 1972
The Payment of Gratuity (Central) Rules 1972
The Pilot Rural Employment Project
The Pradhan Mantri Jan Arogya Yojana (PMJAY)
The Pradhan Mantri Suraksha Bima Yojana (PMSBY)
The Right to Education Act, 2009
The Seamen's Provident Fund Act 1966
The Sick Industrial Companies (Special Provisions) Act 1985
The Unorganised Workers' Social Security Act, 2008
The Workmen's Compensation Act 1923
The Workmen's Compensation (Venue of Proceedings) Rules 1996

Table of Cases

(COMBINED LIST OF THE CASES DECIDED BY SUPREME COURT OF INDIA AND THE VARIOUS HIGH COURTS THAT HAVE BEEN REFERED TO)

The year refers to the year of judgment.

The last number given in the citation refers to the paragraph.

Index

The numbers here refer to paragraph numbers

Index

Index

Index

Index

www.ingramcontent.com/pod-product-compliance
Ingram Content Group UK Ltd.
Pitfield, Milton Keynes, MK11 3LW, UK
UKHW020134290926
15471UKWH00003B/484

9 789403 538716